SOLDIER

AT

HEART

SOLDIER
AT
HEART
Private to General

An autobiography by

Major General Mike Reynolds CB

Pen & Sword
MILITARY

First published in Great Britain in 2013 by
Pen & Sword Military
an imprint of
Pen & Sword Books Ltd
47 Church Street
Barnsley
South Yorkshire
S70 2AS

ISBN 978 1 78159 026 3

Typeset in Sabon by
Phoenix Typesetting, Auldgirth, Dumfriesshire

Printed and bound in England by
CPI Group (UK) Ltd, Croydon, CR0 4YY

Pen & Sword Books Ltd incorporates the Imprints of Pen & Sword Aviation, Pen &
Sword Family History, Pen & Sword Maritime, Pen & Sword Military, Pen & Sword
Discovery, Wharncliffe Local History, Wharncliffe True Crime, Wharncliffe Transport,
Pen & Sword Select, Pen & Sword Military Classics, Leo Cooper, The Praetorian Press,
Remember When, Seaforth Publishing and Frontline Publishing

For a complete list of Pen & Sword titles please contact
PEN & SWORD BOOKS LIMITED
47 Church Street, Barnsley, South Yorkshire, S70 2AS, England
E-mail: enquiries@pen-and-sword.co.uk
Website: www.pen-and-sword.co.uk

Contents

To the memory of
Private Bob Ketteringham
Royal Norfolk Regiment

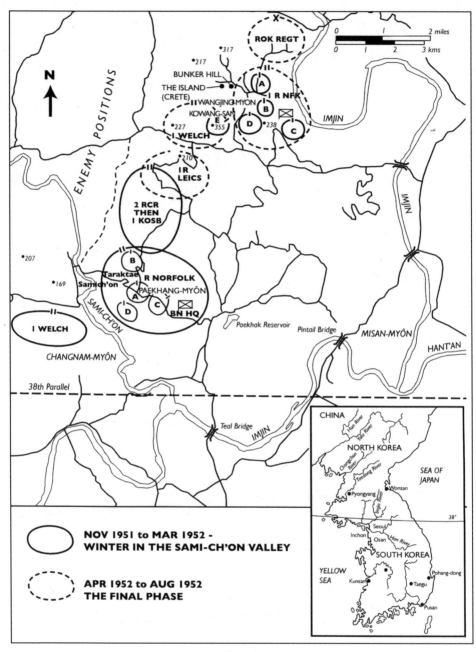

Map 1
Korea

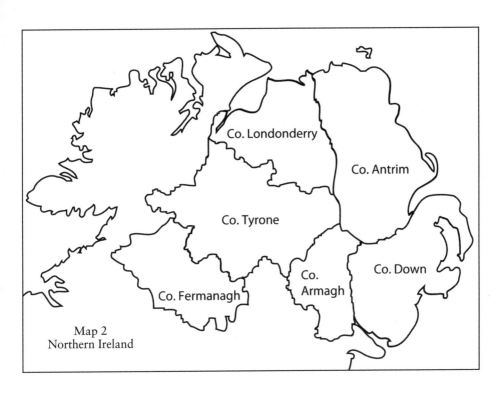

Map 2
Northern Ireland

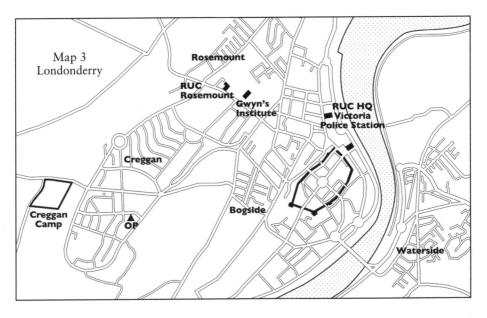

Map 3
Londonderry

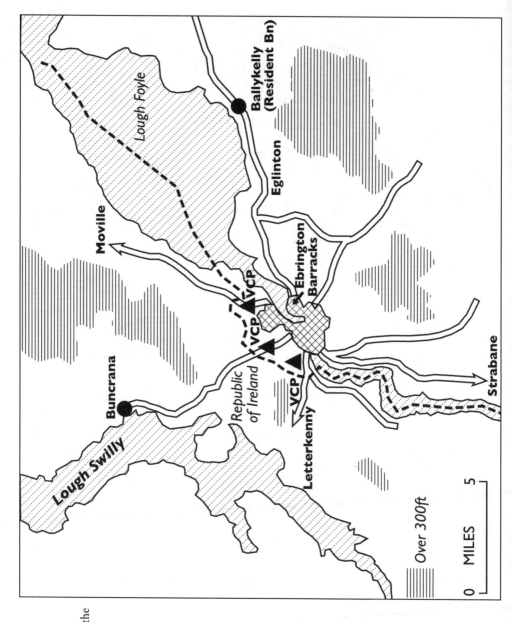

Map 4
Londonderry and the
Enclave

Lough Foyle

Ballykelly
(Resident Bn)

Eglinton

Moville

VCP

VCP

Ebrington
Barracks

VCP

Republic
of Ireland

Letterkenny

Strabane

Buncrana

Lough Swilly

Over 300ft

0   MILES   5

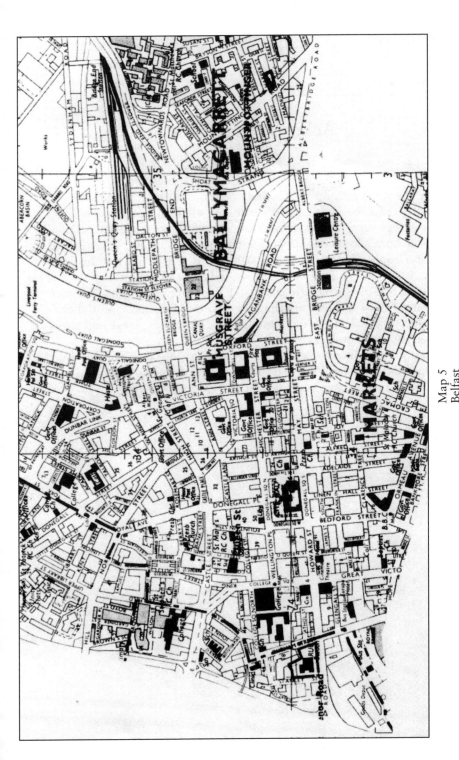

Map 5
Belfast
Ballymacarrett and the City Centre

Acknowledgements

I have mentioned many friends and comrades in these memoirs and it would perhaps be invidious to single any of them out for individual acknowledgement; however, my wife and family deserve special mention. Without Anne's love and support I don't think I would ever have reached two-star rank. She followed me around the world, putting up with constant moves and disruption, and she did much to support the families of those I had the privilege to command. I am forever grateful. And then of course I must mention my children, Victoria, Gabrielle and Deborah and their families. They have brought me great happiness and many laughs. Again, I am so grateful.

Finally, I must mention and thank my original publisher, Jamie Wilson, and my editor, Richard Doherty. Without their help and dedication this book would never have seen the light of day.

East Sussex   MFR
England
2012

Introduction

According to the county and parish records, in 1727 my ancestors lived in the small village of Blankney in Lincolnshire, ten miles south of the county town. The entire village was then part of the Chaplin family estate, but mounting debts forced Henry Chaplin to sell it to the first Earl of Londesborough in 1892.

During the Second World War Blankney Hall was requisitioned for use as billets for RAF personnel and in 1945 was badly damaged by fire, allegedly by a WAAF leaving an iron unattended! Demolished in the 1960s, all that exists now are the remains of the stable block.

Today the entire Blankney estate and village, some 12,000 acres, belongs to the Parker family and it has to be said that, with its lovely medieval church, fine stone buildings, eighteen-hole golf course and cricket club, it is a most beautiful, quintessentially English village. Sadly, the village school, shop, post office and pub have all closed and are now used as private accommodation. The population is less than 400.

So where do the Reynolds fit into this picture? Well, in 1498 the priest in the village church of St Oswald was a Master John Reynold LlB. This may be just a coincidence – and why no 's' on the end of Reynold? I like to think the 's' was added when villagers pointed to a young child and said, 'That's one of Father Reynold's'! Be that as it may, my great, great, great, grandfather, Thomas Reynolds, was certainly living in Blankney in 1727. According to the parish records he was an 'agricultural worker' with six children. The youngest, Mary, was born in Blankney in 1766 and, in 1788, she had a bastard son, James, who was also an agricultural worker. James had eight children and one of his grandsons, Thomas, started his working life as a farm labourer but, by 1862, had moved to Lincoln as an apprentice engine fitter. By 1879 he was a qualified 'iron turner'. His eldest son, Matthew, was my grandfather whom I remember well. He qualified as an engine fitter and, in 1891, he and my grandmother, Sarah, moved to Birmingham. By 1911 they had seven children including my father, Frank, born in 1902. We then see the second big change in my family history because my father gained a place at King

Edward VI's Grammar School in Birmingham and, with the qualifications he earned there, was able to get a junior appointment with Barclay's Bank. In 1927 he married my mother Gwendolen, the daughter of a bank manager, who had also received a good education at King Edward VI's Grammar School for Girls in Birmingham. My family had moved into the middle class and this set the scene for my life – a life that would take me into the middle echelons of the upper class.

SOLDIER

AT

HEART

Chapter One

Boyhood Days

I was born on 3 June 1930 into a world totally different from that of today. We lived initially in a small rented house in a Birmingham suburb but, in 1934, my father bought a new house in Solihull, Warwickshire. It cost him, then a Barclay's clerk, £400 – about £21,160 in today's currency.*

I was an only child and enjoyed a comfortable upbringing, detached from the great problems of the age, such as the 'Great Depression', and unaware of the differences between the various strata of society. My parents were part of a particularly disciplined generation and it was inevitable that this discipline and sense of order would be a major factor in my upbringing. In the 1930s it was unthinkable that children should answer back when told to do something, or complain when our wishes went unfulfilled. We wore what we were given and ate up the food put in front of us. The threat of mild physical discipline was always present, especially at school, but a stern look from mother, father, teacher, bus conductor or even the postman was normally sufficient to ensure calm and order. On the reverse side of the coin, if we were worried or frightened we had no hesitation in running to a policeman or the park-keeper – in fact anyone in a uniform. The police, men only, were much more visible in those days with single 'bobbies' patrolling on foot. We respected everything – the Monarchy and the Church of England, but also the Armed Forces, the Police and our teachers. I knew nothing of the poor, or of unemployment, and lived in an entirely white, Protestant community.

Although middle-class, my parents were not well off. In the fashion of the times, my mother – although as well-educated as my father – did not work. There was no National Health Service and the threat of illness was always a worry to my father. Although he had a brother-in-law who was a practising doctor, he was too proud to ask him for help. Nonetheless, my parents were able to send me to a local private school, Fowgay Hall, where

___
* Today is 2009

1

my classroom was a beautifully converted barn. The education was solid and the Headmaster ensured that we learned about some of the major events of the day, including the Hindenburg disaster, the Japanese bombing of Shanghai and the launch of the German battleship *Bismarck*. That the Germans had a battleship was news to me: I had thought that only Britain possessed these massive ships. The Headmaster also told us of the IRA attacks in Britain in early 1939, as well as the loss of the submarine *Thetis* and the expansion of the armed forces.

I left Fowgay Hall in 1939 for Solihull School, about a mile from my home; I walked there and back daily. The fees were seven guineas a term – about £340 today. My arrival at Solihull School took place in the same month that Britain declared war on Germany. I was playing in the garden with some of my toy soldiers when my father called to me to be quiet in an unusually stern voice. Mr Chamberlain was broadcasting to the nation and no one who ever heard that broadcast will ever forget his words 'Consequently, this country is at war with Germany'. The BBC then played the National Anthem, my parents both stood to attention and the world had changed completely.

Although much of the early months of the war was boring to a small boy there were still moments of high drama – the loss of the aircraft carrier *Courageous* to a U-boat on 17 September, followed by the sinking at anchor of the battleship *Royal Oak* in Scapa Flow on 14 October. Then there was the dramatic battle off the River Plate between the Royal Navy cruisers *Exeter*, *Ajax* and *Achilles* and the German pocket-battleship *Graf Spee* which ended in the scuttling of the German ship in Montevideo harbour.

Petrol rationing had been introduced soon after war broke out and a blackout was imposed immediately. Then, in January 1940, food rationing began – to my great dismay. Clothes soon joined the list of rationed goods and an age of austerity began. My father, a keen gardener, took an allotment nearby to grow vegetables and built a henhouse in our garden in which 'Henry VIII and his six wives' were soon ensconced, providing us with eggs and even some chicks.

On 9 April 1940 the Germans invaded Denmark and Norway and an Allied Expeditionary Force was sent to assist Norway; Denmark had been overrun in a single day. Worse was to follow when the Germans attacked France and the Low Countries a month later and the British Expeditionary Force was driven back to the Channel coast from which, in what was called the 'miracle of Dunkirk', much of it, together with French and other Allied troops, was evacuated to Britain. The force sent to Norway was also evacuated but the aircraft carrier *Glorious* was sunk by the German battlecruisers *Scharnhorst* and *Gneisenau*.

Then came the Battle of Britain but this was far from us. For me the war didn't become personal until August or early September when the air raids began. We were familiar with barrage balloons and air raid shelters. My father had constructed a shelter in our garden to which we used to retire on a nightly basis until it became obvious that it was not waterproof. A decade later, in Korea, I found to my dismay that it is virtually impossible to make a waterproof underground shelter without concrete. With my parents, I watched the bombing of Coventry from the roof of our shelter and, soon after, we hosted for some months an evacuee family, a fat lady and her child. I had to give up my bedroom to them and it was soon obvious that not only had they never seen a bathroom before, they had never taken a bath. I wasn't sorry when they moved on. In November 1940, Solihull was bombed, although this was probably a damaged bomber jettisoning its load. Nonetheless, it was frightening, especially when the last bomb fell on the bowling green close to our house.

Nearby Birmingham suffered heavily during the Blitz with 2,241 citizens killed and another 6,692 injured; 12,391 houses, 302 factories, thirty-four churches, halls and cinemas, and 205 other buildings were destroyed with thousands of other properties damaged.

When my father was promoted to Chief Clerk in Barclay's in Stafford, about fifty miles north of Birmingham, he and my mother chose to rent a beautiful, timber-framed, sixteenth-century house in Haughton, a village five miles west of the county town. In 1940 it had a population of 570, a church of medieval origin, a large rectory built in 1795, two pubs, a small school dating from 1841, a combined Post Office and village shop, a small motor garage and a butcher's shop. I had to leave Solihull School, where I had been doing quite well, and start at a new school, King Edward VI's Grammar School in Stafford, which I entered in September 1942.

I was able to enjoy most of that wonderful summer in Haughton, although I didn't make many friends among the village children. However, I was always very close to my parents and they were great companions – they also bought me a pony. This made things perfect as I could already ride and was able to go off alone to investigate the lanes around the village as well as canter in a nearby field.

In early 1943 we moved again, this time to 'Haughton Villa', an attractive Georgian house at the village's east end. This move was inspired in part because my father had received letters demanding money for unpaid bills relating to the previous occupants of our first house. There were only two snags with the new house – the loo, like the one at the 'Old Hall', was *outside* at the back and, except for the kitchen, it was bitterly cold. I remember being cold even in bed on some winter nights.

Originally, the 'Villa' had been a farmhouse and thus had plenty of sheds and barns as well as a stable for my pony and some pigsties. A local farmer, Mr Len Parker, owned it and the thirty-five acres surrounding it although he, his wife and children, John and Joan, lived in the 'Bell' pub, about fifty yards to the west. John and Joan Parker were my only friends in the village and, since I was the only boy who went to King Edward's in Stafford, I was considered a bit of a 'toff'! That I had my own pony didn't help.

Living in the country eased the food rationing problem. Much bartering went on and the only shortages were of things that didn't grow locally. My father was in his element, immediately starting to plant all sorts of vegetables in the huge garden at the back of the house. This was not to my pleasing as I knew that I would have to help him with weeding, hoeing, digging up potatoes and so on. By contrast, proper harvesting was great fun: I thoroughly enjoyed helping in Len Parker's fields along with John, Joan and others. There were no combine harvesters in the area in those days and, although I think Len had a tractor, horses provided most of the power.

Chickens, ducks, a couple of geese and, finally, 'George' the pig joined us. My mother was very upset when George went for slaughter and refused to have another pig. Although government food regulations forbade us to keep all of George, we soon had some hams hanging from hooks in the kitchen. We had a goose for Christmas and I remember my father plucking and 'drawing' chickens, something I also learned to do. In fact, the animals took up quite a lot of my time when I came home from school and in the holidays.

Father entered fully into village life, playing in the village cricket team, becoming a regular at the 'Bell' and soon getting to know most people in the village. Not so my mother who was much more reserved. In any case, pubs were 'not for ladies' who, in those days, went to hotels while 'gentlemen' used the 'saloon bar' in a pub and not the 'public bar', which was for the working class. No hot food was ever served in pubs before or during the war, and petrol rationing, and the fact that people rarely travelled far in those days, meant that only locals used the Bell. As a matter of interest, anyone under the age of eighteen was forbidden by law to even enter places serving alcohol.

The only middle-class people in the village that I remember were the Rector and his wife, and a couple who had a flat in the Rectory – an Army major and his wife. The major had a 'toffee-nosed' daughter, Anthea, whom I loathed but, fortunately, she was away at boarding school most of the time. Many villagers were slightly in awe of 'the major' until they found out that he wasn't a proper fighting soldier, but the commandant of a prisoner-of-war camp.

One dramatic incident in 1943 will always stick in my mind because it led to me seeing my first dead human body. One weekend I was working in the garden with my father when we heard and saw a large RAF aircraft trailing smoke and diving towards the ground. Shortly after it disappeared from sight we heard a large explosion and so we got on our bicycles and pedalled hard in the direction of a plume of black smoke. Soon we arrived at a field to find some people already there, looking into a large crater containing the remains of an aircraft with smoke pouring from it – I think it was a Lancaster. There was nothing anyone could do. As the smoke cleared we all moved forward and there amongst the remains I saw the body of one crew member. He was lying on his face with the lower half of his body covered with debris. My father took me away and we rode home in silence.

Away from the village we made occasional trips by bus or bicycle to the cinema in Stafford, but usually only on summer evenings or for matinees due to the problems of travelling after dark. Our main source of entertainment was the radio. We listened to many great stars: Bing Crosby singing 'I'm Dreaming of a White Christmas', Vera Lynn, the Forces' Sweetheart, with 'We'll Meet Again' and the Andrews Sisters with 'Boogie Woogie Bugle Boy'. Then there were the big bands, for this was their era, such as Glenn Miller's, Benny Goodman's and Harry James's. Harry James, who married Betty Grable, was the first to employ a new star, Frank Sinatra – 'People Will Say We're in Love' – to sing with his band. I loved the big bands, especially as, unlike today, we could hear clearly every word they sang.

Following Eighth Army's victory at El Alamein, the Germans were on the run in North Africa and, in early 1943, a complete German Army surrendered to the Red Army at Stalingrad. This news, and the fact that our Army was at last winning some battles, led to me giving up any ideas of being a fighter pilot or an officer on a destroyer. I became an Army enthusiast instead and began worrying that the war would end before I could join up.

Meanwhile, my father had certainly been looking to the future as, sometime in 1943, he arranged that I would enter for a Barclay's Bank scholarship to a famous public school – St Edward's, Oxford. We drove down to see it and were very impressed. I sat the exam but failed, causing great disappointment all around. However, my father was determined that I should go to a Public School and arranged private tuition from a retired master from King Edward's, Mr Still, who coached me twice a week in mathematics, English grammar and history. I had to cycle the five miles there and back to his house near the school.

When I re-sat the scholarship exam the scheme had been widened to include many more public schools. On this occasion the exam was followed by an interview in London with the famous cricketer, all-round sportsman, writer and teacher, C. B. Fry. I remember only one question that he asked me. Sitting on his chair as if on a horse and holding the reins, he enquired what was wrong with his posture. 'Your hands are far too high, Sir,' I said. 'Good boy – correct!' Fortunately, I passed both exam and interview and was awarded the scholarship. My parents then had the problem of choosing one of the schools on the list. They consulted Mr Still who recommended Cranleigh in Surrey. It was a very long way from Haughton, but they were prepared to consider it and we travelled by train, through London, to see the school and meet the Headmaster, the Reverend David Loveday. Everything went well, my mother was totally charmed by him and that was that. It was agreed that I would go to Cranleigh as soon as possible, which meant the middle of the school year – January 1944. The fees were just under £200 a year (£6,500 today) and my scholarship was worth £130 (£4,200 today), 'tenable for four years (subject to favourable reports)'. I have no idea what my father's salary was in 1944 although I was warned not to expect any 'extras' such as squash or golf.

Once again my life was to change dramatically. As I would discover many times later in life, what had appeared at first to be a disaster – failing to get into St Edward's, Oxford – turned out to have been for the best. My life at Cranleigh began in January 1944. I was one of 225 boarders and thirty-seven day boys at the school and was assigned to East House which had forty-four boarders and three day boys. It had taken most of a day to travel from Haughton to Cranleigh, journeying by rail to Stafford, changing for a train to Euston whence by Underground to Waterloo, an electric train to Guildford, another change to Cranleigh and a ten-minute walk to the school, carrying my hand luggage – my clothes trunk had preceded me to school.

Discipline was strict at Cranleigh where I was told I was to be a house prefect's 'fag', which meant I had to act as his servant and run his errands. Those arriving late at the dining hall would find that the duty prefect had slammed closed the large oak door at the appointed time. Thus late arrivals not only found themselves without a meal but could also expect a punishment for being late. Prefects administered discipline and there were various 'offences' that now seem so trivial – not having one's jacket buttoned (a privilege allowed only to prefects), whistling (something only 'common boys' did), hands in pockets all drew punishments, as did dirty shoes, untidiness, not making up one's bed properly and any form of cheekiness. Punishments ranged from a beating from the housemaster or house captain to writing out lines or restrictions on free time. And chapel played a large part in our lives – the headmaster and two other masters were ordained – and we attended every weekday morning and twice on Sundays – three times if one went to Holy Communion. I came to love the beautiful chapel and its services and no one seemed to mind attending.

There was little recreation. Those who didn't take part in a team game, play 'fives' or have an 'extra' like squash had to go for a two-mile run. The main games were rugby football, cricket and hockey. I wasn't much good at cricket or hockey, although I liked hockey, had my own stick and played for my House team. However, I was a keen rugger player and played for my House and several times for the 1st XV in 1946; however, I was basically in the 2nd XV and ended up as its captain for the 1947 season. Rugby was very different in those days, the main difference being the *way* in which it was played. Today's exploitation of the rules, and unsporting actions, would have led us to being banned for the rest of the season. And in those days we had an expression which would probably not be understood today: 'better to have played and lost than not to have played at all'!

I did quite well at Cranleigh, sitting and being awarded my Oxford and Cambridge 'School Certificate' in eight subjects at fifteen. In summer 1946, I was promoted to the sixth form and studied English literature and English language and English and European history as 'main' subjects with Divinity and German as 'subsidiary' subjects. In July 1947 I sat and was awarded an Oxford and Cambridge 'Higher' Certificate in all four subjects. (I had switched from French to German as soon as I was allowed to as I was keen to fight the Germans and thought that if I was ever taken prisoner it might come in useful.)

By 1947, the war was over, but it had been a large part of my life at Cranleigh. It made travelling from Haughton memorable: a boy with a third-class ticket was expected to give up his seat to an adult which meant that I often had to stand all the way from Stafford to London. Although the bombing of southern England had finished when I started at Cranleigh, sparing me air-raid drills and going down into shelters, things changed on 13 June 1944, when the first V1 'doodlebug' landed in Kent. These pilotless flying-bombs continued until 1 September with, at one time, 100 a day being launched at London. In all, 1,435 landed on English soil but many fell short or were shot down before reaching London. Returning from our summer holidays, we found that one had landed near Cranleigh gasworks and another on the playing fields near the Headmaster's house, damaging it and, allegedly, covering him with plaster. We all thought this very funny. As we returned to school, the first V2 rocket hit London on 8 September: of 1,402 launched at England,

1,358 landed in the Greater London area. The first you knew of a V2 was a huge explosion as it hit the ground. This was worrying, but fortunately none landed anywhere near Cranleigh. The fact that you could hear a 'doodlebug' coming led to a unique emergency system in the School. On a rota, senior boys watched out for incoming V1s from an observation post alongside the clock tower above the East House dormitory in the old part of the School. If one was seen and its engine cut out, or it was already in a dive, a button was pressed to ring bells all over the school, sending everyone to take cover, preferably in one of the inner corridors or, in the worst case, under a desk. V1 spotting was exciting and something different from the normal routine but, because the tower could only be reached up a ladder, it also enabled the spotters to smoke without fear of detection and many fifth and sixth formers had the odd cigarette when we thought we could get away with it.

While at Cranleigh I wrote to famous wartime figures asking for their autographs. This was quite a successful hobby and I still have those of Eisenhower, Monty, Field Marshal Jan Smuts, Prime Minister of South Africa, and Admiral of the Fleet Sir Bertram Ramsay. I also had those of Air Chief Marshal Sir Arthur 'Bomber' Harris, Guy Gibson VC and General James Doolittle of the US Army Air Forces, but recently gave them to an American friend who is a great air force enthusiast. I wrote to Winston Churchill who didn't reply.

Aircraft recognition was another of my hobbies and there were very few British, American or German planes that I couldn't identify in actual flight or in the silhouette tests which appeared in various military magazines. A Sunday walk from school took us close to Dunsfold airfield where we could watch Boston and Mitchell light bombers, crewed mainly by Canadians, taking off and landing.

Of course, 5 and 6 June (D Day) 1944, were very memorable. Before D Day many military vehicles, mostly Canadian, were parked on some of our playing fields, which were put 'out of bounds', as they waited to go over to Normandy. Then, on the evening of the 5th, we heard the roar of heavy bombers. We started counting but soon gave up as there were simply too many Lancasters, Liberators and Stirlings, all heading for France. We knew the invasion was about to begin and, next morning, were glued to the radio. It was a time of great jingoism. We fifth formers studying Shakespeare's *Henry the Fifth* for our School Certificate exams were allowed to go down to the Cranleigh cinema to see Laurence Olivier playing that part and were thrilled to hear his speech before the battle of Agincourt.

By December 1947 the only career I wanted was in the Army. Greatly influenced by the Second World War, in my naivety I had no real idea of the horrors involved; to me it was exciting, not frightening. An enthusiastic member of the Junior Training Corps (JTC) since my very first term, I was popular with the officer commanding the Corps, and his full-time instructor, RSM Gamble of the Royal Norfolk Regiment. I loved shooting on the 25-yard range and 'Field Days' in the summer terms when we did fieldcraft and platoon and section attacks on Smithwood Common. In May 1944 I wrote home excitedly that 'On Friday we had a Sherman tank, a mortar carrier, three Bren-gun carriers, two armoured cars, a 4.2-inch mortar, a lot of machine guns, and a PIAT for the JTC to look at. We had rides on the carriers and the Sherman and an Auster spotting plane landed on our playing fields.'

I was so 'army-barmy' by this time that I even volunteered to go to Cadet Camps during school holidays. I remember one in the grounds of Arundel Castle when General Sir Oliver Leese addressed us and another with a Royal Artillery regiment at Deepcut where we manned 25-pounders and fired live shells. Because of all this military interest, I easily passed my Certificate A examination on 20 November 1946, which meant that I knew the basics of soldiering. I was very proud. Little did the RSM or I know that one day I would serve in his Regiment in the Korean War or that I would be commissioned into the Regiment whose badge we wore in the Corps, the Paschal Lamb of the Queen's Royal Regiment. Or that, forty-three years later, I would return to school as a retired major general and fire the first official shot down the new indoor range.

VE Day was a very exciting event. During 'prep' on 7 May, someone in a study above our House Room turned a radio up and we heard the BBC announcement that the Germans had surrendered and that the 8th was to be 'Victory in Europe Day'. Although we had known for some time that the end of the war with Germany was imminent this didn't lessen the excitement. Then, to everyone's surprise, we were told that the following day would be a national holiday and we were free to do as we liked, and even go into Guildford. Naturally we took the opportunity, but couldn't think of anything to do when we got there except go to the cinema. Sadly we didn't know any local girls with whom to celebrate. After the cinema we went back to School to wait for the Cranleigh village celebrations that evening: a torchlight procession wound its way from the far end of the village to a large bonfire on the Common where there were fireworks and a ceremonial burning of a Swastika. I can't recall my companions, but we watched the procession from the Onslow Arms where everyone got a free pint. Needless to say we had a whale of a time and I don't remember returning to School.

On 26 July we were all very surprised to hear that Winston Churchill, who had led us to victory in Europe, had lost the General Election to

Clement Attlee's Labour Party. We had no idea of the profound changes this would lead to: the National Health Service and the nationalization of the Bank of England, coal mines, civil aviation, gas, electricity, road transport and the steel industry. All was quite beyond our imagination.

With the exception of a two-week holiday in Weston-super-Mare in 1944, my main school holidays were spent back at Haughton but were not as much fun as I would have liked. My pony had been sold since I wasn't there to exercise her and there was no more riding for me. Nor did I have any real friends. Although John Parker was still around, a public-school boy with a Surrey accent was even worse than a local grammar-school boy. I wasn't popular and this came out in the boxing ring. My father had started a boys' club in the village where John challenged me to 'fisticuffs'. The second round became pretty vicious and the fight more of a wrestling match with the order 'Break!' being ignored. My father had to stop it and we called it quits. Fortunately, John and I made it up and there was no long-term ill feeling.

By the end of 1946 I was more interested in the Indian rather than the British Army. Like Field Marshal Montgomery before me, I was attracted by the better pay, the guarantee of automatic promotion to major and the excitement of serving abroad. This dream came to an abrupt end with Indian independence in August 1947 but I wasn't put off the idea of military service. By the time I left school I was pretty sure I wanted to make the Army my career. Although I could have volunteered, I decided to wait for my National Service 'calling up' papers which I knew would arrive shortly before my eighteenth birthday; in this way I could ensure that Army life really was for me. Meanwhile I would enjoy my new environment by doing as little as possible. Inevitably my father had other ideas.

Before ending this chapter I must mention one particular international event from 1946: Winston Churchill's speech at Westminster College in Fulton, Missouri. Having received an honorary degree, he said, 'It is my duty, however, to place before you certain facts about the present position in Europe. From Stettin in the Baltic to Trieste in the Adriatic an *iron curtain* has descended across the Continent.' This can be said to mark the beginning of the Cold War – a 'war' that would dominate my life.

Chapter Two

National Service

In 1948 my father was promoted to manage Barclay's Northfield branch. In this Birmingham suburb we were close to King's Norton Golf Club which my father joined. A natural 'small ball' sportsman, he soon became not only very enthusiastic, but also a good player but, despite his encouragement, in those days I found golf much too slow and boring.

Soon after moving into our new house my father bought a TV set. We had never seen television before and, although there was only one channel, BBC, and the picture was black and white, we were fascinated. My parents spent most evenings in front of the television, watching it, like many at the time, in the dark.

By joining Moseley Rugby Football Club soon after arriving in Northfield I quickly made many new friends. Moseley, with its rugby club, and Edgbaston, with its Priory tennis club, were definitely the smartest suburbs of Birmingham – almost exclusively WASP (White Anglo-Saxon Protestant), with just a few Jews like Sir Zolly Zucherman and Dame Myra Hess, and Catholics like Professor Thomas Bodkin, Director of the Barber Institute of Fine Art. Certainly, unlike today, there were no Muslims, Hindus or blacks.

My regular haunts in early 1948 were the Kardomah coffee-house in New Street and the Trocadero pub in Temple Street, both in the city centre: the latter still exists. Another favourite pub was the White Swan, better known as 'The Dirty Duck' at the bottom of Harborne hill. Since talking and drinking coffee and beer with my new-found friends, including a number of girls, was about all I did, it wasn't long before my father intervened and told me that he had a job for me – a gap year was unheard of in those days. I was to be a trainee manager with Avery's – a large weighing-machine company that is now defunct. One of Avery's directors had told my father that he could fix a job for me with the company. I was horrified – even more so on learning that I would be working in Digbeth, an industrial area just below the Bull Ring, that I would begin in the repair shop, have to wear blue overalls, start at eight each morning and travel by tram to get there. My only consolation was knowing that, with my call-up for National Service imminent, this menial and, in my opinion, totally unsuitable occupation for a public schoolboy, wouldn't last long. I've no idea now of my weekly wages. Not a lot – just enough for a good night out in the Trocadero or Dirty Duck on Fridays and Saturdays.

My first day was quite a shock. Swaying around on a noisy tram in blue overalls for over half an hour was bad enough but, on arrival, I was greeted by a sour-faced foreman who clearly considered me a 'toff'. To my great relief I soon found out that he rarely left the glass box which was his office in the workshop. He told me that I was to work under the super-vision of Ted, the union shop steward. Amazingly, Ted and I got on well despite the fact that he was an extreme socialist who wanted to do away with the entire British aristocracy. One of his oft-repeated complaints was that Nelson's descendants were all earls or nobles of one sort or another despite never having done anything worthwhile in their lives.

Initially, my job was to assist Ted in repairing weighing machines, or 'scales', which were usually from food shops. The work was extremely boring. I was also irritated by the fact that although we were meant to start work at eight o'clock nobody did. We 'clocked in' by putting our workcards into a machine that 'punched' them to show that we had arrived for work at the right time, but all the workers did for the first thirty or forty minutes was drink tea, read their newspapers and select the horses on which to place bets. The foreman turned a blind eye to all this. After about two weeks I decided that coming in at eight and sitting around was pointless, and so began delaying my arrival by about half an hour. Ted didn't seem to mind but, when the foreman checked our work cards at the end of the week, I was told in no uncertain terms that any repeti-tion of this practice would result in being reported to the senior management. Protesting about my time being wasted resulted in strong verbal abuse. I had no choice but to comply.

After a couple of months I was told that Ted and I were to go out 'on the road', going to factories like Lucas to check their huge industrial weighbridges for accuracy. We would then issue certificates of accuracy, as required by law. Such weighbridges could take loads of many tons but no matter where on the metal surface the load was placed it had to weigh the same. To check this we would place a lot of 56lb weights on each corner in turn, a very tiring and boring physical task. If any inaccuracy was detected we had to go underneath into a dark, smelly and often oil-soaked area and fix the problem. When first I went out 'on the road' Ted told me where the factory was and said, 'Don't get there before ten o'clock', which suited me. I was even more pleased to find that we knocked off at about three o'clock. This was standard practice and I was surprised to find that Ted entered false times on our workcards every day. There was no way I was going to 'bubble' him though – it suited me fine.

After my time in the workshop I was moved to the offices on the top floor and given menial tasks like clearing out old filing cabinets and answering the phone. I hated this and longed for the day when I would join the Army. I didn't have long to wait. In early June I received a letter telling me to report to the Birmingham Ministry of Labour Office to register for National Service. Two weeks later I had to undergo a full medical to ensure I was fit for military service. Then, on 15 July, a railway warrant and four shillings 'advance of pay' (£5 today) arrived with an order to report for duty at the RAMC Depot, Boyce Barracks, Crookham, near Aldershot, on 22 July.

My 'calling-up' papers had told me to report to Boyce Barracks but, as the third letter of the Corps title had been smudged, I had no idea what I would actually be joining. None of the possibilities thrilled me: RASC (Service Corps), RAOC (Ordnance Corps), RAPC (Pay Corps), RAMC (Medical Corps), RADC (Dental Corps) or even RAVC (Veterinary Corps). Anyway I arrived at Boyce Barracks along with a lot of others to find to my horror that I was 22049591 Private Reynolds in B (Reception) Company of the Royal Army Medical Corps, just one of the 1,132,872 boys called up for National Service in the Army between 1947 and 1963. I was eighteen years-and-one-month old, five feet eleven inches tall, weighed 150 pounds and was part of an Army over five times the size of today's.

Boyce Barracks, later re-named Queen Elizabeth Barracks but since sold off by the Ministry of Defence, was a wooden-hutted camp, with single-storey barrack blocks known as 'spiders'. Each 'spider' comprised eight huts with a central ablution area; each hut had twenty beds. The barracks could accommodate 2,500 men and included a large parade area, gymnasium and cinema.

I remember little of my fifteen days in the RAMC except my first army haircut. Then, on the morning of our first full day of service, we were assembled in the cinema where, after the curtains went back, we saw a lieutenant colonel standing on the stage saluting us. He was our commanding officer and told tell us how honoured we should feel to be in his Corps – the Corps with the greatest number of VCs in the Army. I also remember that I never touched a rifle in Boyce Barracks – only stretchers and medical kits. But the main, and most important thing, was my interview with the Personnel Selection Officer, a captain who asked me if I was happy and if I had any problems. I replied that I was very unhappy to be in the RAMC as I wanted to be in the infantry and went on to say that I had been told that, as a Certificate A holder from my time in the Cranleigh Cadet Corps, I was entitled to a choice of arm or service. He agreed that this was true but added that he had never met anyone before who *wanted* to be in the infantry. Anyway, he would see what he could do. Some days later, quite a lot of us were paraded to be told we were being transferred – in many cases to the Royal Pioneer Corps, but in my case to the Royal Highland Regiment, The Black Watch. I was to report to the 1st Battalion, The Highland Light Infantry (HLI) at Fort George, near Inverness, the battalion responsible for training all new recruits, regular and National Service, for the Highland Brigade. Although this was a bit of a shock, at least I was joining the infantry and so, on 4 August, wearing battledress and carrying all my army clothing in a kitbag (my civilian clothes had been sent home during my first few days at Boyce), I said goodbye to the RAMC. Looking back I think I must be the only RAMC private soldier ever to have reached the rank of general officer.

The overnight journey to Inverness was a nightmare. Having travelled to Waterloo by train and then crossed to Euston by tube, I had to stand most of the way to Inverness in the train corridor – all the time with a full kitbag. On arrival in Inverness I found that there were others waiting to be picked up and taken to the Fort. They were also National Service recruits joining the various Regiments of the Highland Brigade – the Black Watch, Seaforth, Gordons, Camerons, Argylls, and HLI. Unlike me they were still in civilian clothes. A 3-ton truck with an HLI corporal in charge arrived to pick us up but we had to stand for the thirteen-mile journey to Fort George.

I found the Fort very imposing. Following the 1746 defeat of Bonnie Prince Charlie's army at Culloden, George II had ordered its creation as the ultimate defence against further Jacobite unrest. Positioned on a promontory jutting into the Moray Firth, it had (has) almost a mile of boundary walls and accommodation for a 1,600-strong garrison although, at that time, I had no knowledge of its history, or indeed that of Scotland, although I was soon to learn in no uncertain manner. On arrival we were marched across the bridge over the moat surrounding the barracks, through the massive walls, past a daunting guardroom to our new home – one of C Company's wooden huts, outside the ramparts to the south-east of the main Fort. I have no memory of what happened next or how long it all took, but soon after our arrival we were shown to our platoon hut, allocated a bed with three blankets but no sheets and then kitted out in the Quartermaster's stores. In my case the latter was very quick as I already had my two battledresses, two pairs of boots, one pair of plimsolls, PT shorts and three vests, three shirts, one tie, three pairs of cellular pants, three (or maybe it was more) pairs of thick woollen grey socks, a thin sweater, my webbing (belt, gaiters, shoulder straps, large pack, haversack and water bottle with holder), respirator and a very uncomfortable steel helmet. All that happened to me was that I had my beret removed and replaced by a tam-o'-shanter (TOS) with a red hackle, the famous feathers of the Black Watch. I was also given the Regiment's cloth tartan badge and told to sew it on my left sleeve after removing my RAMC shoulder flashes. That reminds me that one of the more extraordinary things we were issued with was a 'hussiff', a small cloth holdall containing needles and some cotton and wool with which we were expected to sew on buttons and repair holes in our clothing. I kept my battledress trousers, thank goodness, as kilts were not issued until recruits were classified as 'trained'. At the armoury we were each allocated a .303 Lee Enfield rifle, a weapon that had hardly changed in design since the First World War. We were also weighed, measured, medically examined, given various injections and subjected to a haircut – the second in my case.

In spite of my experience at Boyce Barracks, my new barrack-room was a bit of a shock. Although little different from that at Boyce, it seemed much more stark with its bare floorboards, about twenty beds, no curtains, and a single steel wardrobe and small foot locker each for our kit. Privacy was non-existent, there was no TV and no radio; easily portable and affordable radios were still in the future. The ablution block was some distance away and, when we went to wash and shave, the water usually was cold. There were no baths – only cold or tepid showers.

My company commander was Major Alan Grendon and my platoon sergeant Bill Stobie, whom, I'm told, finished his career as a major quartermaster. A corporal, whose name I don't recall, slept in a partitioned-off part of our barrack room. His role was to keep a strict eye on us.

In 1948 National Service was for a total of eighteen months (later extended to two years) while basic infantry training lasted ten weeks during which we were taught drill – marching in slow and quick time, saluting etc – made fit through daily PT, including running round the top of the Fort's walls, and trained in the use of basic infantry weapons such as the rifle, the .303 Bren light machine gun (LMG) and the Sten sub-machine gun (SMG). We fired all these weapons a number of times on ranges just outside the Fort. The shooting was fun and I classified as a First Class shot on both rifle and LMG. But two aspects of range work were always unpopular – working in the 'stop butts' to mark where other people's shots had landed on the target and cleaning our rifles afterwards. The latter involved lining up to get hot water from a boiling cauldron before pouring a gallon of it down our barrels to expand the metal. We then had to pull a piece of oily 'four by two' flannel on a 'pull-through' (a cord with a brass weight on the end) several times through the barrel to get the wretched thing thoroughly clean. Believe it or not, the pieces of 'four by two' were strictly rationed and we had to wash them afterwards and keep them for re-use.

We also learned to throw hand grenades (two per man) and how to use bayonets. I recall vividly 'bayonet drill': we ran as fast as possible and, with a scream, thrust our bayonets into sandbag dummies to cries from our instructors to 'Get in there! Cold steel is the Hie'landers' weapon!' In addition, we were taught to fire the PIAT (Projector Infantry Anti-Tank), a beast of a weapon weighing 14.5 kg. Spring-loaded, it took all four fingers of your hand to pull the trigger while the recoil nearly dislocated your shoulder. Fieldcraft, patrolling and night movement were other skills we were taught, some of it during a two-day and night camp-out on the moors. Other activities included route marching, often with a piper leading us, and lectures on the dangers of venereal diseases. We were told that in order to suppress our sexual aspirations, bromide was being put in our tea in both the cookhouse and the NAAFI. If it was it didn't seem to work very well.

Much time was spent on 'spit and polish', or 'bull' as it was generally known – polishing our boots until the toe caps reflected like mirrors, blancoing our webbing equipment and shining the brass buckles until they looked almost like silver. We also learned to press sharp creases into our thick battledress trousers by using a piece of brown paper between the material and an electric iron (no steam irons in those days). Ironing was done on the couple of six-foot wooden tables in our barrack room.

Muster Parade began every day. The roll was called and we were inspected from head to toe. Anyone with dirty or scruffy kit could find himself on 'Company Orders' and being given minor punishments such as 'latrine duty' or 'spud bashing' (peeling pounds of potatoes by hand). There was also a weekly 'Pay Parade' during which we stood in line for what seemed like an age before being marched forward to a table where an officer doled out our miserable pittance.

For the first three weeks we weren't allowed out of the Fort. At that point we had to undergo a severe inspection and prove that our drill, especially saluting, was of an acceptable standard. This was done in a procedure called Passing off the Square.

At 0600 each day we were woken by the hut corporal, usually with a vulgar shout. Following cold-water ablutions, we would troop off with our aluminium 'mess tins' KFS (knife, fork and spoon) and brown tin mug to the austere cookhouse with its bare walls and plain wooden six-foot tables. The food was appalling with little or no choice: breakfast was the inevitable porridge with salt, some bread, margarine and jam and perhaps some powered egg or a sausage, or both if we were lucky; dinner at 1230 and tea at 1730 were dull and boring meals and, if curry appeared, we always suspected they had used some bad meat. The NAAFI became our refuge, but on twenty-eight shillings a week (£38 today) less two shillings (£2.71 today) income tax, and a further two shillings for 'barrack damages', we couldn't afford as many meals and snacks as we would have wished. The *average*, not basic, weekly wage at the time was eight pounds, eight shillings and sixpence (£228 today); there was no *minimum* wage then. The 'barrack damages' charge was made just in *case* we damaged some WD (War Department) property. From our remaining money we had to buy razor blades, shaving and washing soap, Brasso for cleaning our brasses, boot polish, blanco, dusters, cigarettes (most of us smoked) and even pay for our haircuts. 'Lights out' was, I think, at about 2230, accompanied by a piper playing some dreary tune whilst he walked slowly round part of the ramparts.

Indoctrination into Scottish, and particularly Highland, history began almost immediately. We had lectures on the HLI's history and a visit to Culloden Moor where we were told how the Duke of Cumberland's English troops had butchered Bonnie Prince Charlie's gallant men before 'suppressing' the Highlands. Our further indoctrination included lessons in Highland dancing and these dance lessons often replaced our normal PT periods. I have to say that I never felt particularly comfortable dancing an eightsome with seven brawny and hairy Highlanders.

So how did an Englishman who had never previously set foot in Scotland fit into this *very* Scottish environment? Strangely enough, amazingly well. I confess that I cheated slightly by saying that I was *half*, rather than a quarter Scottish and, despite a slight problem in understanding the strong accents of some of my fellow recruits, I soon made friends. I must admit, however, that most of them were amongst those who, like me, intended to try for a commission. Some, like Bill Westland, Peter Grant and Bill Donnelly, would come on with me to Eaton Hall, the National Service Officer Cadet Training Unit (OCTU). Of these only Peter was in my Company; indeed, we were in the same platoon. His grandmother had a charming house somewhere between the Fort and Inverness while his father was a serving Scots Guards' lieutenant colonel. After we had 'Passed off the Square', Peter invited me to his grandmother's home for a Sunday lunch party but, as I could hardly turn up as a private soldier in battledress, he had to lend me a suit, shirt, tie and shoes. All went well until I found myself talking to an officer from the Fort. He didn't recognize me but I knew him and when he asked me what I was doing in that area I couldn't resist telling him the truth. He nearly dropped his glass!

Fortunately the late summer of 1948 saw glorious weather in northern Scotland. However, the harvest was late and our training was suspended so that we could help out on local farms. Each morning we drew 'haversack rations' (awful sandwiches) from the cookhouse before being driven to a farm. In addition, we took our water-bottles which, in some cases, turned out to be a wise precaution because some farmers worked us like slaves and refused us even water to drink. Maybe they had to pay the Army for our sweated labour – they certainly didn't pay us. One event in this period sticks in my memory. On a return journey from one of the farms I was in the back of a 15-cwt truck with several others when the driver, a regular HLI soldier, decided to show off by driving very fast. We shouted and banged on the cab but he and the lance-corporal in the front took no notice. Inevitably we came off the road after crossing a hump-backed bridge and were all thrown out. It was a miracle that no one was killed or seriously hurt. I was furious and berated the driver, saying that I would report him for crazy driving. It wasn't a wise thing to do – he and the lance-corporal told me in no uncertain terms that I would be beaten up that night if I did. That closed the matter.

Mention of being beaten up reminds me of my first expedition into Inverness. After a gruelling inspection in the guardroom, several of us caught a bus to the city. There were no pubs as in England, just bars and hotels. Needless to say on our pay we ended up in a fairly grotty bar where there were already several soldiers. Men in khaki, particularly without kilts, were not very popular with the locals and before long an argument started at one end of the bar, fortunately well away from me. My companion, whose name I cannot recollect, but who seemed experienced in bar brawls, immediately told me to take off my web belt and wrap it round my right hand, ensuring that the two rear brass buckles ended up protruding between my fingers. 'This might get nasty – let's get out of here! If anyone comes towards you looking dangerous, make sure you hit him first!' In the event we got out just in time because it apparently developed into a major 'punch-up'. Next day everyone in the Fort was ordered onto the square for an identification parade where we stood for some time before, escorted by civilian police constables, three heavily-bandaged men appeared and started walking down our ranks. Uniform is a wonderful disguise, particularly with hats on, and they were unable to pick out those who had inflicted their injuries. Nevertheless, it was a worrying moment as they passed in front of me just in case one of them suddenly said, 'Aye, this is the guy!'

Sometime in late September a notice went up outside the Company Office saying that anyone who could ride a horse should give his name to the Company clerk. Hoping this might get me out of some boring training, I did so. Shortly afterwards I found myself on 'Company Commander's Interview' and was marched into Major Grendon's office by the Company Sergeant Major (CSM), given the order to 'mark time – halt!' and then left facing the wall, still at attention. To my left Major Grendon then said, 'Reynolds, do you know you've got a big Roman nose and look a little like the old Duke of Wellington?' 'Sir!' I replied. 'OK. Turn and face me, stand at ease and stand easy.' He then explained that the HLI was making a film of the history of the Regiment called 'Proud Heritage' and that, as I could ride a horse and had the same basic features as the Duke of Wellington, they would like me to play the part. I could hardly believe my ears – after all I was only just eighteen. Anyway it all happened. To the intense irritation of the Regimental Sergeant Major (RSM), and every one in authority below him, I was ordered to grow my sideburns to well below my ear lobes and was fitted out with a blue frock-coat with gold epaulettes, red tunic covered with gold braid, cockaded hat, white riding breeches and black riding boots and issued with a sword and scabbard before being introduced to my grey mount and told to practise my riding. I have no idea how much it cost to make this film (a copy of which I have on video tape), but it must have been a lot because it was filmed in colour and all uniforms and equipment had to be hired. Most officers and soldiers of the 1st Battalion HLI took part, as did the Demonstration Platoon of the Parachute Regiment and some Territorial Army personnel. Everyone was correctly dressed in the eighteenth- and nineteenth-century uniforms of the East India Company for the scenes set in India, and in the red coats, kilts and bonnets of later years for those in the Peninsula and at Waterloo. In addition, many horses, muskets and even cannon manned by sailors from a Royal Naval establishment were used in the filming. Many of the horses came from the Inverness riding school and a number of the 'French' cavalry were girls from Inverness and the local area – it's amazing what a breastplate and helmet can hide. I certainly enjoyed my time between 'takes'. I also enjoyed, although he didn't, having the Assistant Adjutant of 1 HLI, Lieutenant Oatts, playing the part of my ADC during some of the scenes. Fort George with its ramparts was perfect for scenes where Indian fortresses were needed and the bare and windswept ranges just outside it were ideal locations for filming battle scenes; even the sea was used cleverly where a river was required.

In my first 'take' I played Colonel Arthur Wellesley, later to become the Duke of Wellington, in the 1799 Battle of Seringapatam. I wore my blue frock-coat with gold epaulettes, sword and sash and, on this occasion, appeared dismounted. However, for the battles of Assaye (1803), and Vimiera (1808) in the Peninsular War, and at Waterloo (1815), I was mounted on a grey mare wearing my red jacket, white breeches and cockaded hat. One of the most exciting parts was in the Battle of Assaye where, as well as playing the Duke in a later scene, I was in the Indian cavalry attacking the Highlanders at full gallop armed with a lance. Lots of bangs and smoke were heard and seen in this very exciting episode for all the participants – the mounted ones anyway. Looking at the film today it strikes me that it might have been quite dangerous as we appear to ride right into the Highlanders' ranks. I didn't have many lines as most battle scenes were filmed to a commentary. However, I did have one quite dramatic speaking part during the battle of Assaye when I said, 'Major Swinton! Well stood Sir, well stood! The enemy are in full retreat. Bring up the Seventy-fourth for the pursuit!' Swinton was played by one of the HLI company commanders, a Major Anderson, and I'm not sure he *really* liked having a private soldier giving him orders.

I must admit I was very proud when a full-colour photograph of me, dressed as the Duke, appeared in *Soldier* magazine with the caption: 'To National Serviceman, Private Reynolds, fell the job of portraying the Duke of Wellington. His features were considered to resemble the 'Iron Duke's.'

Sometime in October 1948 I was moved into a barrack room inside the Fort as a member of the potential officers' platoon where I met others like Ian Leslie and Peter Hoppe who would come on with me to Sandhurst. But that was three months in the future; in the meantime Peter Grant and I were told to report to Catterick Camp in Yorkshire to attend a War Office Selection Board (WOSB) to see if we were suitable for training as National Service officers. We spent the night on the way in Edinburgh in the home of a friend of Peter's family, Robert Bruce Lockhart, who had been a British agent before the Great War and was Britain's first envoy to the Bolsheviks in Russia in January 1912. For a time during 1918 he had been confined in the Kremlin as their prisoner. I remember him as a fascinating man.

The WOSB lasted three or four days during which we were tested physically, made to give ten-minute lecturettes to our fellow candidates, took part in discussion groups and given various, almost impossible, initiative tests like getting an oil drum and our team of half a dozen or so over a stream using ropes and a couple of planks that weren't long enough. We were also subjected to several penetrating interviews. Peter and I both passed and, after a few more days back at the Fort, were posted to Eaton Hall OCTU just outside Chester. And so I said goodbye to Jocks in large numbers – the next time I would see that many Scotsmen again would be twenty-seven years later when I had two battalions of them, the Queen's Own Highlanders (Seaforth and Camerons) and the Argyll and

Sutherland Highlanders, under my command in my Brigade in Germany.

I arrived at Eaton Hall on 5 November 1948, once again carrying all my kit. Eaton Hall, belonging to the Duke of Westminster, had been requisitioned by the War Office. Peter and some of the others were allocated to Companies in the main Hall itself, whereas I was again in a hut in the grounds. At least we were issued with sheets for our beds. I reported to the Company Office and was told by the Sergeant Major to get myself down to the tailor's shop to have white gorgets sewn onto my battledress lapels and a white ribbon round my TOS. As the tailor's shop was at the far end of the camp, I had to cross the main drive leading up to the Hall from the entrance gate. About 200 or 300 yards down this drive was a very tall obelisk in memory of someone or something. Anyway as I crossed the drive I heard a voice boom out, 'Cadet, cadet!' I glanced around and decided that it couldn't possibly be me who was being shouted at. How wrong I was! Again I heard, 'That cadet – come here at once!' And when I looked towards the obelisk I saw a tall figure shaking with rage, clearly directed at me. I doubled down to him, stood to attention and saluted. 'Report at once to your Company Sergeant Major, you are RTU'd [returned to your unit] for failing to salute the Commandant!' he bellowed. 'But Sir, I didn't' – that was as far as I got. 'Don't argue with me boy!' I saluted again and turned to my right. 'And at the double!' he shouted. I arrived in front of my Sergeant Major, perspiring and in shock. I had only been at OCTU for a few hours and had been sacked. The Sergeant Major listened patiently and then smiled and said, 'Don't worry, just keep your eyes open in future. Now, do as I said and get down to the tailor's shop. We want you looking like an officer cadet, don't we? – SIR!'

The Commandant in question was Colonel Dennis Gibbs, a well-known martinet in the Queen's Royal Regiment, into which I would eventually be commissioned. Long after he retired, and I was at least a captain, I told him the story of our first meeting. He smiled and said, 'Oh no, I would never have said that!'

I don't have many memories of Eaton Hall. Certainly I used my first thirty-six-hour leave pass – Saturday lunchtime until sometime on Sunday night – and free rail warrant to go home and collect come civilian clothes. This was the first time I had seen my parents in four months. I also remember being desperately cold in our accommodation hut as there never seemed to be enough fuel for the stoves. And I certainly remember the RSM, Charlie Copp of the Coldstream, and the Adjutant, Captain Hedley-Dent of the Welsh Guards, known as 'Badly Bent'. On one occasion when 'Badly Bent' was inspecting our rifles, he saw a tiny 'money' spider in one poor fellow's barrel. He nearly had a stroke. 'Sergeant Major, Sergeant Major!' he screamed. 'Take his name, take his name! Put him in the book!' 'SIR,' roared the Sergeant Major, which meant the poor chap would appear in front of his Company commander on a charge of 'Conduct contrary to good order and military discipline' and receive some sort of minor reprimand.

Within weeks of arriving at the Hall I was told that I was to be made a Cadet Junior Under Officer (JUO), the equivalent of a platoon commander, a promotion overtaken by my resolve to become a professional soldier and go to Sandhurst. I was sure by then that I liked the Army and wanted to make it my career. I was excused the written Civil Service Examination for Sandhurst as my Oxford and Cambridge Higher School Certificate was sufficient to prove my academic ability, but I did have to pass a Regular Commissions Board (RCB) at Knepp Castle near Horsham – much the same as the WOSB. I was thrilled to be told I had passed and, early next day, 9 December, back at Eaton Hall, found myself with my hand on the Bible, swearing an oath of allegiance to King George VI, 'his heirs and successors and all those set in authority over me'. I was then issued with a Regular Army Attestation paper which I still have. I rang my father that evening to tell him I was a professional soldier and had 'signed on' for five years with the Colours and seven on the Reserve. I think he was a little shocked for it was the first really important decision I had made in my life without consulting him. He didn't say a lot except to wish me luck but, as time went by, he became very proud of me and recognized that I had chosen the right career. Two good results of becoming a regular soldier were that my pay went up to two pounds and eight shillings a week (£65 today) and I became entitled to forty-two days' leave a year.

Thereafter life moved very fast. My chance of becoming a JUO disappeared when I and my other friends from Fort George who had passed RCB were posted to Mons Officer Cadet School in Aldershot. Mons, the OCTU for Royal Armoured Corps and Royal Artillery cadets, had a Sandhurst Company for those waiting to go to Sandhurst. In our case we had to wait until 20 January when our first term would begin. I moved to Mons the day after my return from RCB. Sadly Peter Grant didn't come on to Mons. After being commissioned into the Queen's Own Cameron Highlanders as a National Service officer, he was destined for a very successful civilian career in the City.

I was only on the strength of Mons for forty-two days, about two weeks of which were spent on Christmas leave. Even so, I made more good friends who, along with those from Fort George, would be great companions at Sandhurst and beyond: Geoff Havilland, Tony Gordon, Cedric Mercer, Mike Paxton, Bill Hedges and Colin Scott. I think we received *some* academic and military instruction at Mons, but drill and polishing our kit seemed to occupy most of our time; certainly the famous RSM Brittain of the Coldstream Guards figured prominently in our lives. 'I've never seen anything like it in all my life!' was one of his favourite expressions. Unfortunately for me, he didn't particularly like Highlanders or Light Infantrymen. Why? Because we marched at a different pace to the Guards: they did 120 paces to the minute, whereas we marched slower and the Light Infantry faster. I'm not sure if that was the reason he picked on me on a Saturday morning parade but, as he passed me, he suddenly shouted, 'Dirty hackle, dirty hackle! Take his name! Put him in the book!' I have to admit that my red feathers were by then a bit scruffy, but no one had offered me a new hackle and it had never occurred to me to ask for one. Anyway, my name was taken and I was reported to my Company Sergeant Major but nothing untoward happened.

One day at Mons I found myself on Guard Duty which meant a 'guard mounting parade' with lots of shouting and another fierce inspection, after which we were sent to the guardroom until it was our turn to patrol the barracks for two hours in pairs during the night. We had pick handles as weapons. I'm not sure what we were guarding for, as far as I could see, apart from the armoury, there was nothing of value in the barracks. All I can remember during my patrol was getting very cold and hiding in a dark corner to have a cigarette whilst my partner kept lookout in case the guard commander appeared. Another minor memory of that time was going down to the large NAAFI Club in Aldershot, one of the first in the whole country, which was on a sort of island at the bottom of a hill. We went there in quite a large group, just in case we were set upon by those with no particular liking for future officers. Nothing untoward happened, thank goodness.

So ended my time in Sandhurst Company. On 20 January 1949, along with 103 other cadets from Mons, I arrived at the Royal Military Academy Sandhurst (RMAS), still wearing my 'dirty hackle' but a very proud young man.

Chapter Three

Sandhurst

Arriving at Sandhurst, the 104 Mons cadets joined approximately 120 others who had reached the Academy on the same day through a different system. As civilians, they had had to pass the written Civil Service examination for the Army and Civil Service before passing RCB. Only after succeeding in both tests were they called up as regular soldiers and sent for some fourteen weeks training in their chosen Corps or Arm. My close friend Brigadier Tony Baxter is a good example: following the Civil Service exam and RCB, he spent six weeks in the REME Training Battalion at Blandford, and another six weeks' infantry training with the Lancashire Fusiliers at Knook Camp near Warminster, followed by a two-week REME final indoctrination course at Arborfield, before arrival at the RMA.

Of the 225 or so of us who started at Sandhurst that day, all male, only 214 would be commissioned as second lieutenants eighteen months later. The others were either relegated for an extra term's training or, having failed the course for one reason or another, had been sent back to their Corps or Arm or discharged from the Army. One very unfortunate cadet in my Company finished the whole course, but was not allowed to pass out or be commissioned. We were all shocked and never found out why. Intake V, as we were known, joined roughly 500 other cadets who had already been at Sandhurst for either six months or a year. The full training course in those days was eighteen months. Having just arrived, we were the Junior Intake – known as 'Juniors'; those with six months behind them were 'Intermediates' and those with twelve months 'Seniors'.

Before the Second World War, Sandhurst had been the Royal Military College, responsible for training cavalry and infantry officers. Officers for the technical corps, the Royal Regiment of Artillery and the Corps of Royal Engineers, had been trained at the Royal Military Academy at Woolwich, known as the 'Shop' as it had begun life in a converted workshop of Woolwich Arsenal. In the interwar years Woolwich had also trained officers for the Royal Signals and about half of Royal Tank Corps' officers. Both establishments had been closed on the outbreak of war when officer training had to be accelerated and greater numbers absorbed. After the war, they were combined on the Sandhurst site as the Royal Military Academy Sandhurst (RMAS).

The RMAS was divided into three Colleges, each with four companies of three platoons. With twenty-three other Juniors I joined the seventy-eight Intermediates and Seniors of Dettingen Company, three of whom came from the colonies or former colonies. I should have written *Sovereign's* Company rather than Dettingen because the Company had won the Sovereign's, or Champion, Company competition the previous term and thus was accorded the honour of bearing that name. As such we held, and carried on formal Academy parades, the Sovereign's Banner and wore a red, blue and yellow lanyard on our left shoulder. Red was Old College's colour, blue New College's and yellow that of Victory College.

As a member of Old College and the Sovereign's Company, one immediately felt superior to everyone else. Old College was housed in the attractive Georgian building with the Grand Entrance that appears on virtually every photograph of Sandhurst. Built in 1812, it was the home of the Royal Military College until 1939. New and Victory Colleges were not so fortunate, being housed in much less attractive Edwardian buildings, to the east of Old College. Due to a lack of accommodation, about a third of their cadets lived in Nissen huts behind the main College buildings, well out of sight of the general public.

Dettingen Company was on the first floor on the west side of Old College; Blenheim Company was below us, with Inkerman and Waterloo Companies on the east side. Behind Old College was Chapel Square with some Georgian houses where senior staff members lived. The Commandant, Major General Hughie Stockwell, had a large house in the grounds. We didn't see a lot of him, but he often walked across Old College Square on his way to his office and would always give us a cheery smile and a relaxed salute in return for our rather stiffer and more formal ones. A popular Commandant, I was reminded recently of the occasion when he was driving the Sandhurst coach and four to Royal Ascot and was held up by four cadets dressed as highwaymen. The day ended with him buying them champagne!

The Royal Memorial Chapel behind Old College has a very special place in the hearts of all who have passed through the Academy. It is the second chapel to be built at Sandhurst; the original, from 1813, remains part of Old College, known today as the Indian Army Memorial Room, a magnificent room with a huge central chandelier. Originally Christ Church but now the Royal Memorial Chapel, the second chapel was built in 1879 and later enlarged to commemorate Sandhurst-trained officers killed during the Great War. Externally a rather ugly red-brick building, it has a beautiful interior with about 4,000 officers commemorated on its walls and pillars; its memorials range from campaigns in South Africa, Sudan, Burma, Afghanistan and India, to those of both world wars. More recent memorials recognize the many campaigns in which the British Army has been involved since 1945. Each company had its allotted place in the Chapel; in an amazing coincidence, my normal pew was situated directly below the names of Black Watch officers killed in the Great War. In December 1948, just before I arrived at the Academy, a 'Model Room' at the rear of Old College on the east side had been turned into a Roman Catholic Chapel.

We still wore battledress at Sandhurst – none of today's smart blue uniforms – but with leather rather than web belts for daily use and white for ceremonial parades. The Academy's motto, 'Serve to Lead', was part of the silver badge we wore in our berets; I still have mine. That motto sums up the ethos of Sandhurst and is, in modern parlance, the 'mission statement' of a British Army officer. Although the training programme has changed over the years, as has the length of the course, the Academy's core function remains enshrined in that motto.

My eighteen months at Sandhurst were very busy but very rewarding. Discipline was strict and administered on the drill square by the NCOs and WOs – RSMs, CSMs and sergeants. Within Companies, Senior cadets were responsible for discipline with the most senior cadet carrying the rank of Senior Under Officer (SUO). Below him were three Junior Under Officers (JUOs), a Senior Cadet Sergeant, four Cadet Sergeants and about a dozen Cadet Corporals. The SUO and JUOs wielded immense power and could put the fear of God into the Juniors. My SUO, David Naylor-Leyland, frightened me more than any officer or WO. Commissioned into the Grenadier Guards in July 1949, he later commanded the bearer party at King George VI's funeral in 1952. I saw him two years later in Cassis in the South of France – he was sitting beside a very beautiful girl in a Jaguar XK 120 but, needless to say, didn't recognize me!

The Academy Sergeant Major (senior Warrant Officer) in 1949 was RSM J. C. Lord, Grenadier Guards. Famous throughout the Army, he had been captured at Arnhem and was later appointed MBE for his actions during captivity. Taking control of his PoW camp, his rigid discipline and high standards ensured such excellent morale amongst the prisoners that it was said that their morale and discipline exceeded that of the liberating troops. Immaculately dressed in a tailored uniform and carrying a mahogany pace-stick, he introduced himself to Intake V on the Old College Square. Standing on a table at the top of the King's Walk he said, 'My name is Lord, J. C. Lord,' before pointing his pace-stick skywards and adding, 'He's Lord up there and I'm Lord down here.' Every cadet admired him and, on a recent visit, I was delighted to see that he is commemorated by having an Old College ante-room named after him.

RSM Lord usually took the Academy Parade on Saturday mornings, although sometimes the Academy Adjutant, Major Charles Earle, Grenadier Guards, took command, mounted on his horse called, for some extraordinary reason, 'James Pigg'. He was usually accompanied by the Assistant Adjutant, Captain Desmond Lambert, Irish Guards, riding a black mare. In my day the RMA had its own band under the direction of Lieutenant, later Captain, Thirtle which always accompanied Ceremonial, Academy and Passing Out Parades – the latter being officially titled the Sovereign's Parade.

Below Jack Lord in relation to us was our Old College RSM, Drummy Tankard, also a Grenadier, and below him our CSM, Bill Nash, yet another Grenadier. Nash was liked and admired by all and, not surprisingly, later became Academy RSM. He taught us how to *give* orders on drill parades as well as take them, telling us to use the word 'hipe' instead of 'arms' when shouting 'slope arms' or 'order arms' as this was sharper and would carry farther. Some sergeants also taught us words, often rather rude, to various marches like 'Colonel Bogey' by singing them as we marched off parade, out of the hearing of Jack Lord and 'Drummy' Tankard. I was very disappointed to witness a fall in the standard of drill instructor on returning to the Academy recently. Cadets were practising for a Sovereign's Parade and I had to give way in my car as one Company was being marched towards Old College Square. There was nothing wrong with the cadets, but, oh dear, the very tall Coldstream drill sergeant (Colour Sergeant) in charge was not marching in step with them – he was ambling, loping, along beside them.

My Company commander was Major Jimmy Carr, a Canadian in the British Royal Engineers while our College commander was Lieutenant Colonel Jeff Linton DSO, RA who lived in Le Marchant House, which was attached to Old College by a colonnade on its west side. My platoon commander was Captain the Lord Douglas Gordon DSO, Black Watch, and there were five other captains in the Company; they instructed us in various military subjects. Also attached to Old College were at least four civilian instructors who taught academic subjects, the most memorable being Mr 'Jaw' Priestly MA. Another officer whom most of us liked was Captain Dick Worsley, Rifle Brigade, the Academy Weapon Training Officer, who would be my Corps Commander when I commanded a Brigade in Germany.

Mornings began with Breakfast Roll Call (BRC) on Le Marchant Square in front of the College commander's house to make sure everyone was present and not only properly but smartly dressed. Afternoons were devoted to sport with military or academic instruction resumed after tea. Senior cadets carried out inspections. Retribution for any wrongdoing was instant with punishments including marking time on a nearby slope – very painful on the calf muscles – and close order drill in double time. BRC was followed by breakfast and an Intake, Company, College or Academy drill parade before lessons in military or academic subjects held in Halls of Study. Military subjects included the organization of Army formations and units, map-reading, military law, use of radios and radio procedures, how to make military 'appreciations of the situation', how to give formal orders, administration and resupply within a Division, how to keep accounts, how to write formal letters and accept formal invitations – and other things I have long since forgotten. We were not, however, taught weapon training or higher tactics but given a general knowledge of the Army and how it was organized and run and sometimes felt that we were being trained as divisional rather than platoon commanders. However, we knew we would be sent on 'special to arm' courses after commissioning – in my case, weapons and tactics courses at the Schools of Infantry at Hythe and Warminster. Academically, we had to study mathematics, a language and Modern Subjects or science. I chose Modern Subjects, which included literature and history, with German as my language course.

Drill and polishing our boots, belts and rifles took up a lot of our time; looking back I would say far too *much* time. We were issued with .303 rifles which we kept in our rooms but spent more time polishing their woodwork than firing them (I fired mine only about once each term). They, and our bayonets, were considered essential ceremonial accoutrements rather than weapons. Civilian batmen, usually retired soldiers, cleaned our rooms and made our beds and, if we paid them extra, also polished some of our kit. However, our 'best' boots, leather waist-belt and rifle were our personal responsibility and these, and ironing battledresses, took much time in the evenings. As the Sovereign's Company competition approached towards the end of each term, the intensity of inspections increased accordingly. The drill competition was just one part of the whole competition which included most sports and even our performance in the gymnasium. Dettingen was the Sovereign's Company when we arrived and we were over the moon when we won it again the following July. Although we lost it to Waterloo Company in December 1949, we won it back by the smallest of margins from Blenheim just before passing out in July 1950 – 137 points against 132. As well as the Sovereign's Banner already mentioned, a superb silver centrepiece was also awarded; it stood on one of our tables in the Dining Hall.

For our first term we each had to share a room with another cadet. It was very basic with just a washbasin, two beds, two wardrobes, two desks and two chairs. Mine looked out onto the roof of the Dining Hall at the rear of Old College and part of Chapel Square. Bathrooms and toilets were farther down the corridor and our Company Ante-Room, called the Salamanca Room, with leather armchairs and polished tables, was at the front of the building. Downstairs, in the rear of the building, was a shop, beside which was our large Dining Hall with two tables for each Company. As well as all meals, we attended a monthly formal dinner night there when the Old College officers dined with us, the Academy band played, port was passed and we drank the Loyal Toast. The Dining Hall was, and remains, a very pleasant room with Victorian coloured glass, demi-lune windows.

There was great emphasis on sport at Sandhurst and I participated in most of the major team games. I never made any of the Academy teams but played rugger and boxed for my Company. PT was an important part of our training. We went to the large gymnasium (today the Montgomery gymnasium) at least three times a week for strenuous workouts at the end of which we had a shower. I mention this because there was quite a routine attached to it. Having stripped off and clutching our towels, the PT officer, Major Shuttleworth, would shout, 'In through the indoor, out through the outdoor – TOWELS!' As time in the showers was severely limited, this led to a mad rush for the 'indoor' and a scramble for the showers. Much laughter was involved as we fought our way in and out through the only two doors.

Money was a problem for most, but not all, of us. As well as my forty-eight shillings gross weekly pay (£63.20 today or £3,286 a year), my father gave me a pound per week 'allowance' (£26.30 today) but this was hardly enough to indulge in a 'high life'. Some of my fellow cadets were pretty well off – in Dettingen alone we had a future Marquis and two Lords. I remember one looking up from his newspaper at breakfast one day and saying, 'Oh look, Nigel, she's wearing Mummy's tiara!' The 'she' was in fact our future Queen. Some of the more privileged even had cars, but were not allowed to keep them within three miles of the Academy and so we never saw them 'taking off' for London.

Our first term was designed to reduce any tendencies we had to be individuals and ensure that we became a highly-disciplined group through drill and frequent inspections. The object of drill is not *just* to train soldiers to take part in ceremonial parades, but to ensure that they react instantly to orders. It involves much shouting and, even though the Sergeant Majors always ended their tirades with a 'Sir', one certainly knew one's place. Occasionally punishments were inflicted on those considered 'idle on parade' or not carrying their rifles at the correct angle.

The unfortunate cadet might have to double down to Queen Victoria's statue at the beginning of the King's Walk with his rifle held above his head. On one famous occasion Jack Lord made someone whose 'present arms' he didn't like double down and do another 'present' to Queen Victoria.

Another rather demeaning event in the first term was the Inter-Company 'Junior Steeplechase', a fairly long run through the woods in the grounds. This involved jumping or clambering over fences, splashing through about twenty yards of the 'Lower' lake and crossing the Wish Stream (a muddy stream running through the Academy grounds), which was far too wide to jump. One ended up fairly exhausted and covered in mud, much to the delight of the Seniors and Intermediates who had already suffered it. In uniform, Juniors had to march with arms swinging properly and eyes looking to the front everywhere they went outside the Academy buildings – another way of emphasizing our inferiority in the pecking order.

As at Fort George, we were not allowed out until we had 'Passed off the Square' at the end of our sixth week when we could come and go more or less as we wished during our free time and at weekends after the Saturday morning drill parade. However, if we were spending the Saturday night away we had to have a signed leave pass.

The shortage of money meant that the distance most of us could travel was rather restricted with the Odeon in Camberley and Mr Dunn's 'Wayside Inn' in York Town usually as far as many of us went. Mr Dunn's was a marvellous place where, for about two shillings and sixpence (just under £3.30 today), we could get a mixed grill, toast and marmalade and a cup of coffee. Although Dunn was a miserable-looking old chap and had one of the ugliest waitresses you could imagine, that didn't put us off. Food at the RMA wasn't at all bad but food rationing was still in force (and didn't end completely until 1954) and an extra meal was always welcome.

I went up to London a number of times and, occasionally, by train to Reading. One memorable visit, for the wrong reasons, was to Royal Ascot. A supposedly 'knowledgeable' cadet advised me that if I bet on all the favourites and kept doubling up on any losses, I would end up a winner. I'd never been to a proper race meeting before, only 'point to points' and had never gambled on a horse in my life, so I foolishly took his advice. Needless to say, I lost all my money and have never had anything more than a little 'flutter' since that day.

Among my memories of our training at the RMA are the 1949 and 1950 Kermit Roosevelt Memorial lectures in the Woolwich Hall, the first given by General 'Lightning' Joe Collins, wartime commander of the US

VII Corps in Normandy and the Battle of the Bulge, and the second by General Gruenther, Director Joint Staff, US Forces. And in May 1950 Field Marshal Montgomery spoke to us and gave us one minute to get any coughing over before he began.

One memorable demonstration we attended was at Frensham Ponds for watermanship training run by the Royal Engineers. Another vivid memory is of the exams at the end of each term which Old College cadets sat in a large hall just to the north of the Chapel, which became the first home of the National Army Museum and is now an indoor riding school, the conversion having been paid for by the Sultan of Brunei.

I made many friends at Sandhurst, a number of whom I still see. Our intake has held four reunions (1995, 2000, 2005 and 2010) that have helped us to keep in touch. The first two were held in the superb Royal Artillery Mess at Woolwich and I organized the 2005 Reunion in the Army and Navy Club in London where forty-nine sat down to a good lunch. Our sixtieth anniversary reunion was held back at the RMAS, but illness prevented me attending. Sadly, eighty-three of our intake are known to have died (35 per cent).

My closest friends, in order of seniority in our final term, and the Regiments and Corps in which they were commissioned, were: Robin Cavendish (Greenjackets); Geoff Havilland (Royal Leicesters); Tony (Julian) Gordon (10th Royal Hussars); Colin Scott (Gurkhas); Tony Baxter (REME); Douglas Montague-Douglas Scott (Irish Guards); David Saunders (Welsh Guards); Ben Smith (Royal Northumberland Fusiliers); John Law (Royal Irish Fusiliers); Nigel Napier (Scots Guards); and Bill Hedges (Royal Berkshires). Poor Robin caught polio in Kenya after leaving the Army and died in the nineties while Colin Scott, John Law, Douglas Montague Douglas-Scott and David Saunders have also sadly passed away – as has my very good friend from Fort George, Eaton Hall and Mons days, Bill Westland. Although Bill was in New College we stayed close friends, even spending the summer leave of 1949 together. My oldest *close* friend is Tony Baxter. I was his best man in 1954 and we served together in Northern Ireland in 1974 and in Germany in 1976. We live within forty miles of each other in Sussex and, for some twenty-five years now, we, and our very loyal wives, have met for lunch or some other event roughly once a month.

One of my nicest memories of my early days at Sandhurst is of our present Queen, as Princess Elizabeth, taking the salute at Intake III's Sovereign's Parade at the end of my first term. I was in the front rank of the Sovereign's Company and, as she carried out her inspection and spoke to one or two cadets, I had an awful feeling that she was going to stop and talk to *me*. Sure enough it happened. We were under strict instructions to keep our heads up and eyes to the front when on parade, but I was damned if I wasn't going to look down at my future Queen. I found her to be much shorter than I'd imagined and I looked into the face of one of the loveliest women I've ever seen. Her eyes were absolutely beautiful and her complexion perfect. She asked me which Regiment I was hoping to join and I said, 'The Queen's Royal Regiment, your Royal Highness.' 'Oh,' she said, 'My grandmother's Regiment!' 'Yes, Mam [as in jam],' I replied. The Colonel in Chief of the Queen's was indeed her grandmother, Queen Mary, widow of King George V. I don't think our conversation happened by chance. I'm sure she had been briefed to stop in front of the second chap from the end. Little did I realize that twenty-seven years later I would chair a debate at the Royal College of Defence Studies in Belgrave Square with her sitting less than six feet from me or that, thirty-four years later, she would make me a Companion of the Most Honourable Order of the Bath in Buckingham Palace.

So why did I choose the Queen's Royal Regiment? During my first term my platoon commander, Captain the Lord Douglas Gordon, interviewed me and asked if I wished to be commissioned into the Black Watch, telling me that a cadet in another College, Peter Carthew, whose father and grandfather had served in the Regiment, would certainly get one of the two vacancies, but that I could try for the other one. He said I would be very welcome. Having thought it over for a few days, I told him that, as I wasn't a real Scot, I would probably feel a bit out of place whenever the Battalion was serving in Scotland, or if I was posted to the Depot at Perth, and that maybe I should apply for a good English regiment. He said the lack of Scottish blood was no problem; I would still be very welcome. Shortly afterwards, I was walking down Old College's main corridor wearing a blazer and Old Cranleighan tie, when a major in the East Surrey Regiment, Clive Wallace, stopped me. He said he was an Old Cranleighan too and asked which Regiment I hoped to join. When I said I wasn't sure he responded with, 'Well my boy, you should join the Regiment whose badge you wore at school – the Queen's!' Looking up the history of the Queen's, I found that it was not only the senior English Regiment of the Line, being the 2nd of Foot and formed in 1661, but had a wonderful record. In the Second World War it had two battalions in the Far East and two complete brigades that fought in North Africa and Italy, with one going on to Normandy and into Germany. It didn't take me long to make up my mind. A few weeks later, I was summoned for an interview with General Sir George Giffard GCB DSO, Colonel of the Regiment. After tea and a few questions, he said, 'Well Reynolds, if you can manage to pass out reasonably well, I shall be delighted to have you.'

As I've already said, money was always in short supply, but I supplemented my pay and small allowance with a holiday job my father found for me. He was very friendly with the Managing Director of the Austin Motor Company at Longbridge who arranged for me to work for a small business delivering new cars from the factory to a major distribution centre on Vauxhall Bridge Road in London. This meant driving through the very centre of the capital which was quite challenging for a nineteen-year-old. I was paid £1 a trip (£26.30 today) and, to save money, often 'hitched' my way back carrying the 'trade plates' from the vehicle; they usually ensured that I got a lift fairly quickly. There were no large vehicle carriers in those days, no motorways and even the A-roads were much narrower. If you could *average* 30 mph on a long journey, in any vehicle, you considered you had done well.

At the beginning of our Intermediate term I was surprised to find that I had been promoted to Cadet Corporal. This was good news as it indicated that, barring something very untoward, I was in the running to be, at best, the Dettingen SUO in my final term and, at worst, cadet Senior Sergeant. In the event I was promoted to be a JUO.

I liked being a cadet 'boss' with the power to tell Juniors to do this and that, but I don't think any of us ever bullied them in a nasty way – I hope not anyway. Among our privileges as Seniors in Old College was a private bar which is still there today as 'Topper's Bar'. As a JUO I was very happy to see two Juniors from Cranleigh in Dettingen for my last term. I also noted a tall, good-looking chap called Peter Field who told me that he hoped to join the Queen's Royal Regiment. Little did we know then that he would be my 'best man' and I would be his within a very few years.

One very memorable event of our last term was on 7 May when we marched through the centre of London in the 1950 'Army Day' Parade. A special train carried 430 Seniors and Intermediates and the RMA Band to Waterloo. We were then, according to the *Wish Stream* (Sandhurst's magazine), taken to Chelsea Barracks for lunch. I've no idea how we got there, or to Wellington Barracks, the forming-up point for the march. The magazine says we had to wait a long time before setting off as we were at the rear of a very long column. We finally set off with Charles Earle leading, mounted this time on a horse provided by the Life Guards, followed by the Fifes and Corps of Drums of the Coldstream Guards. We marched with rifles at the slope and bayonets fixed, along Birdcage Walk, past the Palace, up Constitution Hill, through Hyde Park, where Bill Slim took the salute, and then past the Serpentine, along Knightsbridge and back to Wellington Barracks. We arrived back at the RMA late that evening, tired but quite elated.

Our final term saw other notable events and parades. On 24 January and 10 May we performed ceremonial parades for the Indian and

Pakistani High Commissioners respectively, and on 6 June (D Day) another for French General de Lattre de Tassigny, the Commander Land Forces, Western Union. We also witnessed a number of spectacular floodlit Tattoos and Retreats. On 23 May the Royal Marines beat Retreat, the massed bands of the Brigade of Guards beat Retreat and Tattoo on 20 and 29 June and the Pipes and Drums of the Black Watch performed for us on 6 July. They were all superb spectacles that made us immensely proud to be in the Army.

Preparing to be an officer included going up to London to be fitted for Service Dress and Blues and accompanying hats. Although we received a uniform allowance of £120 (£3,060 today), it wasn't enough and we also had to have decent civilian suits once we were officers. Joining a London Club was encouraged: those with enough money, and in the appropriate Regiments, joined the Guards and Cavalry Clubs or one like the Naval & Military ('In & Out'). I couldn't afford anything like that, but was accepted by the United Hunts Club in Grosvenor Street and felt very grand.

The final exams also produced a cliff-hanger. I knew I had done well, but had no idea exactly *how* well. A few days before our Sovereign's Parade, Jimmy Carr organized a Passing Out party at the 'Cricketers' in Bagshot and, during a quiet moment, took me aside to say that I was in the running for the King's Medal. However, I passed out second – there were 237 cadets in my Intake. Although there was great disappointment within the Company, none of us knew that there was to be a nice surprise for me. As the senior future infantryman in the Order of Merit, I would, at a later date, be awarded the Infantry Prize, a beautiful silver statuette of an infantry soldier. My immediate disappointment at missing out on the King's Medal was softened by the news that, as one of the first twenty in the Order of Merit, I was to receive a cheque for £60 (£1,530 today), money left over from the scholarship scheme of pre-war days when one had to *pay* to go to Sandhurst.

One of the more amusing lectures we were given just before Passing Out was by the Chief Medical Officer whose final words have stayed with me to this day: 'Well, you've learned a lot in the last eighteen months, but I'm now going to tell you the most important thing of all. Just remember that no matter how many times you shake it, the last drops will always go down your trouser leg!'

A not so amusing thing occurred on 14 July as we were coming off one of the final rehearsals for our Sovereign's Parade. We always marched off the Square to the east and then round to the back of Old College where we were 'fallen out' in Chapel Square. This took us past the Adjutant's Office in Academy Headquarters, a building attached to Old College by a colonnade on the east side. As a JUO I was marching alongside the main body of the Company and happened to say quietly to one of my friends that I thought it had been a good rehearsal. Little did I know that Charles Earle was looking out of his open office window and had seen and perhaps even heard this terrible crime. By the time I reached our Company lines I had been charged with 'Conduct unbecoming of a Junior Under Officer, i.e. talking when marching off parade'. Later that morning I appeared in front of Jimmy Carr and was 'Reprimanded'. I think I saw a smile on his face though as I was turned to the right to be marched out. I still have that rare document – my 'Officer Cadet Conduct Sheet' signed by Major J. G. Carr RE.

Our final days passed very quickly. On Wednesday 19 July we had our 'Farewell and Dedication Service for the Cadets of the Senior Division' in the Memorial Chapel, a moving service that began with the hymn 'Now thank we all Our God' and ended with 'I vow to thee, my country'. The main prayer was: 'May the strength of God pilot you and the power of God preserve you. May the wisdom of God instruct you and the way of God direct you. May the hand of God protect you and the shield of God defend you.' A number of us would need help and protection from God sooner than we thought.

On Thursday the 20th we had our Seniors' Farewell Dinner. Mr Thirtle and the RMA Band played throughout. It was a super evening but I'm sure we didn't drink too much though, for the following morning, Friday 21 July, would see our Sovereign's Parade.

The Senior Division marched onto Old College Square to the music of 'Here we are again' and 'On the Square'. The rest of the Academy was already there, formed up by half Colleges in line, with Sovereign's Company (Dettingen again) with the King George V Banner on the right. His Royal Highness, General the Duke of Gloucester then arrived and was greeted with a Royal Salute. After he had inspected the parade, we marched past in slow and then quick time with the Seniors leading before advancing in Review Order for a rather mumbled and very short address from the Duke, who presented the Sword of Honour and King's Medal to Peter Burdick and Tom Lindley respectively. Finally, after another Royal Salute, and with the rest of the Academy presenting arms, we marched up the steps of Old College to the tune of 'For Auld Lang Syne', with Charles Earle mounted on 'James Pigg' following us. With a cheer we ran down the corridors to our respective Company lines where we could change into civilian clothes and join our families and friends for lunch.

That evening we had our Commissioning Ball. I don't remember a lot about it except that we danced to Edmundo Ross's famous rumba band in the beautifully decorated gym and that there was a sitting out, or maybe another dance-floor, under the trees outside. At one minute past midnight we certainly all gave a great cheer for at that moment we became Second Lieutenants.

About a week later I received a letter from the War Office dated 27 July. The first paragraph reads: 'His Majesty having been graciously pleased to appoint you to a Second Lieutenancy in The Queen's Royal Regiment (West Surrey), I am directed to inform you that you will ultimately proceed to BAOR [British Army on the Rhine] for service with the 1st Battalion. You will be prepared to proceed overseas by sea on or after 5th September 1950.'

Chapter Four

Subaltern in Germany

Early in the afternoon of 21 August 1950 with nine other RMA graduates I reported to the Adjutant of the 1st Battalion, Royal West Kent
Regiment (1 RWK) in Sir John Moore Barracks, Shorncliffe, the unit
responsible for training recruits for battalions of the Home Counties
Brigade. At Sandhurst we had been told to report in civilian clothes, but
the Adjutant had other ideas and told us to report again next morning in
uniform. Worse followed when we went into the ante-room for tea and
were greeted by a crusty old major who flung his paper down and disappeared, shouting 'The bloody place has turned into a Kindergarten!'
After tea we asked a member of the Mess staff where our rooms were.
Taking us upstairs he showed me and two or three others into an attic
room with single iron beds, no sheets or pillow cases: the only ones they
had were already in use. This was more than enough for me. I telephoned
the Adjutant of the Depot of the Queen's Royal Regiment (officially
abbreviated to Queen's), in Stoughton Barracks, Guildford and told him
what had happened. He asked if I had enough money to get to Guildford
and, when I said yes, told me to get a train next morning and report to
him on arrival. When I enquired whether I should be in uniform he said
'Of course not!' before adding that he would clear my forthcoming
absence from Moore barracks with the RWK adjutant.

After a night that reminded me of my first in the Army, I arrived at
Stoughton Barracks, received a warm greeting from the Adjutant, was
given a nice room to myself in the Mess and made to feel completely at
home.

Recruit training at Stoughton had ceased in 1949 and it was now the
Regimental Headquarters of the Queen's although this changed a year
later when infantry recruit training shifted back to small regimental
depots. With little for me to do during my two weeks in Guildford while
I waited for the order to join the 1st Battalion (1 Queen's) in Germany, I
had plenty of time off to enjoy myself and was certainly happy to be back
in the Guildford/Cranleigh area.

The order to move came on 5 September. Next day, I went by train to

Harwich to join other officers and soldiers for an overnight military ferry to the Hook of Holland where several military trains waited to take everyone to their various places of duty – in my case, and that of a National Service Officer, Dortmund in the Ruhr.

Our journey was particularly memorable. Passing through the Ruhr we were shocked to see mile after mile of rubble with hardly a building that hadn't been flattened or damaged by wartime bombing. Even more surprising were the whiffs of smoke rising from what looked like piles of bricks: people were living under the rubble and in wrecked apartment blocks five years after the war.

At Dortmund station we were met by the Battalion 15-cwt water truck. This was part of our 'initiation' into 1 Queen's set up by the 'senior subaltern'. We had no option other than to pile ourselves and our suitcases into the cab with the driver. Once out of Dortmund, past a number of surprisingly undamaged Nazi-built barracks now occupied by British units, mainly artillery, the sixteen-mile drive to Iserlohn was through very pleasant country. Iserlohn we found to be an attractive town completely undamaged by the war. Aldershot Barracks (now demolished), where the Battalion was quartered, was on a hill north-west of the town centre and had been the home of the 1st Battalion of the 24th Flak (anti-aircraft) Regiment throughout the war and was typical of the excellent modern barracks of the Hitler era. Also in the town were the 1st Battalion Royal Fusiliers and 10th Royal Hussars. The Queen's Officers' Mess was in a separate building over a railway bridge outside Aldershot barracks. We had our meals there but there were only two or three bedrooms in the building which were occupied by captains. The subalterns lived in a block in the main barracks that had been converted to house Battalion Headquarters on the ground floor with our bedrooms on the first. Most married captains and majors, and the Commanding Officer (CO), lived in requisitioned German houses in the town. My room was pleasant enough with a large iron single bed, desk and chair, armchair and occasional table. The walls had military prints on them and I looked out onto the main gate, guardroom and medical block.

Within the first twenty-four hours I had a great disappointment and a real surprise. The disappointment was that the Battalion was seriously understrength. The Korean War had broken out in June and 1 Queen's had been ordered to send a major and 149 other ranks to reinforce the 1st Battalion, Middlesex Regiment which had deployed there. With no platoon for me to command, I found myself with little to do and was just a spare subaltern in B Company. There were three other regular subalterns in the Battalion and seven National Service subalterns.

The surprise came when I discovered that officers in 1 Queen's wore *brown* boots. At Sandhurst no one had mentioned this and, at Stoughton, the Adjutant wore, like me, black boots. Furthermore, in two days' time, 9 September, it would be Salerno Day, one of two Regimental days, with the Colonel of the Regiment, General Sir George Giffard, taking the salute at a full ceremonial parade. Not only that, but I was told I would have to march out in front of the Battalion to receive the Infantry Prize from him. 'What's that, Sir?' I asked the Adjutant. 'Oh, come on, you must know!' Nobody believed me, but I didn't. It was the silver statuette mentioned in the previous chapter.

On 9 September, and in borrowed brown boots, I was duly awarded my prize. General Sir George read out a personal message from our Colonel-in-Chief, Queen Mary, which, rather embarrassingly, included some words of congratulation addressed to me personally. That evening all officers were invited to a Ball in the Warrant Officers' and Sergeants' Mess.

Our CO, Jimmy Sykes Wright DSO, was a charming man, but I didn't see much of him. My Company commander was Major Bill Peet MC, with Captain Geoffrey Curtis MC as second in command. Both were great characters and charming men who had fought in the war. The Battalion's most highly decorated officer was Major David Lloyd Owen DSO MC whom I hardly knew as he commanded a different Company and left shortly after I arrived to be Military Assistant to the Commander-in-Chief in Malaya. I didn't realize it at the time but David would play a major role in my career and become a close friend.

'Dining In' every Thursday and Guest Nights were always great fun. Bill Peet was a great performer on these occasions, singing songs and organizing 'mess rugby'. One of the most extraordinary things in the Mess was a 'vomitorium' in the toilet area, a huge porcelain bowl at waist height, with two chrome handles above it on the wall for the drunken user to grasp. I never saw one used and, before long, they were removed from all British messes.

We were still an Army of Occupation in 1950 and had to wear uniform every time we left barracks. It has been said that when you walked along a pavement at that time the Germans would make way for you but that five years later, when West Germany was admitted to NATO, the largest person stayed on the pavement and that five years after that the British made way for the Germans.

In those days we were paid in BAFVs (British Armed Forces Vouchers) which we could spend only in Barracks, the NAAFI, the Army cinema (SKC) and the Officers' Club. This was to protect sterling and stop us exchanging it for Deutschemarks but we rarely went beyond the 'British' environment. Our pay was pathetic: mine was £260 a year (£6,640 a year today) while a National Service second lieutenant received only £190 (£4,850). Thus we spent most of our time in the Mess or the Officers' Club, which was in a large mansion in its own grounds on the edge of the town. In the Mess and the Club the drinks were duty free – 25p at today's prices for a gin and tonic. Dinner at the Club, run by the NAAFI, was cheap too. Furthermore, on the edge of the Möhnesee, where there was an Army Sailing Club, there was another Officers' Club, with excellent food, in another large requisitioned house. With Möhnesee less than thirty miles away, we went there quite often. This was the scene of the famous Dambusters' raid and one really has to go there to understand the fantastic flying and bravery of those involved in that successful attack.

Our training was predictable and, in the main, boring: drill, PT, weapon training, occasional live firing, route marching and gas drills. The last involved wearing our masks for an hour every Monday morning. We hardly ever saw a tank or artillery piece and never an armoured personnel carrier. As 'heavy' infantry we marched everywhere, except on very rare occasions when 'troop carrying vehicles' (TCVs) were provided for a specific move, such as the one to get us out to our start point for Exercise BROADSIDE, a huge exercise at the end of September involving virtually all of BAOR, then more than 50,000 men strong (total army strength then was 467,000). BROADSIDE was memorable in that all we seemed to do was to 'dig in', move and 'dig in' again. I don't think we ever saw our 'enemy' and most moves were on our feet. In some ways it was just as well that I was not a platoon commander at this time as I had yet to attend my Platoon Commander's Tactical Course at Warminster and would have had to rely heavily on my platoon sergeant. As it was I didn't make a single decision or give a single order on the entire exercise.

I had only been in Germany for seven weeks when I was sent home to attend a Small Arms Course at the School of Infantry in Hythe, Kent. The Officers' Mess was the only centrally-heated building in the barracks but we students lived in separate Victorian accommodation blocks with individual rooms and one bucket of coal a day for our small fireplaces. This was brought in each morning by civilian batmen who also made our beds and cleaned our rooms and any kit we put out. That November and December were bitterly cold and the coal lasted only a few hours with the result that we spent a few evenings in the Mess, where we had to behave, and the others in a pub in Hythe where we didn't – in my case the White Hart in the High Street. Fortunately the landlord's daughter, who served in the saloon bar, was very keen on a friend of mine in the Royal Hampshires which meant that we were able to carry on imbibing after closing time. I'm not sure this did my course grading a lot of good – I ended up with a C (A was the top and F a fail).

Our indoor instruction was carried out in wooden huts on an island between two arms of the Grand Military Canal. All outdoor activities were on the extensive ranges west of the town where we spent hours in the freezing weather, but at least the huts had coke- (or was it wood?) burning stoves. Again, our training was unexciting – the same old Lee Enfield rifles, Bren and Sten guns. The only excitement was firing a 2-inch mortar, an Energa grenade which was fired from the end of the rifle, and an American 3.5-inch recoilless rocket-launcher which we fired towards a hill where the Channel Tunnel terminus has since been built. I think we were allowed one rocket each.

My squad instructor, a very nice Warrant Officer in the Small Arms School Corps, lived in a tiny official quarter on the Dymchurch Road and was kind and generous enough to invite the seven or eight of us in his squad to Christmas drinks in his house. I remember being shocked to find that a warrant officer should have to live in such a tiny house.

I finished at Hythe on 22 December, having made four more friends whom I would catch up with later in my career – one, in the Royal Norfolks, much sooner than I expected. After Christmas at home and a few weeks back with the Battalion in Iserlohn, I found myself in Hythe again, this time on a three-week Weapon Training Officers' (WTO) course, with more freezing conditions in my room and out on the ranges.

Back in Iserlohn again at the end of March 1951, I found some welcome changes, including a new Adjutant, Captain Douggie Snowdon. I was to be his Assistant Adjutant as well as Battalion Intelligence Officer (IO) and WTO. I was thrilled; I had a desk in Douggie's office and felt very important. But there was a snag. Although I didn't know it then, this appointment meant that I would miss my Infantry Platoon Commanders' course at Warminster and have to learn lower tactics the hard way – through practical experience in Korea.

The next four months passed quickly with many memorable events and 'happenings': Battalion training at Vogelsang near the Belgian border; burning out the clutch on the CO's jeep while driving it cross-country on the Sennelager training area during a 5 Brigade exercise; having, on the same exercise, to lay out white tape for the companies to line up for a Battalion night attack and then having to guide them by advancing along the 'centre-line' with a compass (historical stuff today); riding one of the half dozen requisitioned 'patrol' horses allocated to the Battalion; going up to Hamburg to stay at the requisitioned and NAAFI-run Vierjahrenzeit, five-star hotel; the 'Glorious First of June' (Regimental Day), when officers, petty officers and some ratings of the Royal Navy came up from the 'Rhine Flotilla' to play cricket and generally celebrate with us; carrying the Regimental Colour on the King's Birthday Parade on the Schiller Platz (now a shopping centre) in the centre of Iserlohn – designed to show the Germans who were the victors and who the vanquished in their town; and doing well in the BAOR Small Arms Meeting – I came tenth in the Rhine Army 100 best rifle shots and, with a National Service subaltern, Runner Up in the Bren gun 'pairs'. But the most memorable episode is of going up to Berlin. In case of trouble or even riots on May Day in that divided city, 1 Queen's received a warning order to be prepared to move there at short notice to reinforce the British garrison. Douggie Snowdon, the Quartermaster (QM), Sam Sharpe, and I were to go to Berlin for five days to make the necessary arrangements. In my case, as well as receiving an 'intelligence briefing', I was told to 'get to know the city, East and West', for which I was given a Mercedes and driver and left to myself.

We travelled by military train and stayed at the very pleasant and well-appointed British Officers' Club, the Marlborough. While Douggie and the QM got on with their tasks, I set off to explore. Although there was no Berlin Wall at that time, there were checkpoints between the British, American and French occupation zones and the Russian zone. These were no problem as long as I was in uniform – I was just waved through and indeed saluted. It was fascinating to see Russian soldiers and the parade ground where they were due to carry out a big parade. I was also able to visit the huge Russian war memorial at Treptow, the smaller one near the gutted Reichstag building just inside the British sector with its T-34 tanks and Russian sentry, the badly-damaged Unter den Linden, the Berlin Schloss and the Communist Party HQ with its huge portraits of Lenin, Trotsky and Stalin. In the British zone I was briefed in the Garrison HQ beneath the 1936 Olympic Stadium and saw all the main sights in it and the French and American zones – Gatow, Tegel and Templehof airports, the still badly-damaged Brandenburg Gate, the Kafürstendamn, Charlottenburg, the Tiergarten with a huge, damaged, but almost complete Flak tower halfway on its side after a failed attempt by Royal Engineers to destroy it; Spandau prison where Rudolf Hess was incarcerated and the site of Hitler's bunker with some of its above-ground buildings still visible. It was an unforgettable experience. One could almost feel the tension between East and West and I sometimes wondered if I might run into Harry Lime or one of the other characters depicted in the film *The Third Man*.

The evenings in the Club were also memorable with Sam recounting endless stories including the one about how he, as a private soldier in Quetta immediately after the 1935 earthquake, had been forced to wear his tin hat to protect himself from hail stones as large as hand grenades. And, after a few drinks following dinner, going out with some of the younger officers to a nightclub, inappropriately named 'the St Pauli', very near to the Kaiser Wilhelm Memorial Church.

In August 1951 I took three weeks' leave to accompany my parents on a motoring holiday in southern France. I was very grateful to Douggie for letting me go during the run-up to another large BAOR exercise. I didn't know it at the time, and nor did he or the CO but, apart from a very short return visit to collect my kit, I was leaving the Battalion not just for three *weeks*, but for six and a half *years*.

Chapter Five

En Route to Korea

We arrived home from our south of France holiday on 6 September 1951 in great form and with healthy tans, but our happiness was soon marred by a letter waiting for me from the Adjutant. It was a warning order saying that I was being posted to the 1st Battalion, Royal Norfolk Regiment on active service in Korea. I was to report back by the 9th to collect my kit.

I arrived in Iserlohn as ordered and was 'dined out' at the Salerno Day Guest Night. The CO had been ordered to find a regular second lieutenant for the Norfolks and, since the only other one was in a semi-technical appointment and could not be replaced quickly, I was the only choice. I was also reminded that I had talked about volunteering to fight in Korea on more than one occasion.

Three days later I was back at Stoughton Barracks and, on 15 September, reported to the East Anglian Brigade Depot in Bury St Edmunds, only to be told to go back on leave until they called me. This gave me a marvellous opportunity to visit the Festival of Britain with its Dome of Discovery and engineering and shipping exhibitions on the south bank of the Thames in London.

I remember only a couple of things about my few days in Bury St Edmunds in mid-October before embarking for Korea. One is meeting Ian Minto, a lieutenant in the Buffs, who was also being sent out as a regular reinforcement to the Norfolks, and the other is inspecting the draft of men I was to take with me. One was a corporal who, believe it or not, had *three* Military Medals and had been up and down the ranks like a yoyo and 'busted' as often as he had been promoted. I've no idea what happened to him. He never even made the ship, let alone Korea.

On 28 October Ian and I were ordered to take fifty-nine soldiers, mostly National Servicemen, to London where, after spending the night in military transit accommodation in the Goodge Street Deep Shelter (part of the Underground station), we were to catch a morning troop-train to Liverpool and embark on the troopship *Georgic*.

Our train left London at 9.35 and reached Liverpool docks at 2.15. We passed through Stafford which brought back a lot of memories and finally embarked on the *Georgic* to find that an armoured Regiment, 5th Royal Inniskilling Dragoon Guards, nicknamed the 'Skins', had already boarded and, in the case of officers at least, had taken all the best cabins. Ian and I found ourselves in an inner cabin with metal bunks and no porthole, sharing with four artillery and two Royal Leicester subalterns and hardly room to 'swing a cat'. Then I couldn't find my luggage, which had been unloaded from the train by dockers. After three and a half hours I found it in the hold in spite of four labels attached to it reading 'Cabin deck'.

The *Georgic*, of 27,750 tons and a capacity of more than 1,500 passengers, had been launched in 1931 for the White Star line. Requisitioned as a troopship in 1940, a year later she'd been bombed and badly damaged by German aircraft in the Gulf of Suez. It took three years to repair her before she returned to troopship duties under Cunard-White Star management in 1944. She had no air conditioning and, although the public areas, like dining rooms and lounges, were quite well appointed, the cabins and troop decks below the waterline left a *great* deal to be desired. To my surprise, however, the soldiers seemed quite pleased with their accommodation.

After a good dinner of soup, fish, lamb and ice cream, we sailed at 9 o'clock with a band playing on the quay and many people waving us off. It was quite an emotional moment with many of us wondering if we would ever see 'Blighty' again. I kept a diary of the voyage and my entry for the next day, 30 October, records: 'Read all morning. Good lunch. Slept for most of the afternoon. Good film show in the evening – *The Lavender Hill Mob* with Alex Guinness and Stanley Holloway. The kids in the next cabin are driving us mad! No sign of doing any training yet.' Responsibility for training lay not with any of the officer passengers but with the Ship's Commandant and the CO of the 'Skins', both lieutenant colonels. The 'kids' I referred to were with their mother and were just one of many families on board going out to Singapore or Hong Kong to join their fathers and husbands. An entry on the following day says, 'Many of the men are complaining that they've no money and want paying. Most of them were given two weeks' pay before we sailed but spent it all before they even embarked.'

Our third day at sea took us close to Capes St Vincent and Trafalgar and we entered the Mediterranean with Gibraltar on one side and Tangier on the other at 1 a.m. on 2 November. Algiers followed twenty-four hours later, followed by Bizerta and Cape Bon. Some of the more interesting comments in my diary are worth recalling. '3 Nov: Women in nearby cabins kept us awake until 1.30. They are 3rd class and were rude when we told them to be quiet, but we eventually won. 4 Nov: Saw Malta before breakfast. Church bells rang for morning service at 10 o'clock; quite enjoyable. Aircraft carrier *Warrior* passed us in late evening going towards Suez.'

This was the time of the first 'Suez Crisis'. On 8 October the Egyptian Government had announced that it was going to eject Britain from the Suez Canal Zone and take control. On the 21st British warships arrived at Port Said and the British Government announced that more troops were being sent to Egypt. This was the situation into which we were heading.

In the late evening of 6 November a Royal Navy patrol boat escorted us into an oiling berth in Port Said and, very early next morning, we started down the Canal, led by *Warrior*. British troops were present at regular intervals on the right bank and the Royals, an armoured regiment, gave us a gun salute as we passed. All this was in sharp contrast to the Egyptians who made rude gestures, including shaking their penises at us! We reached Suez in the late afternoon, anchoring alongside a destroyer and minesweeper.

As we sailed through the Red Sea the heat really began to get us down. Before reaching the Red Sea we had done a little, but not much, training – PT and firing a few shots at balloons flying over the stern of the ship. Now, however, it was much too hot and training was cut back even further. I complained in my diary about the lack of activity and generally poor organization on the ship. For example on 10 November, 'Practised boat stations this morning – the men had to stand around for over 45 minutes in searing heat.'

At 5.30 p.m. on the 10th we anchored off Aden. That evening I had to pay the soldiers on one of the troop decks in local currency ready for shore leave the following morning. I found the heat on their deck absolutely appalling. We were only allowed ashore for a couple of hours, but Ian and I managed to visit Crater City and the Gold Mohur Officers' Club where we had a swim. The former was 'very squalid and hot' and Ian got very sunburned at the latter. We sailed immediately after lunch – less one of my soldiers: Private Edwards had been arrested by the Military Police for allegedly trying to steal a watch from a street trader.

We reached Colombo, capital of Ceylon, five days later, during which I had TAB and TT injections which made me feel awful and I had £6 (£140 today) stolen from my wallet. I suspected an officer in my cabin, who never seemed to draw any pay, but couldn't prove anything. Half the passengers went ashore in Colombo on the first evening and the rest of us the following morning. It teemed with rain throughout our visit which took much of the fun out of it and my sudden shortage of money didn't help.

Our two days in Singapore were very memorable. The Pipes and Band of the Cameronians played us in and I was greeted at the bottom of the gang-plank by a prefect I had known at Cranleigh, now a lieutenant in the RASC. He told me that there were three other Old Cranleighans (OCs) in Singapore and, within a couple of hours, I met up with two of them for a wonderful lunch at the Cricket Club. After lunch I watched a match in which one of them was playing, attended a ceremonial parade by the 5th Malay Regiment and then met the fourth OC, who had been with me in Intake V at Sandhurst, back in the clubhouse. He drove me to the famous Princes Hotel where I met up with Ian and three others from our cabin and, amazingly, a friend of Mons and Sandhurst days – Cedric Mercer.

We sailed from Singapore at 7 a.m. on the 23rd. The following evening the 'Skins' threw a cocktail party but, as it started, we ran into a typhoon. Many of us felt seasick. The storm lasted well into the next day with waves breaking right over the bow. My diary for that day reads: 'Heard on the news that a ceasefire has nearly been agreed in Korea. This received on board with mixed feelings. Although we want all wars to end, I feel that after travelling all this way I'd like a gong (medal) and the experience. Don't want to have to go back with no medals and say I arrived after it had all finished.'

At 9 a.m. on the 27th we reached Hong Kong where the harbour was full of ships, including British and American destroyers. Unlike today, there were no skyscrapers. All the remaining families and the four gunners from our cabin disembarked, but we embarked some Royal Navy sailors and Royal Marines. After an early lunch Ian and I went ashore. We started by window shopping in Nathan Road in Kowloon before exploring part of the Chinese quarter where 'Ian was a bit worried. Admittedly it was a bit smelly and sordid and we were the only Europeans there.' Then we took the Star Ferry to Hong Kong island and toured the big shops, booked cinema seats and went up the 'Peak' where the view was unbelievable. After tea at the 'Dairy Farm' we explored the Chinese quarter, met two 'Skins' for drinks in the Hong Kong hotel, better known as 'The Grips', and went to the cinema to see *A Streetcar named Desire* before a superb Chinese dinner in a place called the Chinese Emporium. We were the only Europeans there.

We left Hong Kong at midday on the 28th and that evening I wrote in my diary: 'A lot of the life seems to have gone out of the ship now and Ian and I are a bit depressed. It's gone much cooler.' I think one reason we were depressed was because most of us were beginning to feel a little nervous about the future.

On 1 December we dropped anchor off Pusan at the southern tip of Korea. 'Hell of a lot of shipping in the harbour – mainly US. It's turned very cold. All training has stopped. Can't believe we're now off the little country all the fuss is about and of which none of us had ever heard until a few months ago.'

The following day we docked alongside three hospital ships, two American and one Danish, which did little for our morale. However, to lighten our mood, there were two bands on the quay playing us in with jive music such as the 'St Louis Blues' and 'When the Saints go Marching In'. Later the South Korean President, Syngman Rhee, arrived and the ship's Captain and Commandant were both presented with bouquets of flowers. The 'Skins' then disembarked and went off in lorries whilst the rest of us stayed on board, destined for the Joint Reinforcement Base Depot (JRBD) in Japan, whence we would subsequently be sent over to Korea to our various units.

We left Pusan on the 3rd and arrived in Kure, only some twenty-five miles from Hiroshima, in beautifully warm weather on 5 December; the whole voyage had taken thirty-seven days. Disembarking next day, we were taken straight to the JRBD where we spent the next eleven days. My memories of my time there are few, but those I *do* have are visiting Hiroshima to see the 'Dome' – the memorial to the atomic bombing of the city, shopping in Kure and ordering a complete *Naritake* dinner service for delivery to my parents.

On 17 December I packed my tin trunk with my civilian clothes and things I wouldn't need in Korea, like my, although I say it myself, excellent photographic record of the voyage, and handed it in for safe-keeping. That evening we had a farewell party in the Mess and, early the following morning, left Kure in a fast motor launch for Iwakuni airfield and a Dakota flight to Kimpo military airfield near Seoul where we spent the night. It was my first flight in an aeroplane and I found it exciting and enjoyable. Then, on 19 December, after travelling by road along the 'main supply route' (MSR) through the badly-damaged capital, Seoul, and an almost completely destroyed Uijongbu, we arrived at the Royal Norfolks' Battalion Command Post (CP) in the dark at 1900 hours. The CO greeted us and told me I was posted to A Company which was 'in the line' in a forward position and that I would be commanding 2 Platoon. I said goodbye to Ian who was being posted to C Company and got into a jeep for the final leg of my journey.

Chapter Six

Platoon Commander in Korea

By the time I arrived in Korea the war was eighteen months old and armistice talks had already begun. The war of movement had ended with UN forces back more or less where the conflict had begun – on the 38th Parallel. Whilst talks continued, both sides were determined to hold on to the ground they already had with fighting restricted to trying to gain some local advantage. In the case of the British this usually meant dominating no man's land, or capturing a prisoner – both costly exercises, as I would soon find out. During my time in Korea, neither side tried to start a proper offensive to push the opposition back any significant distance. From the purist point of view, therefore, I was about to take part in a 'phoney' war in which the UN had total air superiority. Our virtual monopoly in armoured vehicles and the enemy's lack of tanks led to our anti-tank guns being replaced by American .30-calibre Browning machine guns, thus doubling the number of medium machine guns (MMGs) in the Battalion. However, American 3.5-inch anti-tank rocket launchers were issued to all platoons just in *case* enemy armour suddenly put in an appearance.

The Royal Norfolks were part of 29 Infantry Brigade, part of the recently-formed 1st Commonwealth Division under Major General Jim Cassels. In turn this was part of I US Corps, itself part of Lieutenant General James Van Fleet's Eighth US Army. Also in 1st Commonwealth Division were 25 Canadian Infantry Brigade and 28 British Commonwealth Infantry Brigade, which included an Australian battalion and two more British battalions. All the engineers and most of the artillery were British, but Canada and New Zealand each contributed an artillery battalion. The only armour was provided by 5th Royal Inniskilling Dragoon Guards.

I arrived in the A Company CP fairly late on the night of 19 December 1951 and was greeted warmly by the Company commander, Major Ben Chapman. He was thirty-five years old and had served for ten years in the Army Physical Training Corps (six in the ranks and four as an officer) before transferring to the Royal Norfolks in 1946. Needless to say, he was always superbly fit and 'tough' in every sense of the word. He introduced me to his CSM, Paul Boxall, and the artillery Forward Observation Officer (FOO) located with the Company, Captain Tommy Thompson, a senior captain with an MC, who had served in the Second World War. Paul Boxall, a paratrooper in Normandy on D Day, sported a huge moustache and was known to the men as 'Souptashe' or 'Mutton Chops'.

After a short chat during which Ben explained that the Chinese were about 1,000 yards away, with no one between them and us, he escorted me to the 2 Platoon CP bunker where I met the officer I was to take over from next morning. He was to become the Company second-in-command. I also met the acting platoon sergeant; the official platoon sergeant had suffered accidental burns and was convalescing in Japan. The bunker was dug into the side of a hill, was dank and smelly, and barely big enough for two. It had a blanket for a door, two bunks made of logs, laced across with telephone cable, a small, dangerous-looking petrol stove and a couple of ammunition boxes for storage. It was lit by candles. I was dog tired and, despite the offer of gin or whisky, soon turned in and fell asleep. We had three blankets each but slept more or less fully dressed and with our boots on in case of an enemy attack.

After a very uncomfortable wash and shave, I walked down the hill on which Ben's CP and two of the platoons, including mine, were sited, for breakfast. With the cookhouse and mess tents on the reverse slope of the hill, we could not be observed by the enemy. The cookhouse and mess tents were unprotected but slit trenches were available nearby in case of an artillery or mortar strike. The separate mess tent for the officers and sergeants was known to the men as the Pigsty. Accommodation bunkers, where everyone slept and spent their off-duty hours, were also on the reverse slopes. The fighting trenches and weapon-pits on the forward slopes were manned by only a few soldiers in an observation role during the day. At night manning depended on the current threat which could mean fully manned, fortunately a very rare occurrence, or the minimum level of two men in each section doing two-hour 'stags'.

The third platoon of A Company was sited in front of our main position, on a small hill known as Peter's Pimple – so named after the platoon commander, a National Service officer, Peter Shuttleworth. Exactly why we occupied it I never quite understood – it would have been much better unoccupied and heavily mined, leaving Peter's platoon to reinforce our main position. I often wonder if our Brigadier thought the same after he was mistakenly led by a major from Battalion HQ into one of our own minefields during a visit to Peter's Pimple. They were both injured but, fortunately, not seriously.

At breakfast I met the commander of 3 Platoon, Mike Gunton, a regular officer. The rest of the day was spent meeting my Platoon and looking at the ground we were defending. Two Platoon's strength, including me, was thirty-three – a sergeant, corporal, four lance corporals and twenty-six privates. One complete section, nine National Servicemen, under Corporal Bruce, were former Royal Ulster Riflemen (RUR) who had served less than six months in Korea when the RUR had completed its twelve-month tour and had therefore been transferred to the Norfolks. I also discovered that several others in my Platoon were from the East Surrey Regiment and had, like Ian Minto and me, been sent to the Norfolks to bring them up to strength. Furthermore, and rather worryingly, most of the lance corporals and privates were National Servicemen and due for demobilization the following July. The ratio of National Servicemen to regulars was about ten to one and the average age of my soldiers was about nineteen and a half. I was told that Private Dick Cooper, a former East Surrey, my predecessor's batman and radio operator, would act in the same capacities for me. Whether he was consulted about this neither he nor I can remember.

The 2 Platoon trenches and bunkers didn't look too bad with bunkers dug well into the ground and roofed to a depth of at least a foot, often more, with timber, sandbags, tree branches and turf. To get from a bunker to one's 'stand-to' (battle) position in a fighting bay, communication trenches, dug to at least four feet, were used. Personal weapons were stored in the bunkers and always carried when moving around.

One thing that did disturb me on that first day was the state of my men's clothing. We only had one lined, uncamouflaged, combat suit each and one pair of special boots – 'Cold, Wet Weather (CWW)', better known as 'cobbly wobblies', designed specially for the extremely cold Korean winters with a moulded rubber sole and heel, and wire insoles to help insulate the feet from the ice-cold ground. Temperatures at night often fell as low as minus twenty degrees. The lack of a second combat suit meant that many men had become rather scruffy looking, often with rips in their jackets and trousers from contact with the double and sometimes triple-apron barbed-wire fences surrounding our positions. Another surprising thing was that we had no steel helmets, but wore rather ugly khaki caps with peaks and ear flaps that tied up above the crown. We had good sweaters and scarves but no greatcoats; instead there was a limited number of 'parkas', heavily-padded topcoats with fur-lined hoods; each hood had a flexible wire in the rim, allowing it to be bent into the best position to protect the wearer from the icy wind. Since there were not enough parkas for every man, they were only issued to sentries and, occasionally, to those going out on ambush patrols. Similarly, there were not enough white 'snow-suits' for everyone. 'Flak jackets' or 'bulletproof vests', as body armour was called in those days, were also in short supply;

I think we had about a dozen jackets in my Platoon and, although they gave one some confidence, they were uncomfortable to wear, heavy and only protected one's chest, back and upper abdomen.

The Norfolks had moved into their hillside positions overlooking the Samichon river in late November. Unlike the King's Own Scottish Borderers (KOSB), King's Shropshire Light Infantry (KSLI) and Royal Leicesters, they had seen no serious action since arriving in Korea on 1 October – only one man killed and one wounded due to enemy artillery and mortar fire. Inevitably, this led to a certain amount of mud-slinging whenever the Norfolks came into contact with the personnel of the other Battalions. I had become aware of this during my short time in Japan.

My new Battalion was located some 5,000 yards north-west of the Paekhak Reservoir. The Samichon, which we overlooked, was a fast flowing tributary of the famous Imjin river, which it joined some 5,000 yards to the south. Everyone had heard about the famous stand of the 'Glorious Glosters' just south of the Imjin eight months earlier. The Chinese were sited much closer to the Samichon than we were. Our frontage was some 3,000-yards wide and we had the KOSB on our right and the 1st Battalion The Welch Regiment was away to our left front on a position known as the 'Hook', on the Chinese side of the Samichon and a far more vulnerable position than ours. All battalions were protected by extensive anti-personnel minefields.

The food we ate in Korea was a mixture of British 'compo' (composition ration) and American C-rations, which made a nice change from the British ten-man pack but lacked bulk and contained food strange to British tastes – frankfurter chunks, meat and spaghetti in tomato sauce, pork and beans, corned-beef hash and so on. In my view, they also contained too many fancy things like crackers, jam, a candy bar, coffee, chewing gum and packets of Lucky Strike or Camel cigarettes. The cigarettes were very welcome, but you can't eat them and I often wished that we could have more bully beef, potatoes and tins of rice pudding. Incidentally, we also received occasional free tins of fifty Players or Senior Service cigarettes.

Washing and shaving was a most unpleasant chore during the Korean winter. CSM Boxall constructed a bathhouse over a stream at the bottom of our Company position. Known as 'Boxall's Folly', the water was heated in huge oil drums and usually came out lukewarm or stone cold. No one enjoyed using it and most of us settled for semi-stripped washes in our bunkers. Unfortunately, some men, for understandable reasons, avoided exposing their bodies as much as possible and became pretty dirty and smelly.

I have to say that during my eight months in Korea I had tunnel vision

– I saw very little of people or events outside A Company. I think the CO visited us only once for an inspection of the forward platoons. In fact, officers from Battalion HQ rarely came forward. The only way to meet anyone there was to go to the rear. When we did go back most of us became very irritated over their comparatively luxurious living conditions. But then, as the CO was renowned for saying, any fool can be uncomfortable.

We did receive some comforts from home – gloves, mittens, books and so on, but had to buy our luxuries. The Company Colour Sergeant came up from A Echelon (where our immediate supplies were held) two or three times a week, but didn't stay long and none of us had much time for him. I remember getting very angry when, shortly before the Battalion was due to leave Korea, Ben told me that all company colour sergeants were being recommended for a Mention in Despatches (MiD).

My pay as a second lieutenant at this time was £24-9-4 net a month (£573 today). We were paid in BAFVs, as in Germany, and examples of what we had to pay the Colour Sergeant for our NAAFI goodies in *today's* prices are: 2lbs of sugar £3; ¼lb of tea £2; tin of milk £1; a small bottle of beer £2; Mars and Crunchie bars 50p; bottle of gin (officers only) £10; bottle of whisky (officers only) £12. Our complaints about the 'special prices for our troops fighting overseas' were answered with 'transportation costs'. It may surprise readers that we were buying tea, but the simple fact was that we needed hot drinks throughout all our waking hours in that terrible climate.

Talking of pay, it was everyone's view that it was quite scandalous that National Servicemen, on £1-8-0 a week (£32.80 today), were being paid roughly one-third less than our regulars for doing the same job. National Service had been extended to two years in early 1951 and only in their last six months did conscripts go on to regular army rates of pay. They received a £10 bounty (£234 today) after their first three months in Korea and £1 (£23.40 today) for each completed month after that, but there was still, not surprisingly, much ill feeling. This pay differential wasn't just a way of saving money for the Government, but was also a ruse by the War Office to get National Servicemen to sign on as regulars.

The Samichon valley between us and the Chinese consisted of almost completely flat paddy and rice fields with its only features being three so-called villages and three prominent trees. The villages were only small groups of three or four deserted shacks, built of mud bricks and thatch.

On my second day in the Company, Ben Chapman decided to see what I was made of. Telling me that he was worried that the Chinese might have set up an ambush in the 'village' nearest to us, he said that he, I and a couple of others were going to check it out. Off we set in broad daylight, no doubt to the amusement of the other two platoon commanders and others 'in the know' and, arriving on the edge of the first 'village', Ben said he would cover me as I searched the first shack. I wanted to throw a grenade in first, but wasn't allowed to, so I burst in, my borrowed Sten gun at the ready, only to find it empty – similarly with the other shacks. We returned happily to the Company lines, with me particularly pleased that I had passed my Company commander's first test. Little did we realize that within a couple of months the Chinese would indeed set up an ambush in that same 'village'.

We ate our meals in shifts although there were numerous occasions when most officers and sergeants were together, an indication of how relatively safe it was within the Company position.

My first real test came two days later on 23 December. Ben sent for me in the afternoon and told me that I was to take a strong patrol *across* the Samichon that night. No one had been across before and no one, to the best of my knowledge, ever went again. My mission was to find out exactly how close the Chinese positions were to the only place in our sector where the river could be forded. I can't remember exactly how many men I had in that patrol, but it was certainly in the region of fifteen to twenty. They came from all three platoons and, of course, I didn't really know them – certainly not by name. Composite patrols were the norm for large patrols so that none of our platoon positions would be under-manned.

We set out well after last light on a desperately cold night and arrived at what I thought was the ford. I have to admit that my heart was in my mouth as I put my foot in the freezing water; I'm sure I wondered if any of us would ever survive to get back to the home bank and my worst fears were soon realized when, after only a few paces, I found myself up to my chest in water. We were in the wrong place. The silhouettes of the hills on the river's far side had looked about right, but I soon realized we were too far to the right and so we moved downstream and, after a few minutes, found an obvious crossing place. I splashed across with the rest of my patrol following reluctantly behind me and then, after leaving two sections as a firm base, set off *very* slowly with the third section up what looked like a small re-entrant. We hadn't gone far, probably about fifty yards at most when, to my horror, I smelled garlic and, worse still, could hear people chattering – and not in English. That was good enough for me; I had done my job and found out how close the enemy were to the ford. I indicated a swift 'about turn' to those behind me and we were soon back in the Samichon. That's when the trouble started. Halfway across we came under fire from the home bank – yes, the Chinese were on 'our' bank. Either it was a deliberate ambush or our two patrols had run into each other accidentally – we shall never know. There was nothing else that we, being actually *in* the river, could do other than to advance – so I shouted 'Charge' at the top of my voice. I don't know really what happened next. It was dark and running through water is difficult at the best of times. Anyway I charged as fast as I could, firing my Sten at the unseen enemy and hoping my men would do likewise. They did and, to my amazement, I soon found myself unharmed, standing in the paddy field on 'our' side of that wretched river. Since I had men around me and no one was shooting at us anymore, I asked the three NCOs if they had all their men with them. They said 'yes', so we set off for home at a brisk pace as we were all wet and freezing. The Norfolk History says that one of my patrol had been wounded during the firefight and that I helped him back. I don't remember that.

After arriving back in A Company and sending my exhausted men back to their respective platoons, I reported to Ben in his CP. I too was exhausted and had to thaw out the zip fastener on my combat jacket in front of his hot stove to undo it, revealing an inch-thick block of ice all around my lower chest, back and stomach. A report of this appeared later in a local Norfolk newspaper as an example of how cold it could get in Korea – I still have the cutting. Anyway, I gave Ben a report of what had happened and he then sent me to bed.

The next thing I knew was being woken up by someone and asked, 'Where is Watkins?' 'Who is Watkins?' I replied. 'He was on your patrol last night and he's missing!' 'Oh God!'

About an hour later, in broad daylight, and on Christmas Eve, I set off again with a hastily assembled patrol and a stretcher party with our attached RAMC corporal, 'Doc' Davies. We crossed the valley without any trouble and, on reaching the river, I saw a body lying on a sandbar about a third of the way across. It was clearly a British body and wasn't moving. Again I entered the water with my heart in my mouth, telling Corporal Davies and the stretcher-bearers to follow me. Poor Watkins was lying facedown with his legs still in the water. I turned him over and saw a bullet hole in his forehead. There was no blood. I was relieved that he had died quickly – in that sub-zero climate he wouldn't have survived serious wounds for long. We put him on the stretcher and I covered his face with a blanket. *That's* when the Chinese opened 'extremely heavy fire', as the Regimental History puts it. The stretcher-bearers dropped the stretcher and we took what cover we could behind the sandbar. Fortunately, the bullets passed over us into the home bank. I knew we had no hope of getting out of the river alive unless I could bring down suppressive fire of some sort on the enemy. I also knew that we would have to make a mad dash for home once that fire came in and that there was no way we could take Watkins with us. I called on the radio for artillery fire and, when asked whether we were anywhere near the river, replied, 'We're *in* the bloody river.' 'Roger, wait out!' I shouted to everyone to make a dash for it as soon as they heard the shells coming and, a few minutes later, a salvo of 25-pounder rounds landed a short distance in front of us. We all struggled through the water and I found myself spread-eagled and exhausted against the home bank. I was sure that at any moment I would get a bullet in my back, but the artillery fire did the trick and a short time later, after crawling up the bank, we were all running for home. Corporal Davies had been slightly injured and I helped him back to A Company lines.

Once again I reported to Ben. I hardly needed to – most of the Company had been able to witness the whole episode. The Royal Norfolk History completes the story: 'Later in the day another patrol was sent out under Major B. D. Chapman. This patrol had the benefit of heavy, pre-arranged artillery and MMG fire support and it made possible the recovery of the body. The section commander of the MMG Platoon, Sergeant J.W. Denny, which provided part of this support noted that his two guns fired 6,000 rounds on that occasion.'

Looking back over fifty years later, I have to say that I think the whole episode was a disgrace. *Why* was it necessary to risk men's lives by sending them onto the enemy side of the Samichon? We already knew perfectly well where the Chinese positions were – just as we were on the forward slopes of our hills overlooking the river and its wide valley, so they were inevitably on Hills 207 and 169 and covering the only ford which lay directly in front of those positions – the one I'd been ordered to cross.

Christmas Day was naturally a rather subdued affair from my point of view. I was still very tired and probably in slight shock after the previous twenty-four hours but, in accordance with tradition, my acting platoon sergeant and I took cups of 'char' to our men in their bunkers and, later that day and thanks to the Americans, we had turkey and Christmas pudding for lunch; the Regimental History says the Battalion 'provided everyone with beer.'

I completed three more patrols during the first two weeks of 1952, the first a fighting patrol on another pitch-dark and freezing night to one of the three 'villages'. The aim was to find and kill or capture any Chinese who might be there. We didn't find any Chinese, but I did find quite a nice pendulum clock which I brought back and later managed to get going. Amazingly I also found a silver communion chalice with an English hall-mark on it which, I'm ashamed to say, I used for whisky. My second patrol, also at night, was to the wretched Samichon again to see if any Chinese were crossing. It too proved negative but, as with all night patrols, was highly nerve-racking.

The third patrol was most unusual. On 17 January tanks of the 'Skins' tried a daylight 'swan' across the Samichon valley. Needless to say, the ground proved too soft and the operation had to be aborted. However, one leading tank became seriously stuck and, because it was equipped with a new secret invention called a main armament 'stabilizer', it had to be protected until this item could be removed or completely disabled – at least that was what I was told when I was selected to lead the close protection party. We sat out there for at least a couple of hours in broad daylight wondering when the Chinese would start to mortar us. Fortunately they didn't and we all returned safely. Goodness knows what the aim of the operation had been anyway – no one bothered to tell us.

About this time the original platoon sergeant of 2 Platoon, Sergeant Nobby Clark, returned from convalescence. Two years older than me and formerly of the Essex Regiment, Nobby was a great character with a wonderful sense of humour. We hit it off straightaway, which was just as well as living in a two-man bunker under those conditions wasn't easy. We even had the same tastes in luxuries like Ambrosia creamed-rice pudding and tinned peaches in syrup which we bought at exorbitant prices from the Colour Sergeant and ate with condensed milk.

Our daily routine in Korea was very boring. We manned our weapon pits for half an hour astride first and last light which was when Nobby or I, or sometimes both of us if we hadn't been out on patrol, checked our men and their weapons. Later in the day we cleaned our weapons, repaired or improved our bunkers and trenches, laid more barbed wire round our positions, took the very occasional shower, carried out foot inspections, and dug fresh latrines, or 'thunder-boxes'. These were wooden boxes located over a deep hole, with a hole cut in the top and a canvas screen round them – one for the platoon commander and sergeant and others for the men. We also wrote letters home, played cards, read any books we could get our hands on, devoured newspapers from home no matter how old they were, and rehearsed any scheduled patrols. The only phone I had was an army one on which I could talk to the Company CP and nowhere else while our only news of the outside world came from the US Army *Stars and Stripes* newspaper and a Commonwealth Divisional periodic newsletter called *The Crown*. We knew when the armistice talks were in session at Panmunjom, as a searchlight was always switched on with its beam shining vertically into the sky. We could see it from our winter positions and it helped with navigation during night patrols.

They say that war is ninety per cent boredom and ten per cent fear and that was certainly my experience. In some cases, boredom led to excessive drinking. There were no firm restrictions on the amount of beer a soldier could buy, lack of money being the only handicap. The same applied to officers in relation to spirits. The beer we drank was Japanese Asahi. To everyone's amusement, a well-known Japanese advertisement for it ran as follows: 'Drink Asahi beer! Once you've had an Asahi, you'll never want another beer!'

One exciting event was the arrival in our Company position of a troop of three Centurion tanks from the 'Skins' which ground their way slowly up our hill. The one that ended up in my Platoon area managed to crush a communication trench in the process, which was bad enough but then, to add insult to injury, the commander asked us to help him dig the wretched thing in up to its turret ring.

Other surprises were the sudden arrival in the valley directly behind us of the 81mm mortar platoon of a battalion of the French-Canadian Royal 22nd Regiment who fired a few salvoes at some unknown target before pushing off and leaving us to collect the returns. These weren't accurate and no one was hurt. This was followed by the appearance of some Bofors 40mm anti-aircraft guns on the hills behind us and to our flank. With no enemy aircraft to engage, they were used at night to harass Chinese positions and had tracer mixed in with the normal rounds. Being quick-firing guns they made an almost musical sound – great fun to hear and watch.

Another unusual thing occurred when King George VI died on 6 February. Every Commonwealth Divisional artillery gun fired once a minute for twenty-one minutes. The Chinese must have wondered what on earth was going on. Amazingly, within a few hours of the King's death, every officer was issued with a black armband to wear on his left arm.

My diary records that on the nights of 7 and 14 February we had 'Chinese on our wire.' How did we know? Because the next day we found propaganda leaflets on our barbed-wire fences. These usually included coloured photographs and carried easily-understood messages like: 'British soldiers! Don't risk your life for Yankee dollars!'; 'Leave Korea to the Koreans'; and 'Your families need you back!'. One photograph showed an American soldier in a wheelchair with the caption: 'Hullo Sucker'; on the other side was a 'SAFE CONDUCT PASS'. One of our favourites was a picture of two men and two girls in swimsuits, drinking champagne by a pool and the caption: 'Mr Moneybags is in Florida this Christmas.' Underneath it another photograph showed a column of GIs in parkas on a snow-covered slope with the caption: 'Where are you? In Korea! You risk your life, Big Business rakes in the dough.' These leaflets were greeted with amusement rather than worry; however, the fact that the Chinese could get up to, or at least near, our wire at night without us hearing them was worrying and we soon came to realize that they were much better at silent movement than we were. After all, our battle positions were usually less than ten yards from the wire fences.

At about this time a section from each platoon was taken out of the line each day and driven to the Kansas Line which was located on prominent hills behind the Imjin where new bunkers, trenches and battle positions were being constructed for possible use 'should any change in the current front lines result from the armistice talks'. I went back to the Kansas Line only once in February. After a very strenuous climb we eventually reached the new position where we worked all day. Fortunately we had South Korean porters to carry all the heavy kit we needed. I still have a photograph of a group I took there having lunch. We look a really scruffy lot and of the twelve soldiers in the picture one was later killed, two were wounded and one, as I will shortly describe, was taken prisoner but later escaped.

Each company had a number of porters for carrying food, ammunition and everything else we needed from the jeephead (the most forward place a vehicle could get to without being seen) to the company position.

On 15 February I led an ambush patrol to a feature called Kunson-Dong, but we had no contact with the enemy. We were out there for several hours and the cold was almost unbearable. Then, on the 18th, we took part in Operation POLECAT, a sweep behind our positions to locate and detain any Korean civilians with the aim of catching any North Korean agents who might have infiltrated our lines. We didn't find any although the Royal Norfolk History claims that in an earlier sweep lasting seven hours 'some sixty men' were detained. The following day saw the Battalion's first gallantry award – a private in D Company won an immediate Military Medal. We knew nothing about it until sometime later.

On the 21st it snowed heavily. Before that we'd only had light flurries and usually clear blue skies by day. That night I was ordered to take the Battle Adjutant (there was no such appointment as Operations Officer in those days) on patrol. I can't remember where we went – somewhere near the Samichon I think. Nothing happened, but I didn't enjoy having a senior major breathing down my neck and was worried that he might interfere if we had a contact. Most officers in Battalion HQ came on at least one patrol, more to ease their consciences, I think, than for any other reason. Another reconnaissance (recce) patrol followed on the 26th during which I was able to bring down artillery fire onto a suspected Chinese position. I don't know if it had any effect, but I and the chaps with me certainly enjoyed the 'shoot'.

There was a fairly dramatic event in A Company on 29 February. Ben was at Battalion HQ and I was the senior infantry officer left in A Company. Sometime in the afternoon I suddenly heard machine-gun fire from the area of the nearest 'village' to our position and dashed up to Ben's CP to be told by the CSM that our 'wooding party', which had gone down into the 'village' foraging for wood for our fires, had been ambushed by about twenty enemy. Two of our men had been taken prisoner and were being rushed back across the valley. We had fallen into the dangerous habit of sending a wooding party out every day at about the same time and the Chinese had been quick to spot our practice. I shouted to Tommy Thompson, our FOO, to bring down artillery fire ahead of the group in an attempt to halt them and then, grabbing a few soldiers, set off in hot pursuit. Fortunately the artillery did the trick: the Chinese hit the ground and our two boys, Corporal Ashlin and Private Pantrini, made their escape and, despite some long-range Chinese machine-gun fire, we got them safely back to our lines. My batman, Dick Cooper, with his usual sharp wit, later christened the incident 'The Chinese Takeaway'.

During the night of 3 March a C Company patrol got into trouble when it ran into a group of about twenty Chinese. Three men were killed and six wounded, two seriously. Second Lieutenant Tom Henson was awarded an immediate MC for his coolness and resourcefulness under fire and my old friend Ian Minto led the rescue party.

The following night I took another fighting patrol of twenty into the Samichon valley but found no Chinese. Five days later the Battalion was relieved by the Canadians and we moved into a reserve position near the Paekhak Reservoir, an area known to us as the Peacock Hills. Our relief was quite a nail-biting business though. The Canadians arrived during darkness in the early morning, but we barely had time to cross an open valley which was under observation by the Chinese before dawn broke.

It was a great relief to go into reserve and be able to relax knowing there would be no more patrols for a while. An additional luxury we enjoyed was being able to sleep *inside* our sleeping bags.

One immediate task for the officers was to recce possible counter-attack tasks in the forward areas, which was followed by more work on the Kansas Line. We added to literally acres of double-apron and triple-dannert wire fences.

On 22 March I had a nasty shock. Ben sent for me and told me that reserve battalions were required to take the pressure off those in the forward positions by occasionally carrying out dangerous patrols in their areas. And yes, Mike Reynolds had been chosen for one in the KSLI area. I was to go and live with the KSLI for twenty-four hours, be briefed on my mission and learn the way in and out through the wire and minefields in front of one of their companies. I wondered why, out of twelve platoon commanders in the Norfolks, I had been chosen, but it wasn't 'on' to complain and I joined the KSLI. That gave me another nasty shock as I was billeted with their Battle Platoon which lived in comfort near Battalion HQ, but carried out the most dangerous patrols. I had no choice other than to go out with them that night so that I would know my way around. That led to another shock. The Chinese positions in their area were much closer than ours in the Samichon valley and we had only been moving in no man's land for about ten minutes when a loudspeaker blared out from the Chinese lines in reasonable English, 'We can see you Tommy – go back, go back!' I was completely unnerved, but the Battle Platoon guys just laughed, fired their automatic weapons in the direction of the loudspeaker and carried on. Fortunately, we were back in KSLI lines after a short time and I turned in wondering what on earth I was doing in Korea. Why hadn't I joined the REME like my Sandhurst chum Tony Baxter who was in his second year at Trinity College Cambridge?

Three days later I led a nineteen-man patrol of Norfolks out of the KSLI lines to find out if the Chinese were occupying a feature codenamed 'Woolpack'. It appeared to be unoccupied during the daytime but 'they' wanted to know if the Chinese were on it at night. There were three lines of continuous trenches running about 200 yards along the centre part of 'Woolpack' so I decided to lead one section straight up to the top trench, dropping off my other two sections on the middle and bottom trenches, before turning and running along the top of each trench, firing and lobbing grenades if there was any opposition, before coming down at the far end and heading fast for home. I rehearsed this with my patrol on a similar hill near our reserve position and ensured that every man had an automatic weapon and plenty of grenades.

All went well until we got to the bottom of 'Woolpack'. I turned to Corporal Compton, the section commander due to come to the top trench with me, and asked if he was ready. He whispered, 'You're not really going up that fucking hill are you? I'm bloody not!' For a moment I was taken aback. 'Right,' I said, 'Well I'm off and you'd better bloody well come with me or I'll have you court-martialled.' Fortunately he did and the other seventeen, led in the other cases by Corporals Bruce and Young, followed. Once again my heart was in my mouth and once again we were lucky as there were no Chinese. We headed for home fast and eventually returned elated to A Company. Needless to say I had strong words with Corporal Compton the next day.

I haven't mentioned many of my Platoon by name. In my HQ I had Nobby, Dick Cooper, my radio operator and batman, and Abrahams and Waters my 2-inch mortar men. One section was commanded by Corporal Compton, another by Corporal Bruce with Lance Corporal Marsh as his assistant, and the third by Corporal Young with Lance Corporal Fright as his assistant. Amongst the most memorable soldiers, for various reasons, were the Buchan twins who worried constantly about each other and, in my opinion, should never have been allowed to serve together in the front line; Ketteringham, older than the average and a very strong chap; Ruth, Gorringe, Martin, Webster and Edwards. Edwards was the chap arrested by the Military Police in Aden for allegedly beating up an Arab stall-keeper. He had caught up with us sometime in early 1952 after completing his twenty-eight days' detention and, to my surprise, had asked to come to my Platoon. All in all, they were a great lot of chaps – often cheeky, always moaning and many of them skivers, but one couldn't help becoming fond of them – well, most of them anyway. Dick Cooper, with whom I'm now in close touch, describes them as either Mike's Marauders or Mike's Malingerers. Of the ones mentioned above, Ketteringham and Webster were killed and Edwards was wounded. Amazingly after fifty-eight years, I am still in touch with Dick Cooper and Vic Gorringe. Nobby Clark and I remained in contact until he died of cancer in 2006.

On 6 April I went with a group of all ranks to an American Bath Unit. It was quite an experience. First of all they took all our underclothes and burnt them and then, after our wonderfully hot showers, issued us with new American pants and vests and gave us coffee and doughnuts. It was about this time too that we had our first change of blankets since October for the men and December for me and so it wasn't before time.

Another enjoyable experience at that time was a swim in the Imjin. By now the weather was beautifully warm and was soon to get hot. But it wasn't all relaxation whilst we were in reserve. We did at least one long route march and practised platoon attacks and an assault river crossing of the Imjin.

Some soldiers, including Dick Cooper, were lucky enough to go to a concert party whilst we were in reserve. Dick wrote the following account:

A makeshift stage had been erected on flat ground at the foot of a gently sloping hill. As befits their status the officers were seated on chairs nearest the stage; behind were the senior NCOs and spread and sprawling up the slope of the hill were the 'hoi polloi' from various units. As an introduction we got a 'run of the mill' comedian and then what we had all been waiting for – Hy Hazel, a buxom lady well known to audiences in Blighty. She was dressed in a skimpy costume – very burlesque. To lots of whistling and other appreciative noises she sang a medley of popular songs accompanied by the comedian on an upright piano and then asked if anyone had a request. Someone shouted: 'Yeah, let's have a feel up your skirt!'

Raucous laughter, but some officers and NCOs jumped up and, facing those on the hill who were laughing heartily, shouted: 'Who said that?' More laughter, no one owned up and the show went on.

Our time in reserve ended on 19 April when we took over from the 3rd Battalion, 15th US Infantry Regiment, part of the 2nd US Infantry Division (the 'Can Dos'). Our new sector was some four miles north-east of our old Samichon position, immediately east of the largest hill in the area, Hill 355. We had a large bend in the Imjin river immediately behind us. Our Company was up front on the right flank.

My own time in reserve had ended three days earlier. On the 13th, following a recce of our new position, Ben told me that I was to go forward on the 16th and live with the Americans and learn everything I could about the new position – the enemy we would be facing, the minefields, the wire defences, etc, etc. He would bring the Company forward on the 19th and take over from the Americans. Once again I wondered why I had been chosen: surely he or, at least, the Company second-in-command would have been more suited to the task? I didn't really mind though as my new task sounded quite exciting.

On the morning of the 16th I was driven forward in a jeep and my first surprise was to find that a good 100-yard section of the dirt road leading to the new position was under massive camouflage nets. Yes, the Chinese could observe this part of the road from their position on Hill 317. My next surprise was a blue-and-white sign at the entrance to the American company position which read, 'K Co – Kill 'em, Kount 'em, Kollect 'em.' A third surprise was the size of K Company – 189 men. Since we would be taking over with about 100 at the most I realized we were going to have a problem.

I received a warm welcome from the young captain commanding K Company and was given a bunk in the CP itself. He then took me round his positions, many of which, to my surprise, were sited on flat ground at the bottom of the hill on which the CP was located. This he told me, was so that machine guns located there could produce horizontal 'grazing fire' which, he explained, would kill many more Chinese in a mass attack than 'plunging fire' from hillside positions. With the number of men he had available he could produce both. I mentioned that I would need to recce the way through our own wire and minefields and he immediately invited me to join a patrol going out that night. That was another surprise; I was to join a fighting patrol of no fewer than sixty men. He, a small HQ group and me would set ourselves up on a feature nicknamed 'Bunker Hill' situated at the near end of a ridge, some 2,000 yards long, later known to us as 'Crete', which began about 400 yards from the K Company position, and ran west in front of the main Chinese positions on Hills 317 and 217. These had been held originally by the KOSB, but had been lost in bitter fighting the previous November during which my friend Geoff Havilland with the Royal Leicesters had been wounded and awarded an MC. The main part of the US patrol would move on from 'Bunker Hill' and attack a forward Chinese position believed to be located on the foothills of Hill 317 known later to us, due to their shape, as 'Greece'.

All went well at first and, once established on 'Bunker Hill', we waited to see how the main party would get on. We didn't have to wait long. Suddenly there was some sporadic fire from 'Greece', followed by a wall of fire from the fifty or so Americans who had been advancing in single file up a valley on its western edge. We didn't know it then, but the Chinese had accounted for one American killed and fourteen wounded. Soon after our return there was a debriefing in the CP which I listened to from my bunk. Estimates of the number of Chinese they had encountered varied from fifty to one hundred. Afterwards the Company commander asked me how many Chinese I thought there had been. I said, 'From the muzzle flashes, I would say about a dozen at the most.' He nodded.

On the 17th it started to rain heavily and I borrowed an American jeep and drove back to see Ben. I warned him that many of the US weapon pits on the flat ground were untenable as they were full of water and, anyway, we didn't have enough men to occupy so many positions. I also told him that no one seemed really clear about the exact location of the so-called 'friendly' minefields, which were not properly marked, while much of the wire defences needed re-laying.

My Platoon in the new position was the right forward one, on low ground pointing out towards 'Crete' and the enemy and thus nicknamed 'Finger'. Mike Gunton's Platoon was in the middle of the position near Company HQ and Peter Shuttleworth's was on the high ground to the left. We abandoned all weapon pits on the flat ground at the bottom of our hill, put new wire fences where they had been and then, under cover of darkness, constructed many new bunkers, communication trenches and weapon pits. It was hard and miserable work in horrible weather. Only one of my sections, Corporal Bruce's, actually looked west towards the enemy and we sited a Vickers MMG allocated to the Company with him. My other two sections looked basically north-east across a 300-yard valley on the other side of which was located a Republic of Korea (ROK) infantry company which, fortunately, was soon replaced by a US company. My Platoon was therefore responsible for the right flank of the Company and indeed of the Battalion while all patrols had to go out and in through my position.

One of my first tasks was to 'go over and liaise with the ROKs'. Again, I wondered why me and not someone more senior. I couldn't just walk over and see them though as the valley between us contained wire fences and unmarked mines. I therefore took Ben's jeep and went the long way round. I was warmly welcomed by the Korean company commander in his CP and immediately offered whiskey. We had been warned never to drink Korean whisky and looking at the bottle I could clearly see 'Genuine Scotch Whisky. Brewed in Pusan'. Thinking I would probably go blind I downed my glass, only to have it refilled immediately. As it happened I came to no harm and arrived back in A Company in excellent mood.

I mentioned that we were relieved when the Americans replaced the ROKs on our right flank. This was because the latter were very aggressive and the overspill of the Chinese response to this aggression often affected us. On the other hand the GIs of 7th Infantry Regiment were, like us, more restrained, presumably because of the armistice talks. As usual I was told to liaise with these 'Cotton Balers' which proved useful. Since they were 'dry' a bottle of whisky or gin could buy a lot and I was soon the proud possessor of an American carbine with plenty of ammunition. Their weaponry was much more plentiful than ours and when we cleared one of the rubbish pits in our Company area we were amazed to find about half a dozen 30-calibre machine-gun barrels at the bottom of it which were like manna for our Browning MMG sections which had only one barrel per gun; being air-cooled weapons, spare barrels were essential for continuous firing.

CSM Boxall deciding that we needed a proper officers' and sergeants' mess in the new position, and so had a log cabin constructed with two half-open sides and a log and thatched roof. This beautiful piece of work was inevitably christened the 'Piggery' by the soldiers. Fifty-two years later when I suggested to Dick Cooper that the men must have despised us for our privileges he was aghast and said 'Oh no, we expected you to have things that we didn't – life was like that in those days.'

Soon after settling into the new position I led a recce patrol out to a feature nicknamed 'Tombstone', a prominent 'bump' on the forward slope of a ridge running between the Chinese held Hills 217 and 317. I was very apprehensive but nothing happened – it was unoccupied. Early June saw much activity though. A large fighting patrol from C Company was sent out to capture a live prisoner but ran into trouble. The commander of the Assault Pioneer Platoon, Second Lieutenant 'Whiskers' Wormold, and another man were 'missing', one man was killed and another seven wounded. Poor 'Whiskers' was never found and never returned. Another officer involved in this action, Tony Towell, received an immediate MC for his attempts to find 'Whiskers' and for bringing in the wounded. The following day Private Allman of my Company, who had worked with me on the Kansas Line positions, was killed by mortar fire.

The need to capture a live prisoner now became an obsession with our higher authorities. I never really understood *why* and believe to this day that it was scandalous to risk so many lives and to have men killed and wounded for such an unimportant goal. Did it *really* matter *which* Chinese division was opposite us? According to a relevant US Eighth Army 'Secret' map that still exists today, we already knew they were units of the 190th Division of the Chinese Sixty-fourth Army.

On 13 June my great friend Mike Gunton and another of our soldiers were wounded on a fighting patrol. Three Chinese were killed in the action.

One horror I haven't mentioned was the presence of rats that fed on the waste in our refuse pits and the bodies of dead Chinese and North Koreans that still littered the battlefield. I remember finding one body during our sweep for infiltrators – it was only a skeleton, the rats having gnawed it clean. We tried many ways of eradicating them but never succeeded.

A serious rat incident occurred during one of my ambush patrols on 'Bunker Hill'. On such patrols we connected ourselves to each other with string so that everyone could be alerted silently if the enemy appeared. On this occasion I heard rustling in front of me and, as it became louder, I pulled the strings attached to the chaps on either side of me and pointed forward. More rustling and then, less than a yard in front of me, I saw in the half light an enormous, almost hairless, pink rat. I was almost as startled as if it had been a Chinese soldier.

On 20 June I left the Company to begin my R & R. Every man had five days' leave in Tokyo during his tour of duty. After being issued with clean uniforms at B Echelon, I and the others due for this particular leave period were driven through Seoul to Kimpo airfield to spend the night before our flight to Toyko. There I was accommodated in the Commonwealth Division Officers' Hotel. The rooms and the food were very good and it was sheer bliss to lie in a proper bath, sleep in a proper bed and eat in a restaurant rather than a dugout or shack. Accommodation and food were free and the drinks duty-free and, therefore, cheap.

I had at least a month's pay saved up for this leave and was determined to live it up in every way possible. We started well. Straight after dinner on the first night, a New Zealand gunner I had met on the flight out, Peter Lucy-Smith, me, and the padre of the Welch Regiment called a taxi and asked to be taken to a nightclub. We didn't know it at the time, but many

Tokyo taxis worked for so-called 'geisha houses' – really brothels – and before we knew it we were standing in the reception hall of just such a place. It was only when about ten little girls in yellow kimonos were trotted out for our inspection and choice that we realized where we were. The look on the padre's face was unforgettable. After much laughter we hailed another taxi and reached our intended nightclub which we all thoroughly enjoyed.

The rest of our time in Tokyo was spent sleeping and a bit of sight-seeing by day and 'living it up' by night. It was a brash and ugly city in 1952. American bombing had almost completed the damage caused by the great earthquake of 1923 and the post-war rebuild had done little to enhance it. The only sites worth visiting were Emperor Hirohito's Imperial Palace but we could only see the outer walls and a fairly ornate gate, the Asakusa Shrine, and the Senso-ji temple which had only been rebuilt a year or two before our visit. We went down the famous 'Ginza' shopping street, but I have no recollection of what, if anything, I bought. At night I got into trouble only once. Peter suggested that we should go to a 'beer hall' frequented by Aussies and Kiwis. We paid at an entrance kiosk and received tickets, just as in a cinema, each one of which would buy a beer. I think we were the only officers there and were soon 'ragged' by the soldiers around us – I lost my subaltern's 'pips' within minutes! The trouble really started though when some Americans came in. Before we knew it a fight had started, followed by the rapid arrival of a large contingent of American military police wielding batons and arresting everyone they could get their hands on regardless of nationality. Fortunately Peter and I were near an emergency exit and got out unscathed.

I arrived back in A Company to bad news. Tommy Thompson, our first FOO had been killed whilst attached to the Welch Regiment. And there had been another tragic incident on the 26th immediately in front of our own Company position in which five men had been killed and four wounded. Apparently a patrol led by the CSM of another Company had mistakenly entered our own minefield and set off an American 'jumping' mine. When touched these mines exploded in the air at waist height. Amazingly Ben himself had gone to their rescue, entered the minefield and carried out all nine men to the stretcher parties he'd organized. He was awarded a DSO for this courageous action.

Two days after my return I was not surprised to hear that I was to escort a Royal Engineer minefield marking party to the area where this tragedy had happened. On arrival I deployed my escort party in ambush positions where we could protect the Sappers and all was well until they started work. The noise they made driving the iron pickets into the ground with pickaxe heads was ear-splitting and I dashed over to the sergeant in charge and said, 'For God's sake, can't you muffle that sound?' Fortunately they managed to, using some of their own clothing, and we completed the task successfully without casualties.

A few days later, on 4 July, I took another patrol out and, while returning to our own lines, we were mortared. One round landed quite close to me on my right side and, although I wasn't hit, I lost all hearing in my right ear for about twenty-four hours. The damage inevitably affected me for life.

The next day the notorious Korean summer rains started, forcing us to drain and rebuild nearly all our bunkers. This was probably our most miserable time of all as there was no way to keep the rain out and everything got wet. I can still recall coming in soaking wet from patrols, having nothing dry to change into and having to lie down to sleep on soaking wet blankets. According to the Royal Engineers' War Diary, the wooden bridge across the Imjin codenamed 'Teal', over which our supplies came, collapsed due to the flood waters and, at another steel bridge, 'Pintail', the water rose eighteen and a half feet.

On 7 July the first of my National Servicemen, Widger and Cook, left for home and demob. I was sad to see them go. Two days later I led a patrol to 'The Cutting', a path across 'Crete' in front of 'Bunker Hill' and a day later I had to lead a rescue patrol to find that old rogue Private Edwards who had gone out with another patrol that had run into trouble and had failed to return. I found him lying on a track about halfway along 'Crete', still manning his Bren gun and facing towards the enemy. I put the boys with me out in front to protect us and lay down beside him. 'What happened? Are you alright?' I asked. 'Well, they all fucked off and left me, din't they? I've got something wrong down here I fink,' he replied, pointing down to the top of his legs. I turned him over and saw at once from the dark stains that he'd been shot in the genitals. We took the poor chap back and he was cas-evaced to the rear. I never expected to see him again.

I'm unable to give precise dates but other 'happenings' in early and mid-July included going for stripped washes in a small stream behind our position and changing my batman. Neither Dick Cooper nor I can remember whether I sacked him or he resigned but Ketteringham volunteered to replace him and all three of us were happy.

On a more serious note, I had to order one of my platoon to be 'scrubbed'. I hated doing this, but he just wouldn't wash and smelt horrible. No one wanted to share a bunker with him. In fact, no one wanted to be anywhere near him. I'm sure it was an illegal order but it certainly wasn't unpopular, and two or three of the Platoon carried it out under Nobby's supervision. Discipline in my Platoon was very basic.

Neither me, Nobby, nor any of my NCOs, wanted to charge anyone formally for a misdemeanour. Had we done so, the culprit might well have ended up being given a punishment that would have taken him away from the Platoon and even the Company, which was the last thing we wanted; we were understrength as it was. So discipline became more 'instant' with punishments such as being made to fill in and dig latrines, do cookhouse fatigues, carry out extra sentry duties and 'stags' or even being 'thumped' by the very muscular Nobby. No one ever made a formal complaint though.

Another serious 'happening' at this time occurred after we were ordered to 'fill that damn valley between us and the Yanks with wire'. This meant hours spent erecting double-apron fences. We started doing so at night but were then told to carry on in daylight. 'It will be alright!' It wasn't! One day I was down there with half the Platoon when we were straddled by enemy mortar rounds. Caught out in the open, we hit the deck but one of the Buchan twins panicked, tried to run for the safety of the trenches and got himself seriously entangled in the wire. He was badly cut and it took us some time to free him, after which Ketteringham, one of the strongest men in the Platoon, carried him back up our hill for treatment. He was in a severe state of shock and had to be cas-evaced. I sent his twin back with him. Afterwards when I was thanking Ketteringham, I noticed him arching his back, clearly in some discomfort. I turned him round and his shirt was covered in blood – he had received several small pieces of shrapnel himself, yet had still carried Buchan on his back up the hill. Fortunately for me, as will become clear, 'Doc' Davies was able to remove the pieces of shrapnel and Ketteringham stayed with us.

In mid-July I was told to report to Battalion HQ for an interview with the CO during which he asked me if I would like to transfer permanently from the Queen's to the Norfolks. 'After all Mike, you know us better now than you know your own Regiment.' I was very flattered and it was true that, as well as having become very close to Ben, Mike Gunton and Peter Shuttleworth, I had also come to like most of the other officers I'd met during my seven months with the Battalion. The CO then gave me a carrot – if I *did* transfer I would be given the MMG Platoon in Hong Kong which was where the Battalion was going in two months' time. As command of the MMG Platoon was a captain's appointment it was very tempting. I replied that I would need some time to think it over and it was left like that. In the event the decision was taken out of my hands.

On 23 July Operation CROMER began. Designed, yet *again*, to capture a live prisoner, it proved very costly. The Royal Norfolk History has the following incredible and, to my mind, absurd explanation of the theory behind it:

It was clearly essential that our own HQ knew of changes of enemy units and strengths along the front line to assist in assessing the stance to be adopted at the armistice talks as well as for more routine intelligence purpose.

The basic plan of CROMER was to entice the Chinese to attack a new standing patrol which was to be established close to one of their positions. The spot chosen, Hill 118, was near the west end of 'Crete' and within 500 yards of known enemy positions. In preparation for this ruse, Peter Shuttleworth was told to take a strong patrol and occupy 118 after dark on 23 July. Once in position a C Company platoon would move up and, protected by Peter's chaps, dig weapon pits for occupation by yet another platoon from B Company. The others would then withdraw.

CROMER started badly. As Peter and his men approached 118 they realized it was occupied by the enemy, but nevertheless put in an immediate attack and, despite having one man killed and another 'missing', drove the Chinese off the hill. This allowed the C Company platoon to move in and dig the weapon pits as planned. The 'missing' man was a member of my Platoon, Private Webster. Corporal Bruce, one of my section commanders, was recommended for a Mention in Despatches (MiD) for his part in Peter's attack, but never got it. Before first light on the 24th two sections of John Berney's B Company platoon were therefore occupying the weapon pits on 118 in accordance with the basic plan. The enemy took no action.

That night two ambush patrols were sent out to support the force on 118, one to the north of it and another, commanded by me, to the west. We were to capture any Chinese retreating from 118 after any action there. We didn't have to wait long for something to happen. At about 10.30 p.m. an enemy force hit John Berney's two sections on 118 from the north-west and overran them. Some survivors managed to get back to the firm base established for the operation on 'Bunker Hill', but others were missing. The ambush patrol to the north was therefore ordered to retake the hill, following which mine was to join it and search for survivors. This we did without opposition and recovered four wounded. However, John Berney and two others were still unaccounted for. On receiving a report of the night's activities the Brigade commander gave orders for Operation CROMER to be suspended. The Royal Norfolk History records:

A patrol under 2nd Lieutenant Reynolds later returned to Hill 118 to recover the bodies of those killed in the action. Lieutenant Berney was found dead with his pistol still in his hand. Two other men,

Private Wheeler and Private Haynes, were also killed and their bodies recovered.

My diary entry for the 26th reads: 'Patrol in terrible rain to 2nd cutting [about halfway along 'Crete']. Been raining now for 6 days.' And then for 27th to 31st July it reads: 'Rain. Half my Platoon left for demob.' This was a hard blow; I was losing men I trusted and getting untried replacements.

Operation HARVEST which followed CROMER was even more complicated. I quote the plan from the Royal Norfolk History:

> Operation HARVEST again set out to trick the enemy and lure him into a trap. To do this, an officer and ten men would occupy Hill 118 everyday during the hours of daylight. At night the group would withdraw and four platoons would move out and deploy in the area. Two of them were to strike at the enemy whose curiosity would lure him out onto Hill 118 while the other two were positioned on the flanks to cut off the enemy's retreat.

It goes on to say that two artillery batteries would put down concentrations on 118 just before the striking force reached it and also mentions all approaches to 118 being covered by trip flares, but *not* a large battle simulation panel that had been put together by the Sappers to be detonated remotely to give the impression of a section opening fire. It was to be left on 118 when the daylight group withdrew just after last light. And guess who was to lead the first daylight group? Yes, Mike Reynolds.

At 8.30 p.m. on the 30th I set out for 118 with a full section and a couple of Sappers with an NCO and the simulation panel. Two sections from the Battalion HQ Defence Platoon, took up a position on 'Bunker Hill' as a support force and four more patrols from other companies set up ambushes on my flanks. We spent the rest of the night improving the very basic weapon pits on 118 and putting out trip flares and then, at 4 a.m. on the 31st, the flanking ambushes withdrew, leaving me and my group to sit it out for the rest of the day. It wasn't easy to show yourself deliberately to your enemy for some fourteen hours and I was convinced that we would be mortared, but once again we were lucky and nothing happened. At 8.30 that night, after twenty-four hours out in no man's land, and with the battle simulation panel set up, my mission had been completed and we withdrew, passing two platoons of C Company which were getting into position further to the east as the strike force. The Chinese didn't take the bait though and 'before first light [on 1 August] the platoons slipped back into the FDLs [forward defended localities] to be replaced by ten men who returned to the hill for the daylight hours once more to act as bait.' Peter Shuttleworth commanded the bait group this time and among those with him was Dick Cooper of my platoon. Again nothing happened, but during the day they discovered and later recovered poor Webster's body and that of another soldier killed earlier.

Operation HARVEST, which involved some 130 men, was repeated on the 2nd, but this time B Company, under Captain Ted Eberhardie, provided the two-platoon strike force and A Company provided the northern ambush platoon – and yes, I got the job! I was pretty tired by now, but there was nothing for it but to rehearse my platoon ambush party during the afternoon of the 2nd and brief them carefully on what to do in certain eventualities. One slightly worrying aspect was that, as had happened on my very first patrol across the Samichon in December, I didn't really know some of the men I was taking out. About half had only arrived in the Company a few days before to replace those who had left for demob.

We reached our ambush position at about 9 p.m. and I deployed my three sections in a triangle so that we were covering in every direction. I was in the centre with Ketteringham and the radio. Almost immediately after deploying, and just as I was rubbing some mosquito repellent on my face and neck, the section facing north-west suddenly opened rapid fire. I crawled over and peered through the half light to see a group of at least twenty or so Chinese moving towards us at a half double. I got up onto my knees, threw a grenade and opened fire with my Sten. We had rehearsed that, in this situation, the sections not engaged directly would swing round into line and bring fire to bear. The next few minutes were noisy and confusing with both sides firing rapidly, throwing grenades and with Corporal Bruce and me shouting our heads off to encourage our men. I don't know how long the firefight lasted but before long I found myself with no grenades and only one magazine left and realized we couldn't stay in that position much longer. The Chinese seemed to be in amongst us and the whole situation was chaotic. I shouted something like 'Collect the casualties and get back up the hill!' During the afternoon briefing I had told the men that if the worst should happen and we became dispersed they were to regroup at a designated rendezvous (RV) on the hill behind us in the direction of the strike force. No sooner had I given this order though than my right leg juddered away from me, as though I'd been kicked by a carthorse. I decided to find out if I could walk on it and slammed it onto the ground. I'm not sure exactly what happened but I think it buckled between the knee and the ankle; I certainly found myself on the ground and thought 'Oh God, now I've had it'. I remember shouting 'For Christ's sake, don't leave me here' or something like that, and then putting my arm up to someone crouching over me and saying 'Good boy Ketteringham!' The next thing I remember is finding him lying beside me. He wasn't moving. He was dead.

My memories of the next nine hours are intermittent and fleeting. I remember hearing the sound and seeing the flashes of considerable artillery fire and hearing the crack of our MMGs firing over my head at targets I couldn't see. The Battalion War Diary records:

> 2135hrs: OC B Coy calls for DFs [defensive fire plans each fired by four 25-pdrs] ORANGE, GIN, PINKERS. These DFs are all to the north of CRETE [designed to hit or at least deter any Chinese moving towards the B Company strike force and in fact not very far from where I was lying]. 2150hrs: ORANGE, GIN, PINKERS fired again. 2200hrs: DF BURGUNDY [sixteen 25-pdrs] fired on Hill 118.

No wonder I heard and saw a lot of artillery fire!

I also recall hearing a number of Chinese chattering loudly, fitting magazines to their weapons and removing their dead and wounded and began to wonder how long it would be before they found me. Things then seemed to quieten down a bit and I heard some Chinese talking; they were quite close and, I think, as confused and frightened as I was. It was only when things went completely quiet (at about midnight according to the Battalion War Diary) that they moved off. Sometime later I found one of the A Company corporals next to me. I had already tried crawling, but my lower leg seemed almost detached from my knee and the pain was such that I think I must have passed out a number of times. I knew that I couldn't possibly crawl over a mile back to A Company lines through the thick undergrowth and that the farther I moved away from my original ambush position the less likely it would be for any rescue party to find me. I told the corporal that it was pointless him staying with me and to get back and tell them where I was. He left reluctantly. I tied my Sten gun strap tightly round my thigh in the hope of staunching the flow of blood, but I had discomfort in various places down my right side and came to the conclusion that I must have caught the odd piece of grenade shrapnel as well. After some time on my own I began to panic. I was much closer to the Chinese than to friendly troops and visualized myself dying there alone. Rather than that, I would try to give myself up. I therefore began to whistle 'Rule Britannia' in the hope of attracting their attention. However, within a very short time, and to my amazement, I got a couple of 'Rule Britannias' back and realized there were at least two other wounded members of my platoon nearby.

I must have been unconscious for quite a lot of the nine hours I was there. When I *was* conscious I remember being desperately thirsty, due to the loss of blood I suppose, and I remember sucking the dew off leaves.

With daylight came the rescue party. The Battalion War Diary records:

3rd August 0555hrs: A missing corporal [the one who had been with me] has now returned to A Coy position. He gave whereabouts of an officer and one man who were still in the area of the A Coy ambush position. 0615hrs: Patrol reports they have located one man dead [Ketteringham] and two wounded [one was me]. 0705hrs: One more wounded man located by patrol. 0740hrs: Five enemy dead still on the position.

Peter Shuttleworth led the rescue party which included the Battalion Medical Officer, Captain (later Major General) Trevor Hart, a friend of mine who had insisted on coming out to look for me. Fortunately it was a very misty morning and they managed to recover us unseen by the Chinese.

The only thing I recall about the return journey is being mortared as we crossed 'Crete' somewhere near 'Bunker Hill'. Everyone hit the deck, they dropped my stretcher and I went rolling off down a steep slope. I've always thought that did as much damage to me as being shot. Anyway we arrived safely back in A Company lines where Trevor Hart had established a forward Regimental Aid Post and I was given a much-needed shot of morphine and a cigarette. Then, after a short journey on a stretcher-jeep, I was placed in a plastic bubble on the outside of a helicopter and airlifted to the American 8055 MASH (Mobile Army Surgical Hospital).

Operation HARVEST had worked more or less as planned and four wounded Chinese prisoners were taken, but all died before reaching our lines. The Battalion War Diary reported, 'An official estimate of enemy casualties was thirty-five killed and sixty wounded.'

And the terrible cost of this operation? Three killed, twenty-one wounded and one man missing, nearly half of them from my patrol. We suffered one killed, ten wounded, including me, and one man missing – Private Burrell who, it was later established, was a prisoner of the Chinese. My patrol's casualty rate was a devastating 48 per cent. The B Company commander, Ted Eberhardie, received an MC for Operation HARVEST, his radio operator, who was wounded in the foot early on in the operation but kept going, got an MM and one of his platoon commanders, Captain McBride, got an MiD. His FOO, Captain James Baxter, also got an MC. All were 'immediate' awards. And A Company? Nobody got anything, not even a MiD.

This has not been an easy chapter to write. Memories of people and events I haven't thought about for many years have come flooding back, but I'm afraid the sad ones have outweighed the happy ones. Whilst writing it I've had disturbed nights and many of the events described have made me angry. Watkins, Allman, Tommy Thompson, 'Whiskers' Wormald, Webster, John Berney, and, of course, brave Ketteringham – oh, what a waste of good lives! And I think, too, of some of those I knew who were wounded, many of whom have suffered for the rest of their lives. Total British casualties in the Korean War were 1,078 killed in action, 2,674 wounded and 1,060 missing or taken prisoner.

Chapter Seven

Hospitals and Recovery

I have very few memories of the forty-eight hours or so I spent in the MASH. I remember being in a tented ward and that once, as I washed my face, I found a small, but very sharp piece of shrapnel between my fingers. It had come out of my right cheek. The most important thing that can be said about those forty-eight hours is that the American surgeons did a wonderful job saving my leg and patching me up generally. Some older readers may remember the wonderful American TV series *MASH*. I can assure them that I never saw anyone like 'Hotlips' – in fact I don't remember *any* female nurses at all.

On 5 August I was moved, along with 110 others to the American 121 Evacuation Hospital in Seoul, housed in what had been a pre-war school. All I remember happening there was a visit from dear old Ben. Operation HARVEST had been the last action of the Battalion which was now out of the line and in reserve before being moved to Hong Kong. I remember asking Ben to make sure Ketteringham and Corporal Bruce got medals. He said he would try his best, but that as Ketteringham had been killed the only awards he could get were a Victoria Cross (which required witnesses other than me) or a MiD. Neither of them got anything. When Ben said goodbye that day I never expected to see him again.

On 7 August I was flown to Kure in Japan where I was admitted to the British Commonwealth Military Hospital and, a day later, had a visit from my old comrade Private Edwards. He was in a wheelchair, but in great form. When I enquired, 'How is it?' looking at his crotch, he replied, 'Oh fine Sir. I've only got one ball but the Jap girls love it. Tried it out the other night and it works a treat!'

I had four more operations, on the 9th, 18th, 25th and 29th, and one skin graft whilst I was in the BMH. The operations didn't worry me, but the removal of the skin graft dressing was almost as painful as being wounded. I'd had about a square foot of skin taken from my thigh and grafted onto my wounds in little one-inch squares – 'postage stamping' they called it. The British ward sister on duty the day the dressing had to come off my thigh gave me five minutes to do it myself. It was excruciatingly painful and I'd only got about two or three inches of it off when she returned. 'Right!' she said and ripped it off in one stroke. I nearly died – it bled a lot, but I suppose she was right.

Life in hospital really wasn't at all bad. At least we were alive and had super nurses, including one New Zealand sister named Cassidy with whom I immediately fell in love. Several times a week Australian officers based nearby used to visit the wounded Aussies in our ward and always brought in beer which we hid under our sheets and drank when the nurses weren't looking. I remember it was desperately hot in Japan that August and our discomfort (no air conditioning) was aggravated by the fact that next to the Officers' Ward was a swimming pool for the hospital staff. It was agony to lie there sweating and listen to them through the open window splashing about and laughing. Kay Starr's 'Wheel of Fortune' was the number one on the 'Hit Parade' in August 1952 and will always remind me of the Britcom Military Hospital Japan.

Not long after reaching the hospital I was reunited with the tin trunk I had left in Kure eight months before. When I opened it I was upset to find the photographs and negatives recording my journey out on the *Georgic* were missing. Although I say it myself, they were very good photographs and it was a unique record of a world that has gone forever. I was very upset.

My parents had received a telegram for the War Office dated 4 August, reading: 'Regret to inform you that report received from overseas states that your son [then full details of my name and Regiment] was wounded in action in Korea on 2 August. The Army Council desire to offer you their sympathy. Letter follows.' That letter arrived two days later stating that my wounds were 'severe' and enclosing two concessional telegrams so that my parents could communicate with me: 'For your information and guidance, the text of the messages should be kept within twelve words.' Another letter followed, dated the 15th, stating that I 'was located at the British Commonwealth General Hospital', that my condition was now 'quite good' and that 'in view of your son's satisfactory condition, no further reports are expected from overseas.' Ben had also written quite a long and moving letter to my parents on the 15th. After describing roughly what had happened, he went on, 'I have always had great admiration for Mike's abilities and considered him the officer most likely to succeed.' He went on, 'I must mention that Peter Shuttleworth who was due to leave for England and demob the very next morning after that night's show, insisted on going out for Mike'. I discovered later that this was indeed true. Over a year later Peter received an MC for this action – why on *earth* it took so long for it to be awarded I have no idea.

On 5 September, thirty-four days after being wounded, I was told I was fit enough to go home and, next day, was moved to a nearby airfield to begin the eleven-day journey. My last Medical Board Report (F. Med. 24) in Japan read, '2/Lt Reynolds will require prolonged convalescence and neurosurgical treatment. He should therefore be evacuated to the UK.'

On 6 September 1952 I was flown in an RAF Hastings to an American naval hospital in the Philippines. The seven-hour flight carried a number of 'walking wounded' and the aircraft had been adapted to carry at least a dozen, probably more, stretcher cases. We were well looked after by a Princess Mary's RAF nursing sister and a couple of nurses, but the stretchers were stacked one above the other in threes (or was it fours?), with our noses only about six inches from the stretcher above us or, in the case of the chap at the top, from the aircraft's roof. It took up to half an hour to stack us up for take-off and a similar time to unload us and we were in different positions in the stack for each leg of our journey back to England.

On the 7th we flew on, another seven hours, to Singapore and the Royal Naval Hospital at Changi. We remained there for six days because our aircraft was needed for another task. Anyway we were not unhappy to be in Changi. The officers' ward had single rooms with half walls that only came up to bed level at the sides which meant we could feel the sea breezes, keep cool and watch the ships passing between Singapore Island and the mainland. I got messages to my old Cranleigh school friends who visited and brought me a nice bottle of gin.

On the 13th we flew for over eight hours to a hospital in Nagombo, near Colombo, in Ceylon (now Sri Lanka). We were all exhausted after the flight which had been marred for some of us by a young Scottish soldier who kept calling out, 'Oh, sister, sister – help me, help me!' Eventually I said to the sister, 'For God's sake, can't you give him something to shut him up? If he's *that* bad why on earth didn't they keep him longer in hospital in Japan?' Sometime later she came back and said, 'You won't hear him again. I gave him a shot of sterile water and when he went quiet I knew there was nothing *really* wrong, so I've had a few harsh words with him.'

Another seven-hour flight on the 14th took us to Karachi in Pakistan and the following day we reached RAF Habbaniya near Baghdad in Iraq, the most uncomfortable stop of all. As luck would have it I was nearest the aircraft roof on this flight and nearly passed out with heat exhaustion during the half hour or so it took to unload us and get us into the shade. The next day saw us in Malta and then, after a final eight-hour flight, we landed at RAF Brize Norton in Oxfordshire to be taken to Wroughton RAF hospital near Swindon for the night. It was great to be home.

I was transferred to the Cambridge Military Hospital in Aldershot next day where I was to be a patient for a further eleven months, although not always an in-patient. My parents came down to see me within a couple of days. My parents had spent the previous night in London and by sheer chance had run into Tony Baxter near Paddington station. He recognized them and they told him about me. Tony, then in his last year at Cambridge, came down to visit me and our friendship was renewed.

The Sister in overall charge of the Officers' Ward was Sister Harris who looked a bit like the comedian Arthur Askey, had a reputation as a martinet but in fact had a heart of gold. During our long acquaintance I became very fond of her. Matron was the real martinet. I remember having to lie virtually to attention in my bed, without so much as a crumpled sheet, for her daily inspection. However, she too had a kind heart beneath her stern exterior and ran an excellent nursing staff.

My first surprise at the Cambridge was to find that the surgeon who had operated on me four times in Japan had come home just a little before me and had been posted to the Cambridge. He was therefore still *my* surgeon. A lieutenant colonel named John Watts, it was my good fortune that he was one of the country's foremost experts on gunshot wounds; he later wrote a book called *Surgeon at War*. His expertise was demonstrated within my first week in Aldershot. The senior British Army surgeon at that time, an Australian colonel called Marsden, and known as 'Butcher Marsden', came down from Millbank Military Hospital in London every so often to look at new cases and review old ones. He took one look at my leg, turned to John Watts, said, 'We'll have that off on Thursday!' and walked away. I was devastated. John Watts returned on his own a short time later and said that, although the Colonel was probably right in that I might be better off in the long term without my leg, it *could* be saved if I was prepared for a long haul. I replied, 'I've kept it now for over six weeks, I'm keeping it Sir!' He smiled.

I don't know how many operations I had in the Cambridge or for how long my leg was in a full-length plaster. It was certainly towards the end of the year or the beginning of 1953 before the cast was removed finally. I'd been home several times on crutches; my father used to come down and collect me and it didn't take long for me to join my old friends for nights out. One night wasn't so much fun though. I suppose today it would be called Post-Traumatic Stress Disorder but, suddenly I started crying and shouting at my friends that they didn't understand life or death and how much better Ketteringham was than any of them. They eventually calmed me down and, thank goodness, it never happened again.

I had a very nasty shock when my leg plaster was finally removed. I was sitting on my hospital bed and had finally managed to bend my knee when

I found that my right foot didn't seem to reach the floor alongside my left one. 'Oh, didn't they tell you?' asked Sister Harris, 'That leg is bound to be shorter after the damage to your tibia and fibula – in fact you've really only got one lump of bone there now instead of two separate bones.' I was pretty shattered and immediately thought, 'Well that's the end of my military career.' The shortening turned out to be two and a half inches. The other shock was to find that a major nerve, the posterior tibial, in my leg had been severed and, as well as having no feeling in the sole of my foot, I had very restricted toe movement.

To compensate for my short leg, the Physiotherapy Department raised the heel of my shoe by three-inches. This was painful to walk on and I had to use a stick to keep my balance. When my father saw me hobbling around on this high heel he arranged for a private consultation with the head orthopaedic surgeon at the Queen Elizabeth Hospital in Birmingham, who was shocked when he saw the heel and, literally, threw my shoe into a corner. After a full examination of my leg and foot he got out some small wooden strips, each about an-eighth-of-an-inch-thick and started putting them at right-angles under my foot, instructing me to tell him when I was really comfortable. When I had an inch under the heel, half an inch under the ball of my foot and a quarter under the toes, I knew he had found the answer. I showed his prescription to John Watts when I got back to Aldershot and within a week my shoe had been given the required 'raise' by a specialist shoemaker. A few days later I threw away my stick and, although still having quite a pronounced limp, found I could walk more or less normally.

Early that year I decided it was time to try driving again. However, I was told that, due to my permanent disability, I would have to take another driving test, to be arranged for me with a Royal Army Service Corps unit at Farnborough. I was a bit worried to see that my test vehicle was a 3-ton lorry and even more worried when the examiner was a civilian. I complained that I thought it was a bit tough to give me a vehicle like that with a heavy brake pedal, but was told there was nothing else available. Somehow I passed and within a few weeks was the proud possessor of my first car, a second-hand Austin 8.

Sometime in April I was sent to the King Edward VII Rehabilitation Home for Officers, in Osborne House on the Isle of Wight, so-named after the King gave the building and grounds to the nation. Designed by Prince Albert in the Italian palatial style, Osborne had been Queen Victoria's favourite house, and her rooms and Albert's were kept as they had left them. It was a fantastic place in which to convalesce with a staff of sixty to look after twenty male patients from the armed forces and civil service. I had a huge room with en-suite bathroom and superb views over the

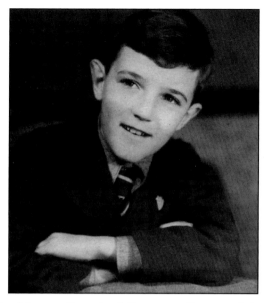

Aged 8 at my first school, Fowgay Hall, Warwickshire

On my pony 'Beauty' - aged 12

My second home in Haughton 1943–48

Cranleigh School 1944–47

School rugby champions 1945 – me front right

Private in the Black Watch 1948 – with my mother

As the Duke of Wellington in the Army film 'Proud Heritage' – 1948

Our future Queen takes the salute at Sandhurst, July 1949

On commissioning, July 1950

Korea – Cpl Compton and poor, brave Ketteringham

Korea, 3 August 1952 – after lying out in no-man's land for 9 hours;
Peter Shuttleworth in background

Our wedding 4 June 1955

Our Simca at Kyrenia, Cyprus

Pilgrimage to the Holy Land, October 1957

Adjutant to Lt Col David Lloyd-Owen, Major Jock Haswell, 2IC,
on left – 1958

Clewborough Camberley 1961–63

With my officers, CSM Jack Chaffer (2nd from left) and sergeants in Canada,
June 1965

Our house and car in Ottawa, 1966–68

Our girls – Palm Beach Florida, November 1967

Burami Fort in Trucial Oman, July 1968

Leading the Advance Party to Ulster, August 1969

CO 2nd Queen's, 1 July 1971

Ground floor CO's flat in Unna!

With my personal staff in 2nd Queen's – Pat Gwilliam, Brian Morris, Nigel
Harris & Mike Jelf at Soltau

Handing over the 'Trimm Dich Fahrt' to the Mayor of Werl, Frau Dr Rohrer

My Battalion at full strength after 10 days at Soltau in 1973

Promoted Brigadier December 1974

Talavera House, Osnabrück

One of many inspections – the Argylls.

Elected Schinken Senator of Osnabrück!

Queen's Jubilee visit to the Royal College of Defence Studies, 1977

ornate gardens and the Solent. On top of that we were honorary members of the Island Sailing Club and were warmly welcomed wherever we went in Cowes. Life was good. I soon made friends with a couple of the other patients, both recovering from polio.

My treatment at Osborne consisted of physiotherapy for part of the morning, followed by occupational therapy – making jigsaw puzzles using a foot-operated fretsaw machine to exercise my knee, ankle and foot. We were free in the afternoons to do as we liked – sightseeing and, occasionally, sailing. I went out three or four times with a famous yachtsman called Martin Sharp and the even more famous boat designer Uffa Fox. The Isle is a beautiful place and I enjoyed seeing where my parents had spent their honeymoon at Shanklin and visiting places like Carisbrooke Castle. After supper, our evenings were usually spent in the 'Anchor' pub in Cowes. We were meant to be back in Osborne by 9 p.m. but soon found a way in through an unlocked ground-floor window. The only real impediment to our adventures was that the last ferry across the estuary between Cowes and East Cowes, where Osborne was situated, sailed at 10 o'clock. Even if we missed that, we could still drive the long way back through Newport.

My girlfriend during my time at Osborne was Molly, a nursing sister who was *very* Irish; we had great fun together both on and off duty. The on-duty part was possible because her night-duty station was only a short distance from my room.

My idyllic life at Osborne came to an abrupt end in May when we were told suddenly that we were all being returned to our base hospitals. This was because the Cowes Week sailing regatta was coming up and the Governor, a retired head of Army Medical Services, wanted our rooms for his friends!

A tearful Molly insisted on coming on the ferry with me all the way to Portsmouth and I duly reported back to John Watts in Aldershot who was angry that I'd been sent back. He said there wasn't much more they could do for me in the Cambridge and suggested that, as time was now the best healer, I should go home to Birmingham for a couple of months. That suited me fine. And so I said a final goodbye to the Cambridge Military Hospital. I had been very happy during my time there and was greatly saddened when I visited it in 2007 to find it abandoned, boarded up and derelict.

The next memorable event in my life was the coronation of Queen Elizabeth II on 2 June. As a wounded veteran of the Korean War, I was given the 'privilege' of two wooden seats on the pavement opposite the left main gate of Buckingham Palace. I decided to take my mother and, after spending a night with an aunt in Sussex Gardens, we took our places at some unearthly hour like eight o'clock in the morning. I wore my

Service Dress and my mother dressed the part – and it rained and it rained. However, I did get to see and salute the Queen on her coronation day. The other thing that sticks in my mind is a Royal Mail man on a bicycle riding down the completely traffic-free Mall and straight through one of the main gates of the Palace; he got huge cheers from the masses of people lining the route. We didn't stay for the Queen's return from Westminster Abbey – we were soaked and hungry, so we returned to Sussex Gardens and watched the rest of the event on TV.

Shortly after returning from a superb holiday in Spain and France with a couple of my male friends, I decided that I should leave the Army and find a civilian job. I had been told that my disability made it unlikely that I'd be allowed to stay in the infantry, or transfer to any other combat arm. This depressed me and so I was quite pleased when my father arranged for me to have an interview in London with the Castrol Oil Company. Although I was accepted for training as a junior manager I then had second thoughts. When, a short time later, I was told that the only way I could stay in the Army in the long term was to transfer to the Royal Military Police or the Royal Pioneer Corps, I decided to dig my heels in. I was going to stay in the infantry. I wrote to my father, 'If my leg holds out and is still good in six months time I shall try to stay in the Queen's.'

I had a full medical under John Watts in early August and was thrilled when he said I could return to duty, although medically downgraded to 'LE'. That meant I could serve only in the UK or BAOR and even then not in an operational battalion, but at least I was on the road back to proper soldiering. I duly reported to the Officer Commanding (OC) the Queen's Regimental Depot in Stoughton Barracks, Guildford on 12 August 1953, just over a year after I'd been wounded. I was now a lieutenant and my pay was £354-18 a year (£7,610 today) gross.

Chapter Eight
Back to Duty and Marriage

Built in 1876, Stoughton Barracks in Guildford was the Depot of The Queen's Royal Regiment and its imposing entrance, with the Regimental badge over the main gate, and huge Keep, which housed the Guardroom, Quartermaster's stores and Regimental Museum, made it a local landmark. So much so that, although the Ministry of Defence sold off the barracks in 1983 with much of it turned into residential accommodation, the Keep, Officers' Mess, CO's house, Depot HQ building and one of the soldiers' accommodation blocks (Peterborough) look almost exactly the same today as they did when I served there in the early 1950s.

Depot Queen's, as we knew it, was a very small unit with a total military staff of thirty-seven to train drafts of, mainly, National Servicemen for ten weeks. The OC in August 1953 was Major Edward Clowes, a veteran of the Burma campaign who had commanded a Chindit column. He was an old Cranleighan which gave us an immediate bond. Other officers included the Adjutant, Quartermaster, Museum Curator, a retired Quartermaster, and an Administrative Officer, a retired Queensman who looked after the accounts and generally helped Edward with Regimental affairs. Other memorable characters were ex-Private 'Chuck' Sheffield, who had joined the Army in 1907, had an arm full of long-service stripes and looked after the boilers, and Private Bellord who cared for eighty pigs, housed in nearby sties, that were an important source of income for the Regiment.

I was posted to the Training Company, commanded by Captain Peter Durrant and joined a National Service Second Lieutenant, David Hughes, as a Training Subaltern. We each had two platoons of recruits commanded by sergeants – in my case Sergeants Wildgoose and Jessop. Surprisingly, I already knew the 'Goose' from Korea. A Second World War Royal Marine, he'd re-enlisted after the war in the Queen's and had, like me, been sent to the Norfolks as a reinforcement. Jessup had also served in Korea with the Middlesex Regiment so we were a pretty strong and experienced team. Under these sergeants were two or three corporals for each platoon. *Carry On, Sergeant* was filmed at Stoughton but well after my time. Although a comedy and a parody of what life was really like for a National Service recruit at the Depot, it brings back many happy memories every time I see it.

Recruit training was very repetitive for the permanent staff but, nevertheless, rewarding. All we could really do in ten weeks was to 'tame' the 'Teddy Boys' of that era by teaching them discipline, self as well as military, get them fit and teach them how to shoot and throw grenades. The discipline part was instilled through drill, cleanliness and kit inspections. The latter took place every day, but with the big one on Saturday mornings. The platoons were in competition with each other to win the title 'Champion Platoon'. For the Saturday inspection blankets and sheets had to be 'boxed up' with cardboard strips, and every piece of personal military equipment laid out on the recruit's bed in a specific layout. Everything had to be spotlessly clean and polished if appropriate. It took so long to do this that many recruits slept on the floor rather than get up at an unearthly hour to lay it all out. The competitive spirit led to some ludicrous situations such as the time Sergeant Wildgoose said to me, 'You haven't looked up the chimney Sir!' 'What on earth are you talking about?' I replied. 'They've whitewashed it!' Sure enough, on their own volition and to get extra points, his recruits had whitewashed the inside of their large barrack-room chimney as far as I could see.

Passing-Out Parades at the end of the ten-week training period were also organized with the aim of instilling pride. A band always played, parents were invited, and the most senior officer we could find, often a general, took the salute. There is no doubt that all this worked well for the vast majority of the National Servicemen who usually left us feeling proud of their unexpected achievements. The parents were also often extremely complimentary saying they could hardly believe the improvement in their son's appearance. Of the 300 recruits trained in my first year at Stoughton, we persuaded twenty per cent of the National Servicemen to become regulars – a record in Southern Command.

The big 'happenings' at the end of 1953 were meeting my future wife, Anne, and on the military side the 1st Battalion leaving Germany and being sent to Malaya. Although called an 'emergency' by the British government, the campaign being fought there at that time was in fact a full-scale guerrilla war between the 'Malayan Races Liberation Army' (the military arm of the Malayan Communist Party) and the armed forces of Great Britain, Australia and Malaya.

On Maundy Thursday night 1954 I proposed to Anne. It wasn't a particularly clever day to ask a devout Catholic, but nevertheless she said yes. I did, however, make it clear that a Queen's officer was not expected to marry before he was twenty-five (I was only twenty-three and a half), that I wouldn't be entitled to a married quarter until I reached that age and that I couldn't possibly afford to marry until I was a captain anyway. This meant we would probably have to wait for two and a half years. She didn't seem to mind.

On 5 April 1954 I appeared before Colonel 'Butcher' Marsden again for a re-assessment of my medical grading. I produced a certificate signed by Edward Clowes confirming that I had recently completed an eleven-mile march, followed by the assault course in the barracks. The Colonel examined my foot and leg and then said, 'OK, well done – you're FE' (fit for operations anywhere). 'But what about the Medical Board Sir?' 'I *am* the Board boy – get out!' He in fact wrote on his report. 'This is a first-class officer who makes the best of his disability in that he plays games and tries to do full duty. Therefore I recommend that he is given a trial tour of duty in Category of FE.' The official 'Board' rubber-stamped this recommendation on 6 June. In fact, although graded FE, the skin-grafting on my leg, which was paper-thin, meant there was no way I could join the 1st Battalion and go into jungle or swamps.

The next important event was when Edward asked me to take over from his Adjutant who was due to join the 1st Battalion in Malaya. I was thrilled and took up the appointment on 7 October. I'd only been in the job about a week though when I learned that Peter Durrant was also being posted to Malaya and that they were planning to send back a captain to take over the Training Company. I saw my chance and went in to see Edward. 'Sir, it's crazy to send someone back,' I said. 'They need all their captains out there. Why can't *I* take over the Company? After all, I have combat experience and after more than a year here I know the Company, its staff and the training programme like the back of my hand.' Edward smiled. 'You've got a cheek young man!' he said. 'But you might be right – I'll have to consult the CO of the First Battalion and the Colonel of the Regiment of course, so don't get too excited just yet.' But I didn't have to wait long – on 28 October I was confirmed as the Company commander and promoted to the rank of captain. When I told Anne she said, 'Good! So we can get married next year when you're twenty-five!'

In 1954 I visited Ketteringham's parents in nearby Godalming. I was very nervous when I knocked on their door, but after I introduced myself and said I'd been with their son in Korea they immediately invited me in. I didn't tell them that he'd died saving me until we'd had a few drinks, but I finally summoned up courage and came out with it. To my amazement his father turned to his mother and said, 'Well that's the sort of thing Bob would do, isn't it?' They showed no anger or ill-feeling whatsoever and the evening ended on a happy note. They told me that Bob had been a keen cyclist and that the local club had instituted an annual memorial race in his memory.

Later that year, in August and September, I accompanied my parents on a fantastic – for those days anyway – motoring holiday around Europe. We drove through Belgium into Germany and then south to Munich and into Austria and Italy. We visited Dachau Concentration Camp, still with refugees living in it, Berchtesgaden and Salzburg, which we all loved. From Venice we travelled through Bologna, Florence and Siena to Rome. My mother, who had become a Catholic whilst I was in Korea, was very excited at the prospect of seeing the 'Eternal City'. I was also very much looking forward to it for I had already accompanied my mother to her local church a number of times during my convalescence and was becoming quite interested in the Catholic faith.

On the military side, 1954 was an interesting and important year for me. The Depot shooting team under my captaincy won the China Cup and Falling Plate Competitions in the Home Counties District Rifle meeting at Hythe, thus beating all the regular and Territorial Army (TA) units in the south-east.

The winter of 1954–55 saw some spirited exercises with the Home Guard. Our local unit really was a 'Dad's Army' outfit with a mobile HQ in the form of an open-topped Rolls Royce and a formidable lady who operated the radio back to the static HQ. On one occasion we had to provide 'flying columns' of platoon strength to go down and reinforce the Home Guard who were guarding a radar station on the South Downs somewhere near Brighton. A Territorial Army (TA) SAS unit was the 'enemy'. However, when we arrived, the Home Guard wouldn't let us into their bunker as we had a different password and they were convinced *we* were the enemy! Somehow the misunderstanding was sorted out, but it would have made a good episode on the *Dad's Army* TV programme.

Soon after I took command of the Training Company there were some important and essential additions to the Depot staff. Three regular subalterns, Peter Field of Sandhurst days, Mike Doyle and Brian Faris, all with experience in Malaya, and an additional National Service officer joined us. Peter took over as Adjutant, but I was still left with enough training subalterns for up to eight platoons. I therefore demanded, and after a short time was given, additional NCOs with experience of Malaya to join this strong and experienced team. One of the new NCOs who arrived was a corporal named Lea – seventeen years later he would be my RSM.

By early 1955 my interest in the Catholic Church had increased to a point where I had decided to take weekly instruction in the faith from the local priest in Guildford. I freely admit that I was strongly influenced in this decision by my mother as well as Anne. The result was that in May

1955 Monsignor Dickie Foster, Rector of Oscott College, a seminary in Sutton Coldfield and a great friend of my parents, received me into the Church. Anne and my mother were thrilled.

The most vivid memory during my last days as a single man was the 1955 'Glorious First of June'. The weather was good and a large party came up from HMS *Excellent*. As well as the cricket there was a 'Social' in the Sergeants' Mess, an All Ranks' dance and a splendid Guest Night in the Officers' Mess, which was particularly memorable as we had most of the senior officers of the Regiment to support us and it was the first time after the war that we wore scarlet mess kit. As Mr Vice I had the Commander of *Excellent* on my right. At some stage during dinner the Commander said to me, 'I simply don't believe what I see!' 'Oh dear,' I said, 'What's wrong?' 'I've just counted eight DSOs and six MCs round this table, not to mention five CBEs or OBEs,' he replied. He was right: the Queen's had a remarkable war record and just seven of our officers were wearing all these medals!

I married Anne at the Oratory in Birmingham on 4 June and the reception was held in Anne's parents' late-Georgian house in Ampton Road, Edgbaston. My responsibilities were minor: all I had to do was provide a Guard of Honour – and turn up on the day. The priest who married us, Father Geoffrey, had been a friend of Anne and her family for many years. Also present on the altar was Dickie Foster who gave a homily based on my Regimental badge, the Paschal Lamb, which went down very well with the Guard of Honour, all Protestants and including Edward Clowes, my first Company commander, Bill Peet, and my platoon commanders from Stoughton. Peter Field was my best man.

I had suggested a possible honeymoon itinerary to Anne some weeks before our wedding. We would head down through France to Rosas in Spain and, provided she liked it, spend about a week there before returning home through Switzerland and Paris. We were hoping for a three-week honeymoon, but knew that when the money ran out we would have to come home.

After disembarkation in Calais, we drove in glorious sunshine through Boulogne, Abbeville and Beauvais to Chartres. From there we set off next morning on the journey to Spain and arrived in Rosas in very hot weather at about midday on 9 June and enjoyed an idyllic week before leaving for Switzerland. From Switzerland it was back to France and Paris where we saw the sights and Anne did some shopping. Then it was home, via Calais, to a borrowed flat in Guildford.

We were in borrowed accommodation as there were no official officers' quarters in Guildford, except the Depot commander's, and I had been unable to find a suitable place to rent at an affordable price. However, in early September we found a very nice, well-furnished house to rent just above the Tunsgate in the centre of Guildford. There was only one snag – it had no central heating and only two open fireplaces, one in the drawing room and one in our bedroom. We nearly froze to death during the following winter.

The biggest change on the military side of my life in 1955 was the arrival of a new Depot commander, Lieutenant Colonel David Lloyd Owen, who had been a company commander in Iserlohn when I joined the 1st Battalion in September 1950. A remarkable man, he had left the Queen's in November 1941 to serve with the Long Range Desert Group and, three years later, aged twenty-six, was commanding this elite force in Italy and the Balkans. He had been badly wounded in the Desert and injured his spine severely during a night parachute drop into Albania in September 1944. By the end of the war he had been awarded an MC, a DSO and been Mentioned in Despatches. After the war he served in the War Office on the Military Operations staff, became Military Assistant (MA) to Bill Slim, the CIGS, and went on to be MA to Gerald Templer in Malaya. He came to command the Depot from the Staff College in Camberley where he had been on the Directing Staff.

As far as I was concerned as Training Company commander, the change of COs made little difference, although David's ability to talk informally to anyone meant that I often found him in one of my barrack rooms chatting to my soldiers – but they were *his* soldiers as well. We also had a change of Quartermasters in 1955 – Jimmy Kemp, a very experienced soldier was to prove a useful and wise counsellor in one of my later appointments.

During 1955 and the early part of 1956 major work was carried out on the soldiers' accommodation in Stoughton. This could not have happened at a worse time since, to keep the Battalion in Malaya at full strength, we had a larger than normal number of recruits passing through. At one stage in early 1956 I had over 200 recruits and some twenty-five instructors under my command; I was only twenty-five years old and I remember thinking one day on a muster parade that I would never command that number of men again unless I rose to command an infantry battalion. The Regimental Journal notes that more than 1,000 recruits passed through the Depot during my time there – over 700 while I was OC Training Company.

With my time at the Depot coming to an end, I was thinking of trying to be an army helicopter pilot but David Lloyd Owen had other ideas. 'You don't want to be the driver Michael,' he said, 'You want to be the VIP in the back! Don't worry. I'll get you a *proper* job!' And so in April I learned that, the following month, I was to be a General Staff Officer

Grade III (GSO3) Plans at GHQ Middle East Land Forces in Cyprus. Anne and I were thrilled at the thought of going to Cyprus and the Middle East, although the fact that Greek Cypriot nationalists, better known as EOKA (National Organization of Cypriot Fighters) had begun a terrorist campaign to force the British to leave the island and for union with Greece was a little worrying, not least for her family and my parents.

Chapter Nine
Staff Officer in Cyprus

Anne and I flew to Cyprus from RAF Stansted and, after a stopover in Malta, landed at RAF Nicosia at six o'clock in the morning of 10 May 1956 to be met by my future boss, General Staff Officer Grade I (GSO1), Lieutenant Colonel Dick Vernon of the Rifle Brigade. He drove us to our hotel and told us that, in view of the security situation, we should stay put. My immediate superior (GSO2), Major 'Tubby' Arnold, a Sapper, would collect me and take me to GHQ the following morning. The diary that I kept for the first three months of our time in Cyprus reads, 'Have never seen so many soldiers and police – all heavily armed and stopping traffic etc'. Apparently we had hanged two Greek Cypriot terrorists that morning and 'trouble was expected. All shops closed in protest at hangings.' My diary for that day ends, 'Good dinner. Early bed and listened to piano in ballroom below. Also heard drunken British paratroopers, one of whom accidentally discharged his rifle – thought the round was coming through our floor. A Royal Marine officer was killed last night and a soldier wounded today.'

The background to the Cyprus emergency into which we had entered was as follows: after securing independence from the Ottoman Empire in 1831, Greece claimed Cyprus due to its majority Greek population. In 1956, 80 per cent of a total population of 520,000 were Greek with the remaining 20 per cent virtually all Turks. 'Enosis' (union) with Greece was sought by the vast majority of Greek Cypriots and when Britain made Cyprus a Crown Colony in 1925 the political campaign intensified. The Greek Orthodox Church led the Enosis movement and, after the Second World War, Archbishop Makarios personified it. In 1951 he secretly invited Cypriot-born retired Greek Army colonel Georgios Grivas to form EOKA (the National Organization of Cypriot Fighters) as the military wing of the movement. In February 1956, Makarios rejected a British plan for gradual independence and was exiled to the Seychelles. In July Turkey rejected another British plan for eventual Cypriot self-determination. Three incidents in 1954 then precipitated the trouble: a ministerial statement that Cyprus would never be granted independence; the move of

British forces, including GHQ Middle East Command, from Egypt to Cyprus, thereby turning a colonial backwater into a major military strategic base; and a United Nations refusal to consider the Cyprus question. Through a terrorist campaign, begun in April 1955 and aimed chiefly at British military targets, and a propaganda campaign, EOKA sought to control the local population, sway world opinion, and wear down the British. In November 1955 the British declared an official 'emergency' and, by December 1956, troop levels had increased from 17,000 to 40,000. Overall strength of the Army that year was 383,848. The British Army suffered 763 casualties during the 'emergency', including seventy-nine killed; sixteen British civilians also lost their lives. There were 234 Turkish Cypriot militia casualties, including eighty-four killed and, on the other side of the fence, 366 Greek Cypriots died, of whom 166 were members of EOKA; the remainder were killed by EOKA for not supporting 'Enosis'.

On our second morning in Cyprus Tubby collected me at 8.30 and took me to GHQ in a heavily-guarded Wolseley Barracks. Dick Vernon's office was in the main building, but Tubby and I were in a caravan on a dusty concrete square at the back, as Wolseley Barracks was far too small for a major HQ. Our caravan was as hot as a furnace with only a couple of electric fans to cool us. The rest of the Plans staff consisted of our chief clerk, Staff Sergeant Perry, and one clerk, Private Fox. They worked in a separate caravan next to ours.

Our job was to prepare defensive plans for a war with the Soviet Union which would involve moving major reinforcements into Jordan to meet a Soviet advance towards the Persian and Iraqi oilfields. As the plans had already been prepared all we had to do was to keep them updated; we would therefore not be very busy. Our working day was from 0730 to 1230. When I enquired about the EOKA emergency, Tubby explained that it was nothing to do with us as it was being controlled by HQ Cyprus District.

My immediate concern was not the Soviets or EOKA, but finding somewhere to live. Since I was not senior enough to qualify for an official quarter in a protected area we would have to rent from a Cypriot. Colonel Dick took us to see possible houses and we finally found a furnished bungalow after viewing another eight properties with Tubby. The owners of the bungalow, a Greek Cypriot couple with their teenage son and the husband's mother, 'Granny', lived directly below us in what had been designed as the cellars.

Life in Nicosia was dominated by the EOKA campaign. Seventy-five British soldiers and civilians died at the hands of the terrorists during our time in Cyprus with, according to my diary, forty-eight being killed or wounded during our first thirteen weeks. One of the worst incidents in our early days occurred when a bomb was thrown at soldiers returning from a Queen's Birthday Parade rehearsal – three died and twenty were wounded. As a result of the threat I carried a gun, a .38 revolver, throughout my time in Cyprus; I even had it with me when we went to the beach and always slept with it beside me.

The only times we had any friction with our landlords were when EOKA shot or blew up a 'Brit' or when we hanged a Greek-Cypriot. In the first case I ignored Granny and in the second she ignored me. These stand-offs usually lasted only a couple of days.

Shopping for Anne was very simple – the NAAFI and an occasional visit to a market for fresh meat. All wives were banned from the city's main street, Ledra Street, known to us for good reasons as 'Murder Mile', and I was furious when I discovered that Anne had been down there one day shopping with an American neighbour. Our eggs were delivered two or three times a week to our door by an Arab on a donkey and fresh vegetables and fruit were delivered daily by a young Cypriot.

Our daily routine was also very simple. I was picked up by a military bus every morning and delivered home by about one o'clock. We only worked in the mornings due to the high temperatures. They hit 96 degrees within two weeks of our arrival and by June were often over 100. This led to a water shortage and supplies being cut off from 6 a.m. to 6 p.m. After lunch Anne and I usually rested until mid-afternoon when we either drove to the north coast to sunbathe and swim or explored those parts of Nicosia located outside the city walls, or Turkish villages around the capital. Quite often we went farther afield to places like Famagusta and Larnaca and to visit historic sites like the Crusader castle of St Hilarion, the Roman remains at Salamis, the nearby tomb and monastery of St Barnabus and the beautiful twelfth-century abbey of Bellapaise. We could swim at Larnaca where the beach was guarded by soldiers of the Middlesex Regiment, but Kyrenia was by far the most popular place for virtually everyone in the Headquarters.

Soon after our arrival we found several old friends on the island, including the couple whose flat in Guildford we had borrowed when we were first married. Also there was my best man, Peter Field, who was with 2nd Battalion, The Parachute Regiment, based just outside Nicosia. I had been *his* best man when he married Diana just before we flew to Cyprus. Then, one day, Ben Chapman, my Company commander from Korea, walked into my caravan at Wolseley Barracks – he was the District Officer PT at HQ Cyprus District. One of the first things Ben did was to get me invited to a party at the residence of the General Officer Commanding Cyprus District who turned out to be my Brigadier in Korea, now Major

General, 'Abde' Ricketts, and the party was for anyone who had fought in Korea. I met five members of the Norfolks I had known and ran into Colonel 'Butcher' Marsden in the District Mess in Kykko Camp. Taking me off into a quiet corner, he asked to see my leg; to my great relief he said it looked good and congratulated me. The other thing I remember clearly about that evening is Ben telling me I had been extremely unlucky not to be awarded an MC for my actions in Korea.

About once a month during my time in Nicosia I was 'Duty Officer' at GHQ which involved spending the night in Wolseley Barracks. So that Anne wouldn't be on her own at night I arranged for our Branch clerk, Private Fox, to sleep in our house. He was armed with a Sten gun, but Anne always said that if anything had happened she would have grabbed the gun and used it herself! Fortunately nothing ever did.

One incident that did rather shake us though also occurred while I was Duty Officer. I came home after breakfast on 15 June and told Anne that a Royal Warwick sentry had shot dead a Greek Cypriot in Metaxus Square just as he was about to throw a bomb. They had found the primed bomb near his body. We thought nothing more about this until a day later when we enquired of our landlords why our vegetable boy hadn't been for a couple of days; to our horror we found he had been the one shot in Metaxus Square. Our landlords claimed he had been forced to take the bomb or EOKA would have shot him or a member of his family. This was probably true as he could easily have shot me on a number of occasions when he was taking Anne's order in our kitchen and I was sitting or standing with my back to him.

On 21 June Anne kept an appointment with the gynaecologist and to our great joy we were told that she was already five months pregnant and could expect her baby about 10 November. We were both relieved that the pregnancy was already halfway through. However, the intense heat of Cyprus soon took its toll and, after another visit to the doctor, I was told to get a couple of weeks' leave and take Anne up to the 'Pine Trees' leave centre in the Troodos mountains. This centre was based on bungalows used before the Cyprus emergency by members of the Diplomatic Corps on leave from Egypt and other Middle Eastern countries. By the time we got there the centre had been vastly expanded with the bungalows being reserved for very senior officers – we found ourselves in an army tent and on camp beds. It was beautifully cool though and we ate in a nice restaurant in the Pingos Hotel. We had great fun walking in the pine forests and visiting places like Mount Olympus, the asbestos mines at Amiandos, the Berengaria Hotel at Prodhromos and the village of Platres where the Gordon Highlanders were based. They were busy in the hunt for Grivas and his EOKA terrorists, but also provided security for the general area of the leave centre.

Not long after our arrival in Cyprus King Hussein of Jordan cut off relations with Great Britain. It soon became clear that our war plans were in shreds and that there could be no conventional defence by the British Army against Soviet expansion in the Middle East. In other words we were left with nothing to do other than read the daily 'diptels' (diplomatic telegrams) from the Foreign Office and other intelligence sources. Some of the most interesting were from King Hussein's mother, Queen Sein.

With the collapse of our plans for a conventional war with the Soviet Union it came as no real surprise to be told that I was to be given a new job. An RAF Wing Commander, Wally Cadwallader, a New Zealander, and I were to form a 'nuclear target selection committee'. We were given incredibly detailed intelligence and aerial photographs of Soviet installations in the Caucasus and asked to recommend which were suitable targets for nuclear strikes and even the size, in kilotons, of the weapons to be delivered. We spent several weeks on this project, at the end of which our recommendations were passed up the chain of command and then back to London. We never knew though which of our recommendations were accepted.

On 28 July my diary records that I 'worked late due to the Suez crisis'. On the 26th Nasser, the Egyptian leader, had nationalized the Suez Canal Company, which operated the vital trade route to the east and in which British banks and business held a 44 per cent stake. Between July and October 1956, the United States tried unsuccessfully to reduce tensions between the UK and France and the Egyptians but, in the meantime Israel, France and Britain held secret meetings and reached agreement that Israel should invade the Canal Zone, Britain and France would intervene and instruct the Israeli and Egyptian armies to withdraw their forces to a distance of ten miles from either side of the canal. An Anglo-French intervention force would then deploy in the Canal Zone around Port Said. The operation was to be called MUSKETEER. Looking back, it seems quite incredible that no one in GHQ, certainly below the rank of major general, had any idea of the political collusion and skullduggery behind this operation.

On 29 October Israel, as planned, invaded the Gaza Strip and Sinai Peninsula and made rapid progress towards the Canal Zone. As per the agreement, Britain and France offered to re-occupy the area and separate the warring armies. Nasser refused the offer, which gave the European powers a pretext for a joint invasion to regain control of the canal and topple the Nasser regime. Britain and France began to bomb Egypt on the 31st. Nasser responded by sinking forty ships then in the canal, closing it to further shipping.

On 5 November, 3 PARA dropped on El Gamil airfield, clearing the area and establishing a secure base for incoming support aircraft and reinforcements. French paratroopers landed on the east side of the Canal. At first light on the 6th, Royal Marine Commandos stormed the beaches, followed by other British troops, including my friend Peter Field, who came ashore in Second World War landing craft. From a military viewpoint, the operation to take the Canal was highly successful. From a political viewpoint, however, it was a disaster, for the United States was also trying to deal with the Soviet/Hungarian crisis. Faced with a public relations embarrassment of criticizing the Soviet Union's military intervention in Hungary whilst not also criticizing the actions of its two principal European allies, and fearful of a wider war after the Soviet Union threatened to intervene on the Egyptian side, the Eisenhower administration insisted on a ceasefire which came into effect at midnight on the 6th. Part of the pressure that the United States used against Britain was financial, as Eisenhower threatened to sell the United States' sterling reserves, thereby precipitating a collapse of the British currency. The British government and the pound thus both came under pressure and Prime Minister Anthony Eden was forced to resign.

How did all this affect Anne and me? I was very frustrated as GHQ Middle East had nothing to do with MUSKETEER; a completely new HQ under General Hughie Stockwell, my Commandant at Sandhurst, was brought out to command the operation. All Tubby and I did was set up a War Room for Stockwell's staff in a new but unfinished complex at Episkopi on the south coast that was to be the new location of GHQ. Having set up the War Room I found myself with nothing to do, so asked my brigadier if I could join the 1st Battalion, The Royal West Kent Regiment, which had just arrived in Cyprus for MUSKETEER. I received a curt 'no'! A couple of days later I asked to be sent to HQ Cyprus District in Kykko Camp, just outside Nicosia which was being overworked due to the arrival of thousands of extra troops being brought in for the invasion. My brigadier agreed reluctantly and I found myself in the Staff Duties branch of this subordinate HQ responsible for authorizing the issue of 'G controlled stores', including telephones and sandbags. As every unit arriving in Cyprus wanted both for security, as well as communications, I became a very popular officer.

Shortly after the abrupt end to the Suez crisis, at 8 p.m. on 12 November, Anne gave birth to Victoria Jane. We were over the moon and, as a present, I gave Anne a diamond brooch in the form of a Paschal Lamb made at Garrard's.

I stayed at Cyprus District until March 1957 but, with the end of the Suez crisis and the Cyprus garrison reverting to its normal size, there was no real work for me to do and I returned to GHQ. Dick Vernon left in June and I was transferred to the Operations' branch under a new boss. My final report from him reads:

> Captain Reynolds has made a promising start to his staff career. During the last year he has been GSO III Plans at GHQ MELF for 5 months and attached to HQ Cyprus District as GSO III (SD) during the height of the EOKA troubles and during the time of our intervention in Egypt. He has now returned to GHQ MELF as GSO III (Ops). He has tackled all these jobs with common-sense, initiative and energy, yet has remained calm and unruffled throughout.

He graded me 'above average'. Not bad, I thought, for someone who had yet to attend Staff College.

The next dramatic event in our lives was the move of GHQ to Episkopi in early May which meant that we had to look for somewhere to live near Limassol since there were no houses in Episkopi itself, apart from the CinC's Residence and I was not senior enough to be allocated a nearby quarter. We eventually found quite a nice, new house belonging to a fairly wealthy Turk, a good two miles from the northern edge of the old town but today in the *middle* of Limassol.

Life in Limassol was very different from that in Nicosia. We were much more isolated and the GHQ Mess was much too far away to attend at night while our new baby prevented us going to events like curry lunches on Sundays. There was no TV and even the Army cinema at Episkopi was beyond our reach.

In early September we faced a crisis. Anne was pregnant again, but had an ovarian cyst. The doctors decided it had to be removed, but warned us that she might lose the baby. With no hospital in Episkopi, I drove Anne back to BMH Nicosia whilst friends looked after Vicky. I spent the night, but had to return to Limassol and Episkopi and was unable to be with Anne for the operation. Fortunately, it was a complete success and the baby survived unharmed.

I was now approaching the final few months of my time in GHQ and had been told that I would be attending a Company Commanders' Course at Warminster in the New Year. However, on 16 October, I received a signal from David Lloyd Owen asking me to be his Adjutant. He was to command the 1st Battalion on its return from Malaya to Iserlohn in Germany. I was thrilled. I remember running down the main corridor of G Branch, waving the signal and shouting, 'I'm going to be the Adjutant of the 1st Battalion, The Queen's Royal Regiment!'

My elation was dampened a few weeks later though when major cuts were announced in the size of the infantry. To my utter disbelief, I learned that the senior English Regiment of the Line, the Queen's, was to be amalgamated in two years' time with the 1st Battalion of the East Surrey Regiment. David would therefore be the last Commanding Officer of 1 Queen's and I would be the last Adjutant.

Knowing that we had only a few weeks left in the Middle East and having a couple of weeks leave in hand, we decided to join a ten-day pilgrimage to the Holy Land later that month. It was a wonderful and most memorable experience. As well as seeing all the Holy Places in Jerusalem like the Via Dolorosa, Garden of Gethsemane and Church of the Holy Sepulchre, we visited Bethlehem, Jericho, the river Jordan and the Dead Sea. It was all very moving and did much for our faith.

On leaving Cyprus we had to sell our car and leave behind the few items of furniture we had purchased during our time there because we couldn't afford the civilian freight charges. Everything else was packed into six MFO boxes and, that done, Anne, Vicky and I sailed in the troopship *Dilwara* on 7 December. The voyage was very pleasant with a good-sized cabin and stops at Tobruk and Benghazi. We arrived at my parents' new home in Harborne, Birmingham, in time for Christmas. My Company Commanders' course had been cancelled and I was told to report to the 1st Battalion on 27 January. Anne would not be able to come with me though as Army wives within a few weeks of childbirth were forbidden to travel – Gabrielle Anne was due before the end of February. And unbelievably I wasn't able to apply for a quarter until I actually arrived in Iserlohn!

Chapter Ten
Adjutant in Germany

On 27 January 1958 I left for Germany in my brand new Morris 1000 Traveller. I knew Gabrielle Anne was likely to be premature and so I was not surprised to hear she had been born on 17 February; however, the bad news was that she had jaundice which meant that Anne could not travel out to Germany with the children. I had to continue living in the Officers' Mess until early April when they were finally allowed to join me. This separation, although very upsetting, proved quite useful as I was able to give my full attention to my duties as Adjutant. It also gave me a chance to get to know all the officers and many of the warrant officers and sergeants. Amongst these I was delighted to find old friends from the Depot – officers like Edward Clowes and Jimmy Kemp, now QM of the Battalion; and members of the WOs' and Sergeants' Mess like Wildgoose and Jessup and my Depot Training Company CSM. Sadly the latter didn't last long. Soon after his arrival his English wife refused to say goodnight to the RSM's German wife after a Mess dinner, calling her a 'German cow!' When the poor chap appeared in front of me the next day he knew what was coming and asked, 'So where am I being posted to, Sir?' I did my best for him with a nice job with the TA.

The RSM in question was George Mileham and, fortunately, he and I hit it off from the moment we met and soon became a strong team. As well as the Orderly Room staff, another of my responsibilities was the Regimental Police. They were under a great character, Provost Sergeant 'Moyses' Stevens. I had known him back in 1950 when he was a bit of a troublemaker, but now he was a tower of strength. He claimed to be related to the London florists of the same name, so that's how he got his nickname.

The next eighteen months proved to be a very happy period for both Anne and me. We had our two beautiful little girls with us, we lived in a very pleasant army quarter in an attractive town, we had nice friends and I was the right-hand man of a charismatic leader admired by all ranks. David Lloyd Owen was not only a brave soldier, but he was a brilliant leader and I learned much from him – perhaps most important of all that you cannot have a militarily efficient unit unless it is a happy one; also, that a good leader should always appear relaxed and be prepared to delegate. David did both superbly – even to the extent of normally going home for lunch and not coming back in the afternoon! Fortunately he got on extremely well with our Brigade commander who understood him and his eccentricities. I was also fortunate in that I got on well with the Brigade Major (Chief of Staff).

The West Germany I came back to in 1958 was very different from the one I had left in 1951. In the first place it was a sovereign nation and part of NATO and, in the second, its economy had been rebuilt and was beginning to boom. There was now almost no sign of the devastation caused by the Second World War. East Germany was a very different matter. I had seen evidence of this huge change as I drove out to Iserlohn through the Ruhr – factories belching smoke and fumes everywhere I looked. Fortunately Iserlohn had no heavy industry.

The Battalion was in a different barracks this time, one much nearer the BMH. Our previous one was now occupied, coincidentally, by the Royal Norfolks and, even more surprisingly, the quarter I was allocated was next door to the chap whose Platoon I had taken over in Korea just over six years previously; and I knew a number of their officers from my time with that Battalion.

Mons Barracks had also been built in the Hitler era and was spacious and well suited to its purpose. I re-visited it in 2003 and found the accommodation and administrative blocks had all been converted into private flats and houses and a supermarket had been built on the old parade square and where the various messes had been.

As well as David's wife Ursie and Edward and Louise Clowes, other officers and wives I already knew on arrival were Ian and Sally Beattie and Douggie and Judy Snowdon from my original Iserlohn days, and Toby and Muriel Sewell from Stoughton and Cyprus days. Toby had stood in as Adjutant until I arrived and was now commanding a Company. He would one day be my CO and he and Muriel are still close friends. Louise, Sally and Judy are still alive but, sadly, all the others have died. One of my biggest and most delightful surprises was to find that my old friend Lieutenant Colonel John Watts of Cambridge Hospital Aldershot fame was now the resident surgeon at BMH Iserlohn. This was good news indeed – as will shortly become evident. He and his wife Elizabeth became good friends.

One slightly depressing thing I found on arrival was that the Battalion was seriously understrength – 400 as opposed to our official strength of 580. We were due to receive some new drafts before our amalgamation with the East Surreys towards the end of 1959, but we knew we would never be brought up to full strength. Bearing this in mind it is remarkable what we achieved in those final eighteen months – extremely high morale, excellent training reports, imaginative exercises and superb ceremonial parades. Not only that, but we won the BAOR hockey in 1958 and in 1959 the BAOR and Army swimming championships and the Duke of Connaught's Shield for the most highly-trained stretcher-bearers and medical staff in BAOR. This latter award was due to the enthusiasm and skill of our doctor, Captain Geoff Clinton-Jones (an old Cranleighan nicknamed 'Clinking Bones') and his right-hand man, a very senior sergeant, 'Doc' Watret.

The quarter I was allocated – our first army quarter – was a three-bedroomed, semi-detached house in Rubenstrasse. Most Iserlohn quarters were located on a hill on the north side of the town with good views over a valley leading to Schwerte and, eventually, Dortmund. Some senior officers, like the CO of the Norfolks, and John Watts lived on the road above us, Rembrandtstrasse, and Other Ranks, needless to say, lived below us. David and Ursie with their three boys lived in a very nice quarter much nearer the barracks and the BMH.

Our quarter was fully furnished and equipped with everything you could possibly want – even to an aluminium fish kettle for cooking whole salmon! All we had to do was put up our pictures and arrange our few pieces of silver and ornaments. What is more, for the first time in our lives, we had central heating looked after by an old German provided free of charge. He stoked our coal-burning boiler in the cellar each morning, bringing with him 'Brötchen' (bread rolls) for our breakfast, and did the same again in the evening. The house also had something we had never even heard of, let alone seen before – double glazing! We were also provided with a daily *Putzfrau* (cleaning lady) free of charge and a batman. My batman was a National Serviceman called Knight, a volunteer and an extremely nice and gentle person. We quickly discovered that he was married and that his wife Rosemary was working as a 'mother's help'. Inevitably, we asked if she would be prepared to come out and work for us. They readily agreed and 'Roro' arrived towards the end of May. I'm sure we didn't pay her much, but she lived free and had her own single room. It may seem incredible, but as National Servicemen were not allowed to have their wives with them (very few were married), I would not allow Knight to 'live in' on a full-time basis. Except when we were away and left the children with them, he was only allowed to spend Friday and Saturday nights in Roro's little room!

The first exercise David organized ended with a sixty-mile march back to barracks. This was done in three days. Despite his war wounds, David was a great marcher and insisted on leading his Battalion all the way.

There was no way I could complete such a distance and so I was told to drive back and organize the Band to 'play in' the Battalion when it arrived at the barrack gate; the Corps of Drums was to 'speed march' the last thirty-six miles in fifteen hours to join up with the Band.

The lifestyle we entered was simple and highly enjoyable. Anne was very tied up with the children, but a Putzfrau, mother's help and batman made life relatively easy. Shopping for basics was always done in the NAAFI, but there was a good market several days a week in the town centre and, to our delight, we found a MacFishery in the main street. We still used BAFVs in the NAAFI and at the SKC cinema next door, but it was a new experience to use Deutschemarks. Sadly, the Officers' Clubs I had known in 1950 in the town and on the Mohnesee had both closed.

Having Roro and Knight to look after the girls allowed us quite an active social and recreational life. There was no television in those days so we were regular cinema goers. I remember *The Big Country* with Gregory Peck and *Cat on a Hot Tin Roof* with Marlon Brando and we even went to the German cinema to see *Gigi* in German with Leslie Caron and Grossmuttie Gingold. Another great recreation was listening to gramophone records: 33rpm long-playing records had now arrived and, after buying a Pye 'Black Box', we spent many evenings listening to Frank Sinatra, Bing Crosby, Nat King Cole etc. But the late Fifties were also the days of the cocktail party and rarely a week went by without one – usually followed by a meal at the 'Haferkista' restaurant in Iserlohn or the 'Zum Bären' near Hemer. Small dinner or supper parties were also in vogue – small because the dining rooms in even the majors' quarters wouldn't seat more than six in comfort. Formal Mess dinners were held weekly and living-out members had to attend the monthly 'Guest Nights'. These were always great fun.

The Canadian army had a couple of infantry battalions (the 'Vandoos' and Queen's Own Rifles of Canada) stationed in nearby Hemer, a pleasant little town just to the east of Iserlohn and we soon had trouble with British and Canadian soldiers brawling and fighting after too many beers and rough German brandies in the many pubs in both towns. In the end, the Adjutant of the Queen's Own Rifles of Canada, Charlie Belzile, and I agreed to designate various pubs to each nation and that solved the problem – it was certainly fun visiting them all to agree which went to them and which to us. Charlie Belzile ended up as the four-star head of the Canadian Army and we recalled those wonderful days when I, as a major general, visited him in Montreal in 1982.

Traditionally, in the Queen's at least, the Adjutant always commanded the Drums Platoon and I soon made it my business to increase the strength of the Corps of Drums. Within three months we had twenty-six drummers. Few of the new boys could blow the bugles they carried, but that didn't matter; their drumming and 'stick drill' was soon of a high standard and they merely pretended to blow so that they didn't ruin the sounds of the experienced buglers. I also dressed the Corps in scarlet tunics as opposed to No. 1 Dress and made them wear white gloves and told Drum Major Bennett that I wanted him to model our Corps on the style of the Royal Marines with proper 'stick drill'.

The Battalion hockey team under John Davidson's captaincy won the finals of the BAOR cup on 19 April and this led to wild celebrations. A day later Gabrielle was christened in the RC chapel of the BMH and naturally we had a big party afterwards for all our close friends.

The next big event in the Battalion's calendar was the Glorious First of June. The Colonel of the Regiment, Major General John Whitfield, came out for the weekend celebrations and David ordered a full ceremonial parade with the Colours, followed by Beating Retreat by the Band and Drums in the evening. These events were basically my responsibility, but with the help of the RSM, Bandmaster Lynes and Drum Major Bennett they went extremely well. I was very relieved that my expanded Corps of Drums performed superbly. That evening there were formal dinners in the Messes and when I arrived I found a letter from David in my pigeon-hole. It read, 'This is just a note to thank you for all the splendid arrangements you have made for this weekend. And also to congratulate you because everything has gone quite beautifully. You must be pleased because so much depended on you. Thank you awfully and well done.' The following day we had a very successful 'Fun Fair' for all ranks and their families.

Twelve days later we moved up to the Soltau training area for combined arms training with C Squadron, 3rd Hussars. David sent me another note dated 13 June, 'An excellent order for the move to Soltau. Well done.' The PS said, 'I hope it all works!' It did and we had a great time, training quite hard with the tanks by day and whooping it up at night. The Hussars were facing amalgamation too and were so short of men that we had to provide radio operators for their Centurion tanks. We lived under canvas, but in some comfort with armchairs and tables and waiters in the Officers' Mess marquee. Soltau is not far from Hamburg and, against all the rules most of the captains, including me, and the subalterns had a night on the infamous Reeperbahn. In one of the nightclubs there was a circus-type ring and girls did their striptease mounted bareback on gently cantering horses. As the act finished someone in our party, probably John Davidson, shouted, 'Hey Adj, you ought to be mounted!' Not to be outdone, I quickly entered the ring and mounted one of the horses. All went well until I decided to turn the horse to go anti-clockwise. He didn't like that and I ended up dismounting rather sooner than I had planned – to the cheers of all present, including the strippers!

In July we faced two crises. The most serious was that we were suddenly ordered to send a complete company of five officers and 100 men to reinforce the East Surreys in Cyprus. Naturally, we chose our best and A Company was brought up to the required strength and left on 14 July. In typical David fashion we saw them off from Hamm station with champagne. This left the Battalion desperately short of men until the Company returned just before Christmas.

The second crisis arose when Drum Major Bennett announced he was leaving the Army and joining the Blackpool police force. There was no one in the Drums who had the figure or the presence to take over and so I looked around for someone else. My eyes lighted on Sergeant Brian Morris, one of the Mortar Platoon sergeants – tall, good-looking and a good leader. I well remember calling him off the range at Sennelager and telling him of my plan. He would have about six weeks to learn the job from Bennett, but if he was successful he would be a Warrant Officer Class II within a couple of years and the way would then be open to further promotion. He was shattered, but accepted and went on to become a superb Drum Major. He was later promoted to RSM and, after commissioning, had various jobs like MTO before becoming QM of the 2nd Battalion of the Queen's Regiment. Needless to say he was always very grateful to me and kept in touch with numerous letters until he died tragically of a heart attack whilst playing basketball in Gibraltar in May 1978.

That same July we left the girls with Roro and Knight, who incidentally they adored, and took off on a ten-day tour of southern Germany. I can't remember exactly where we stayed, but we travelled in glorious weather down the Rhine to Heidelberg, then on to Baden Baden, Lake Constance, Oberammergau, Ettal, Wies, Mad King Ludwig's castles of Neuschwangau and Linderhof, then to Salzburg and back via Munich. It was a superb holiday.

Looking back, the Battalion's role in the event of Soviet attack was a strange one. We were well into the Cold War and everyone knew that our only hope of stopping the Red Army was by the use of nuclear weapons. There was no plan to try to rush to the border with East Germany; instead, we would ensure the line of the river Rhine was secure. Accordingly, 1 Queen's was to defend a major crossing site on that river at Uerdingen, near Krefeld. There were far fewer bridges over the Rhine in those days and the Uerdingen bridge stood in the middle of flat open fields. When David and I went down there to look at our mission, we were appalled. All we could do to defend the bridge against an airborne assault was to put our companies at each end of it in what was known as a 'close bridge garrison' – hardly an exciting task.

From 3 to 5 February 1959 I sat the Staff College entrance examination. Soon after I took over as Adjutant, David told me that I should sit this exam as early as possible and that meant 1959. I said I couldn't possibly do the necessary study for it and be a good Adjutant at the same time. Eventually we reached a compromise – I would sit the exams, but only if he gave me three weeks off immediately beforehand – and they wouldn't count as leave. This I did and I worked damned hard at home for those three weeks – 6 in the morning to 6 at night, with Anne and Roro doing a great job keeping the girls quiet. Most candidates spent a whole year preparing for this exam and attended several short courses in the various subjects.

I sat the seven exams (three tactics papers, military law, military history, current affairs and administration and morale) with a lot of others in a gymnasium in a barracks on the edge of Paderborn. My back was playing up a bit at this time and I remember having to leave my desk on a number of occasions and do press-ups on the floor beside it in order to relieve the pain. Somehow I got through though and, a month or two later, learned that I had not only passed all the subjects, but that my overall average was 66 per cent – the pass mark average was 50 per cent. This meant that I had not only qualified, but that I had earned a 'Competitive Vacancy' and would therefore enter the Staff College the following January – normally one had to wait at least a year for a vacancy. I could hardly believe it for it also meant that I would be one of the youngest officers ever to go to Camberley.

Later in February we embarked on our final BAOR training year. However, my bad back was now becoming quite a problem and rather than 'report sick' through the normal channels, I decided to approach my old specialist, Colonel John Watts, privately and avoid the possibility of being downgraded medically. John fully understood and could not have been kinder. Advising me to sleep with strong wooden boards under my mattress, he told me that if this didn't help I would probably have to undergo surgery with the risk of being downgraded. Fortunately it did, and for many years after that I had a six-foot army table under the mattress on my side of our double bed.

Our last training year started with two weeks at the Sennelager Training Centre, near Paderborn – a place I always enjoyed with its excellent ranges and wide manoeuvre areas. I had first been there in 1950, just five years after the war, when there were still wrecked German tanks to be seen and one could almost feel the presence of Nazi ghosts in the Mess and in some of the barrack blocks. Indeed I discovered then that some of the Mess waitresses had been working there during the days of Hitler's Third Reich.

Not content with normal range work, David came up, as usual, with an imaginative exercise to end our time in Sennelager. I can't remember the details, but I know it took Battalion HQ slightly out of the official training area and, in doing so, we discovered a beautiful trout farm with its own small restaurant, the 'Forellenhof'. The latter was run by two fat sisters who were tremendous fun and allowed each of us to choose our trout, which they would then hit over the head with a pin-pong bat before coating it in butter and throwing it into a hot frying-pan. Every time I visited Sennelager after that, right up to the late 1970s, I used to eat there.

The next amazing incident in the life of 1 Queen's was an order to take the whole Battalion down to Hubbelrath, near Dusseldorf, and move in with 3rd Coldstream Guards for three days. We were about to take part in a typical time-wasting exercise quite common in those days. The Tory Minister of Defence, Duncan Sandys, had demanded to see what a typical BAOR infantry battalion looked like on parade beside a battalion at full strength (Higher Establishment [HE]). We would provide the 'typical battalion' and the *three* battalions of the Guards Brigade would combine to produce the HE battalion. The Royal Engineers had to build a 40-foot tower so that he could view the scene. The whole thing caused a lot of amusement and we had a great time with the Coldstream who were generous hosts.

Easter saw one of David's most imaginative ideas – an initiative test in which pairs of officers and soldiers were challenged to get as far away as possible from Iserlohn but return within five days. They were allowed only a limited amount of money and no private cars: 160 volunteered and pairs reached places as far away as Sweden, Switzerland and the Isle of Wight. The winners, a couple of lance corporals, managed to spend a full day in Casablanca. Needless to say, a number of those who entered simply used the test for a short break at home in the UK.

It was during 1959 that other old friends re-joined the Battalion – Geoffrey and Mary Curtis from the previous Iserlohn tour and Mike Doyle from Depot days.

April saw 1 Queen's at the Haltern training area carrying out combined arms training, this time with C Squadron, Royal Scots Greys. The Duke of Kent was one of the troop leaders and I had the 'honour' of looking after and sitting next to him at a Mess dinner. He was very nice, but his conversation seemed to be limited to cars and motor racing.

John Davidson left at about this time on posting to the Far East. He had been a great asset to the Battalion, an excellent assistant Adjutant and a good friend. In a farewell letter to me, John wrote:

The purpose of this letter is to thank you really sincerely for putting up with me so tolerantly over the last year. I can honestly say that I have enjoyed the last year more than any other, and this is largely due to the tremendous fun I've had working and playing with you and Colonel David.

It was during April that we left the girls again with Knight and Roro and took a few days' leave in Paris. I had discovered that we were entitled to stay in the French Officers' Club in the heart of the city and that the cost was minimal. We had a wonderful visit, seeing all the sights and eating really well in the Club restaurant – again very inexpensively. One big surprise was running into Cerdic Mercer from Mons, Sandhurst and Singapore days. He and his wife were attending a wedding reception in the Club. He had joined the Royal Signals and was stationed at SHAPE HQ at Fontainebleau. We're still in touch to this day.

The major event of 1959 was the celebration of the 'Glorious First of June'. It was to be the last in the Regiment's history and David decided that it would also be our official farewell to Germany. The first event in the programme was inevitably a full Battalion parade with Colours. David originally wanted all three Colours on parade, but I suggested instead that we should Troop the Regimental Colour. This hadn't been done, certainly since the war, and would be a major challenge. David immediately agreed and it wasn't long before I realized that I had given myself, and the Battalion, an immense task. Trooping the Colour is a very complicated parade and none of us knew how to do it. I therefore despatched the RSM down to the Guards Brigade to find out. Once we knew the format it came down to a *lot* of rehearsals. George Mileham had a couple without the officers on parade and then I had three or four, or maybe more, with everyone except the CO present. The only two majors on parade, Ian Beattie and Geoffrey Curtis, very kindly agreed to accept me, a captain, giving the orders on these parades. Then finally David took two rehearsals himself. Jimmy Kemp, our QM, somehow managed to obtain No. 1 Dress (Blues) for the Escort to the Colour – a Guard of over sixty officers and men. The other three companies wore normal battledress. In those days only officers, warrant officers and sergeants normally wore No. 1 Dress. We had nearly 300 on parade, an amazing achievement out of a total strength of less than 400. In the event the parade, with the salute taken by the Colonel of the Regiment, was a huge success. The weather was good and over a hundred guests attended, including a Royal Navy admiral from Kiel, the Captain of HMS *Excellent* and four of his officers, the CO of the Greys and some of his officers, all with their wives, and many members of the local German population. Most of us had lumps in our throats as we watched the Colour leave the parade ground for the last time. David wrote to me afterwards:

Today's parade was a tremendous personal triumph for you and I am so glad that it went so superbly. Thank you so much for all that you have done to make it what it was. I for one, will certainly never forget it. I hope it was worth all the butterflies you had in your tummy before it! Well done and thank you.

The following day there was a very successful All Ranks' dance that included a barbecue with a whole pig roasted over an open fire and on the Friday we gave a cocktail party for a couple of hundred people, followed by a highly amusing variety show called 'Jack's All Right' performed by some of the officers and sergeants. That was followed by an informal supper and a floodlit Tattoo. This latter event was again my responsibility. We started the Tattoo in complete darkness. Then the Corps of Drums with illuminated drums and tiny torches on their drum sticks led the Band onto the square. It was a fantastic spectacle and drew long applause from the spectators. The whole Tattoo was a great success and a marvellous 'feather in the cap' for Brian Morris and Bandmaster Bill Lynes. It ended with fireworks and then Corporal 'Gungy' Seager, my best bugler, blowing the Last Post from an illuminated catwalk on the roof of the Battalion HQ block. I was a bit worried about this as Seager was renowned for having a drink or two, but all went well.

On the Saturday we had a most successful funfair followed by the officers and senior NCOs serving a special turkey lunch to the men, accompanied by a plentiful amount of free beer, and that evening the WOs and Sergeants invited the officers and all the guests of the Battalion to a most successful Ball in a beautifully decorated gymnasium. One of the highlights of the evening was a display by the Pipes and Drums of the Greys.

Sunday saw a Drumhead Service in the evening after which the Colonel of the Regiment presented four Long Service and Good Conduct medals. Finally, on the Monday evening, there was a tombola and draw with many prizes for the men and a black-tie dance in the Officers' Mess for our UK guests and other special friends in the Garrison.

It had been an incredible six days. The Colonel of the Regiment described what he had seen as 'surpassing in standard and excellence all my previous experience in the Regiment.' David wrote to me again: 'Ref your A/13/1 dated 14 Apr (my written instructions for the whole six days). It has all been a Herculean task but the success of it all must be your only reward. My thanks are far too inadequate however sincere they are.'

On 11 June we moved to Soltau again to train with the tanks of the Greys. I don't remember much about the training but I do recall one of our young officers buying a quite high-powered water-pistol in the nearby town. Soon we all had them and the poor mess staff suffered accordingly. That was until one of the mess corporals bought a water machine-gun with a range of about twenty yards and a large magazine. After he dealt with us in revenge for several soakings he'd received, we called a truce. That didn't stop us taking our pistols up to Hamburg though and enjoying a few 'shots' in a couple of bars before hitting the Reeperbahn. I remember sitting beside one of the catwalks enjoying a striptease when one of our party suddenly drew his pistol and shot one of the girls in a delicate spot. She wheeled round and nearly took his head off with one of her high heels. We thought it wise at this point to beat a retreat.

After our return from Soltau we took three weeks of well-earned leave and set off with Vicky and Gabrielle for Grado in Italy. It took us two full days to get there, but the house I had rented turned out to be very nice and the weather was lovely; it was a super holiday.

Not content with a most memorable Glorious First of June, David decided that our last exercise would be equally so and rather different from the norm. His predecessor in command was serving in Holland as a liaison officer to I Netherlands Corps and David decided to make use of this contact. He was determined to get away from the normal BAOR-type exercise and, after delicate negotiations with our own HQ in Germany and the Dutch authorities, Exercise ZWAAN SONG was agreed. It involved not just 1 Queen's, but other units with whom we had established a close relationship. In essence, the exercise saw four 'mobile columns' – our A and B Companies, C Squadron of the Greys and a fourth provided by our affiliated Royal Artillery battery – driving into Holland with the object of finding and destroying four well-protected Dutch nuclear-missile-launch sites. David was the Force commander and my job was to run Force HQ. We were blessed with lovely weather and, as we were the first British combat units to enter Holland since 1945, we received a lot of attention from the Press – all of it, I'm relieved to report, very favourable. In fact, the Dutch people as a whole could not have been more welcoming. The exercise itself was a huge success with both sides claiming victories.

Our last few weeks in Iserlohn were marred by illness. Anne developed stomach pains which after admittance to the BMH were diagnosed as a kidney problem. It must have been pretty serious because she was told that it was likely to lead to an operation to remove the troublesome kidney and that this should be done at the Military Hospital in London. Knight, Roro and I, therefore, quickly packed up the house and after a very sad farewell to them, I drove the family home, leaving Vicky and Gabrielle with my parents and taking Anne on to the Hospital. To our great relief a final test on the kidney showed that it had cleared itself and Anne could go home. She and the girls then moved in with her parents and I returned to Germany for the Battalion's last few weeks there. I had to move into the Mess, and although we had some fun evenings it was a rather painful time as we moved towards the end of the Regiment's life. This ended with a final parade on Salerno Day, 9 September, during which over 330 all ranks formed a 'hollow square' and were addressed by David. He told us what a great privilege it had been to command such a splendid and successful Battalion and congratulated us on everything we had achieved. One could almost feel the pride in our breasts. The day ended with Beating Retreat, followed by cocktails parties in both Messes, to celebrate. We invited all our friends in the Iserlohn Garrison and our parent Brigade and Division. The weather was good and I was quite relaxed when the Band and Drums marched on; however, they had no sooner done so than David turned to me, sitting behind him, and said, 'Why isn't the Drum Major carrying the silver mace?' 'But it's too fragile Sir, we've never carried it before.' 'Well Michael, I want it on parade for this last time.' I duly ran up to the Mess where the mace was kept, took it off the wall and ran back to the rear of the parade ground. Then, as the Drums with the Band behind them counter-marched, I handed an astonished Brian Morris the silver one in exchange for his much lighter wooden mace. To his great credit he managed to carry it as though he'd been doing it every day. That silver mace can still be seen today in the Queen's Surreys' Museum at Clandon Park, near Guildford.

The main body of the Battalion, a mere shadow of its former strength, arrived in Blenheim Camp (no longer in existence), Bury St Edmunds on 7 October and David and I established a small HQ to carry on routine administration until Amalgamation Day, 14 October. The decision to set up this small HQ was David's and I strongly disagreed with it. It merely prolonged the agony, but David was insistent that we should complete the 298th year in the Regiment's history.

That last week was miserable for I had hardly anything to do. I remember clearly being told by the CO-designate that he wanted my Drums for a special rehearsal at a certain time on a certain day. I instructed Brian Morris accordingly, but discovered shortly afterwards that the CO had visited my Drums and repeated the order himself directly to the Drum Major. I asked for an interview and told him that we didn't do things like that in the Queen's and that I was very glad I was going to the Staff College and therefore would not be in his Battalion. I don't think anyone had ever spoken to him like that before. Amazingly, within a couple of years we were playing golf together and getting on very well.

After the Queen's flag was lowered on the evening of the 13th for the last time I went out to dinner with a few friends. On my return to my room I found a letter from David. It was addressed to 'Michael' and began 'Adj.' It went on:

> I shall never have the fun of writing that again. I suddenly realised it in my bath tonight. For me it's very sad. I shall be very lost without you for I am not only losing a magnificent Adjutant but I shall miss a wonderful friend. You have done so much for me and, although I may not have shown it always, I can assure you I have always been terribly aware of it all and immensely grateful. I can never thank you enough and won't attempt to. All I will do is to tell you that, if ever I can help you in any way, you only have to ask. Before too long I shall probably be coming to you for employment! You have a great future. I shall watch it with tremendous interest and remember that we were once privileged to serve together. Good luck and thank you, so very much.

Neither David nor I attended the Amalgamation Day parade on 14 October. As we said goodbye that morning my CO of the past eighteen months presented me with a beautiful solid-gold Paschal Lamb tie-pin. It was all I could do to murmur a quiet 'thank you'. He gave me a gentle pat on the shoulder as I turned away.

Chapter Eleven

Staff Colleges

I arrived at the Royal Military College of Science, Shrivenham, along with thirty-three others, a few days after leaving Bury St Edmunds and found myself on the three months 'idiots' course', designed to ensure that all officers going to the Staff College in Camberley had at least a *basic* scientific knowledge.

Anne and the girls were still with her parents in Edgbaston and I, like my fellow students, took a room in the Mess. The first couple of nights were quite fun, but community living soon palled and I missed my 'girls' very much indeed. A phone call to Anne soon revealed that they were missing me too and I immediately resolved to find somewhere near the College where we could all be together. It didn't take long and within a week we were living in an old seventeenth-century furnished cottage in a lovely village called Great Coxwell, about six miles from the College. It had at one time been the village pub and, although reasonably comfortable, the furniture and fittings were very basic and the only heating was provided by an open fire in the living room and a stove in the kitchen. Nevertheless, we were very happy and both the village and the surrounding area were delightful.

I remember little of the 'idiots' course'. It was summed up for most of us by a very laid-back Guardsman who, when asked if there were any questions at the end of an early lecture, asked 'What on earth's the difference between a watt and an amp?' We had a lot of very interesting lectures though, and made a number of fascinating visits, including one very dramatic one to a coal mine in south Wales. After descending nearly a mile into the mine, we had to crawl the last fifty yards to the actual coal-face. There we found men striped to the waist and covered in sweat as they hacked the coal out with picks and shovels. From that moment onwards I always had the greatest sympathy and respect for miners.

We moved to an official Staff College married quarter in Camberley in early January 1960. It was a three-bedroomed house with an open, bare front-garden and an equally bare back-garden. The house was 'heated' by a coke-burning stove in the kitchen; this fed a single radiator in the hall, right opposite the front door, and a towel rail in the bathroom. We can both remember waking up to find ice on the *insides* of our bedroom windows that winter and of Anne being thrown across the bed by a lightning strike on the house next door. Fortunately she survived unharmed.

The Staff College in 1960 was divided into three 'Divisions', each made up of sixty students and seven Directing Staff (DS). A and B Divisions were located, and received their instruction, in the main Staff College building in Camberley, within the grounds of Sandhurst, whilst C Division was located in Minley Manor, a chateau-styled mansion seven miles to the west of Camberley. David Lloyd Owen had 'arranged' for me to go to Minley – 'all the nicest people go there, Michael' and there was no doubt that we considered ourselves far superior to those in the Main Building. We only went to the main Building to listen to visiting lecturers and participate in the occasional indoor exercise.

I checked in at Minley on 14 January and found an American, a German, a number of former Dominion officers, a sailor, a Royal Marine and an RAF officer amongst the other fifty-nine students. Our Divisional Colonel and five of our six DS later became generals. The German, Eberhardt Retzlaff, had served on the Eastern Front, including Stalingrad, during the war. He was the first German to attend our Staff College and was slightly out of place, being a lieutenant colonel; the rest of us were much younger and were mainly captains with a sprinkling of majors. His favourite expression was 'Ver ist der Schwerpunkt?' The American, Jerry Collins, was the son of General 'Lightning Joe' Collins of Second World War fame. The naval officer later became an admiral. I well remember him on a TEWT (tactical exercise without troops) on a hill near Basingstoke; it was pouring with rain and, as he stood there in his naval uniform, carrying a multi-coloured umbrella, he muttered, 'What on earth is a lieutenant commander RN doing here trying to site a bloody Bren gun?'

There were many enjoyable military highlights in my year at Camberley, but it wasn't a particularly happy period. There were several reasons why I didn't enjoy it. First, unlike the bachelors who were not only financially much better off, but could 'live it up' at Minley in the evenings, Anne and I were short of money and very restricted by our children. We couldn't afford any help in the house and when I came home with a military paper to write or something to study for the following day I often found Anne tired out and the girls, who were still far too young for school, still very active and demanding attention. It was no surprise that my work suffered. Second, as the winner of a 'Competitive Entry', I was undoubtedly judged more harshly than my brother officers and criticized accordingly. This came to a head after one of my military papers was 'torn to pieces' by one of the DS. David Lloyd Owen was now a College commander at Sandhurst and I asked him to take a look at it – he had after all been a DS at the Staff College himself. He told me he thought it was a very good paper and not to worry – 'that's the way some DS are', he said with a smile. Nevertheless, it didn't do my morale much good. And third, I found a lot of the 'staff work' boring and petty and some of the tactical instruction unimaginative and dated. This may sound arrogant, but I could see little point in studying how to carry out an assault crossing of the Thames near Dorchester! Were we *really* going to hold the Russians on the river Weser in Germany and then counter-attack them? And were we *really* going to carry our infantrymen into battle on the backs of tanks behind a massive artillery barrage? It seemed to me that we had learned little or nothing from the lessons of the Second World War.

Highlights of the year included lectures by Lord Louis Mountbatten, the Chief of the Defence Staff, and Monty, visits to the Schools of Infantry, Armour and Artillery, and especially, a battlefield tour in June to Normandy. This latter event was very memorable. We stayed in a hotel in Cabourg and visited the British landing beaches, the Merville Battery and Pegasus Bridge, and studied Operation GOODWOOD in detail. In each case we had veterans describing their parts in the various actions. I remember one RSM breaking down in tears at the Merville Battery – it was the first time he'd been back since 1944. German veterans were not allowed by the French to participate in these Normandy tours at that time, so we had a tape recording of the famous Panzer commander, Hans von Luck of 21st Panzer Division, describing his part in GOODWOOD. Little did I realize that twenty years later he would be an overnight guest in my house in Germany.

The visit to the Royal Armoured Corps School at Bovington was very memorable – not for the tanks and so on, but for the journey back. We went in our own cars and I had three fellow students in mine including Eberhardt Retzlaff. As we neared Winchester on our return he asked if we could stop there for a drink. 'It has the oldest bar in England!' he said. Sure enough it had and he went straight up to the bar and ordered four gin and tonics. We were all in uniform and it was clear that the barman was surprised and a little shocked to see a German colonel wearing an Iron Cross in his pub. Anyway, across came the typically British gin and tonic of that time – no ice and no lemon. Eberhardt looked at them, pushed them slowly back and said 'Und now ve vill have der ice und der lemon, bitte!' I thought the barman was about to hit him, but he reluctantly complied. It turned out that he'd been in the Eighth Army – or so he said.

As already mentioned, our social life at Camberley was very restricted:

we couldn't afford to eat out or hire babysitters very often, and I don't think we went to the cinema at all that year; however, we did have a television set.

One highlight of 1960 was golf. My father had bought me a set of clubs and taught me the basics, and the big bonus of being at the Staff College was that we were automatically members of the famous Royal Berkshire Golf Club near Bagshot. More than that, if there was a competition at the Berkshire we were allowed to play for nothing at the Sunningdale and Wentworth. I took up the game quite seriously and soon had a handicap of twenty.

For our summer leave that year we spent a week with my parents and then, after leaving the girls with them, booked into the Bull at Long Melford in Suffolk. This was a Trust House Forte hotel and we paid £27 (£463 today) for seven nights' full board for the two of us. The advantage of the Trust House system was that you could take meals in other Trust Houses and so we were able to enjoy lunches at attractive places like the Swan at Lavenham. I also took out temporary membership at the local golf club near Sudbury and while Anne rested after lunch I would play nine holes.

A memorable event that year was meeting Monty. I've already mentioned that he lectured the whole College, but each Division had a 'Dinner Club' to which we could invite a guest of honour. It was a black-tie affair and, after dinner, the guest would make a short informal speech and then answer questions. We chose Monty who lived nearby at Isington in Hampshire and he was a great success. I remember him telling us that only *he* knew the true situation in the world since only *he* had met Stalin, Mao, Truman, Eisenhower, de Gaulle, Adenauer etc, etc!

The year ended with the publication of our future appointments. I hadn't done particularly well and certainly wasn't in the running for a top job. To my amazement I found myself posted, as a temporary major, to the Army Operational Research Establishment just down the road in West Byfleet. This was a highly technical establishment manned mainly by civilians, but with a brigadier as a 'military advisor' and a handful of lieutenant colonels and majors to staff the War Gaming section. My initial disappointment at not having been given a 'proper' military job soon turned to delight though when I discovered that I was to spend the next three years 'War Gaming' with plenty of time off.

Chapter Twelve

War Gaming

The years 1961 to 1963 turned out to be amongst the happiest of our lives. We lived in a beautiful house, were surrounded by good friends, had a beautiful addition to our family, there was no terrorist threat and the major changes to the traditional British way of life had yet to happen. And, most importantly for me, I thoroughly enjoyed my job which was both fascinating and challenging.

My first task after receiving my posting to the Army Operational Research Establishment (AORE) was to find somewhere to live. There was no Army quarter for us in West Byfleet or Camberley so once again I had to find somewhere myself. Fortunately, an officer I had known in the Queen's, way back in Iserlohn in 1950, was about to move out of a flat in an old house in Camberley and one look told us it was just the place for us. The MoD paid most of the rent but I had to pay a small shortfall myself; however, now that I was on a major's salary, this was not too much of a burden and proved to be well worthwhile.

'Clewborough', as the house was called, was situated at the end of a 200-yard, rhododendron-lined drive off the Portsmouth Road on the south-east side of Camberley (sadly the drive is now a proper road with modern houses on each side), and its garden backed on to the sixth green of Camberley Heath Golf Club. It was a large house built in the early 1900s but, by 1960, it had been divided into five flats. We had the best one: on the ground floor on the west side. It faced the forecourt and was the only one with direct access to the spacious garden with its huge lawn. The flat had oil-fired central heating and was beautifully furnished with mainly antique furniture and had three bedrooms, two bathrooms, a large kitchen complete with an Aga, and a garage. We could hardly believe our luck. The senior officer at AORE and his wife came to dinner in May 1962; she wrote afterwards: 'Thank you for a delicious dinner. It seemed so civilized after these quarters' – and she was talking about a brigadier's quarter!

Not being entitled to a batman or domestic help, we decided to have a living-in 'mother's help' – not an 'au-pair'. Pregnant again, and with two very active little girls, Anne certainly needed help. Accordingly, Friedel Sieg, a very plain but charming German girl, soon arrived and settled in without any problems.

Another great 'plus' about our time in Clewborough was that we were near to some of our oldest friends as well as a number we had known at the Staff College and who had continued to live in the Camberley area. The oldest friends were Tony and Pat Baxter who arrived for their year at the Staff College in 1961 and Peter and Wha (Diana) Field who were living with her widowed father in his house in Farnborough. Peter had resigned from the Army in 1958 and worked in his father-in-law's sports equipment business for a short time. It was not really the life for him though, so in June 1959 he applied to rejoin the Queen's. Amazingly, he was told that there were no vacancies for someone of his age and so he applied to the newly-formed permanent cadre of the Parachute Regiment where he was welcomed with open arms. He had earned an MC with the Paras in Cyprus during the EOKA campaign. By the time we moved to Clewborough Peter was serving in Aldershot and then attended the 1962 Staff College course.

Camberley in the early sixties was a very different place from today. Frimley, Bagshot and Farnborough were completely separate villages and towns, and there was no M3 motorway. The A30 running through the town was a pleasant road with some nice shops including a Moss Bros and a nice hotel, the 'Cambridge', and the High Street had some very good shops including a Sainsbury's. Life moved at a much slower pace and shopping was still very much as it had been before the war – there were no supermarkets.

Fortunately for us another officer from my Staff College course was posted to the AORE at the same time and he also found a hiring in Camberley. This meant that we could share cars and, as it turned out, one of the lieutenant colonels at AORE lived near Camberley, so he often gave me a lift to work too. Without these lifts Anne would have been completely stranded as the town shops were a good mile away and one had to climb quite a long and steep hill to reach them on the other side of today's M3. There was simply no way we could afford a second car.

The fact that our garden was right next to the golf course was a godsend for me. I joined the Camberley Heath Club straight away and, against all the rules, was able to practise my chipping and putting on and around the sixth green early in the morning and late at night. By May 1962, my handicap was down to eighteen and by the time I left, at the end of 1963, it was sixteen. A lot of this improvement was due to a new friendship with a former National Service East Surrey officer named Peter Mason. He was a good-looking bachelor with an Austin-Healey sports car and was sole heir to a large nursery near Egham. I met him through the Queen's Surreys' golf society meetings at Sudbrooke Park and he quickly detected that my short right leg was affecting my performance. I needed to take more lofted clubs than normal for most of my shots.

Three years in south-east England meant I was able to play many of its courses with John Davidson, Peter Field, Peter Mason and my father after he retired and moved south to Sussex in April 1962. A regular opponent on Camberley Heath in my last year was the first CO of the amalgamated Battalion with whom I had fallen out at Bury St Edmunds. He wasn't a popular man but he could be fun on the golf course – as long as he was winning! One of my proudest moments was being asked to play for the Queen's Surreys against the Royal Marines at the Royal Cinque Ports Club in May 1962. I beat a Marine Colonel 4 and 3. Sadly, continuous postings abroad meant that, after I left Clewborough, I was never able to play golf regularly again.

The great event of 1961 was the birth of our third daughter, Deborah Mary, at the Louise Margaret Hospital in Aldershot – the maternity wing of the Cambridge Military Hospital. Debs as she soon became known, was christened at the Sandhurst RC Chapel on 18 June and the next two and a half years of her life were idyllic – pampered by her parents, sisters, grannies and grandpas and two mother's-helps, she never cried and seemed to have a permanent smile on her face. I mention two mother's-helps because Friedel left us after eighteen months and was replaced by a marvellous English girl called Judy. Friedel had been efficient and was nice, but Judy was much more fun whilst being equally, if not even more, efficient.

The fact that I had a lot of time off in my new job was another important factor in my enjoyment of this period. So what exactly was my new job? I won't go into a lot of detail, but essentially we were wargaming I British Corps in Germany resisting a full-scale attack by a major part of the Group of Soviet Forces Germany (GSFG) and trying to find out how long the British could delay the Soviets before having to resort to the use of nuclear weapons. I was the permanent Chief of Staff (COS) in the Red, or Soviet, Room and the other Camberley graduate was my equivalent in the Blue (British) Room. Each 'side', Red and Blue, was commanded by a visiting general or at least a brigadier. Amongst the more memorable commanders I served as the Red Room COS were Lieutenant General Sir Dick Craddock, Major Generals John Nelson and Neil Foster and Brigadier Charles Armitage. They had all served with distinction in the war and were highly decorated. Dick Craddock was a fascinating person – a former Buff who had lost a leg on D-Day, he later became the first Colonel of the Queen's Regiment, formed in 1969 and in which I would command a Battalion and later hold the same honorary appointment. He was a great raconteur and would mesmerize us with stories of his wartime and other experiences.

My commanders, although very senior officers, had very little idea of exactly how the Soviets would organize their forces and so I would have to advise. To do this I had to make a detailed study of the Red Army and its tactics. By 1962, after a year of war gaming, the commanders knew I was experienced and were often more than content to leave the initial deployment in my hands.

The game was both fascinating and mentally taxing. I would often wake at night and think of something we *ought* to be doing – putting more weight on the northern flank or something like that and then in the morning try to persuade my commander to do it. I won't go on, but rather quote part of Brigadier Hope-Thomson's Confidential Report on me after my first eighteen months:

> I consider this officer comes close to being outstanding for his rank and service. During the period under review he has acted as COS on the Soviet side to War Game commanders of rank not below that of brigadier. In addition he has specialized in Soviet organization, tactics and weaponry and produced most valuable aide-memoirs in these fields for the War Game organization. He has on all occasions gained the complete confidence of the commanders he was serving. He is prepared to assume responsibility for planning and tactical decisions but does not unduly obtrude his views on his commander. He has an overall grasp of the capability of a large complex force of all arms quite unusual for his rank.

At the conclusion of each game, which normally lasted about six weeks, we would tidy up, prepare for the next game and then go on leave, usually for at least two weeks, leaving the civilian scientists of the AORE to assess the results and write their reports. These reports may have been very useful for the 'Director of Combat Development' at the War Office, but they were of little interest to me. I was drawing my own conclusions about *how* the battalions and regiments of I British Corps should be deployed and used and where the weaknesses in the Soviet structure lay. Big-headed perhaps, but very useful later on when I became a brigade commander in Germany and subsequently commander of NATO's Allied Command Europe Mobile Force. Having said that, I did play the main role in a presentation we gave to the Joint Planning Staff (JPS) in London at the end of 1962. General Sir William Pike, Vice Chief of the Imperial General Staff, wrote later to our Director:

We got the Chief of Staffs yesterday to approve the JPS paper 'The British View of Strategy for the Defence of Central Europe'. This paper is very satisfactory to us, particularly in its soundness on the need for tactical nuclear weapons for the Shield forces. I do not believe that we would have succeeded in getting this paper through but for . . . the invaluable presentation which you gave . . . [This] was evidently even more educational than we had dared hope. I would like you to know the value we attribute to the AORE in general and this presentation in particular.

In April 1962 David Lloyd Owen was promoted and appointed to command 24 Infantry Brigade in Kenya. He immediately asked the War Office to cut short my tour at the AORE and send me out as his BM (COS). The Brigade was heavily involved in anti-terrorist operations and it would have been a wonderful opportunity for me. I was highly flattered that he should want me, but the War Office said no: brigade commanders were not allowed to choose their BMs in the way that COs could choose their Adjutants – not even influential brigadiers with lots of friends in high places like David. In his usual style he wrote to me later, 'My new BM arrives next week and I wish to goodness it was to be you!'

I was in demand again later that year. This time it was the CO of the Queen's Surreys, Mike Lowry (he'd been the Adjutant at Stoughton when I'd first joined the Queen's in 1950). He wanted me to join his Battalion in Hong Kong in January 1963, but again the War Office turned him down and decreed that I must complete my three years in West Byfleet.

1963 began with heavy snow. By the beginning of February the drive to Clewborough was completely blocked and we had to walk to the Portsmouth Road through snow three-feet-deep; sledging on the golf course and tobogganing from the ninth tee provided many happy hours for our girls. The scenery around the house was breathtaking.

In the autumn of 1963 I applied for a vacancy on the All Arms Battlegroup Leaders Course at Warminster. This was designed for those who had *not* been to the Staff College, but I got a vacancy on the grounds that I had been away from regimental soldiering for four years and that, as I was about to rejoin the 1st Battalion of the Queen's Surreys in Germany as a company commander, I needed an update. It was a hugely expensive course in that a complete infantry battalion (the Black Watch), a tank squadron, an artillery battery and an engineer troop were available for our training and familiarization. It was so expensive in fact that it was discontinued after six courses. The Commandant was a Colonel (later full General), Jackie Harman, a superb soldier and leader: I was privileged to serve under him again in several future appointments. I loved the course.

During it I commanded a Centurion tank, a tank troop, directed guns as a Forward Observation Officer and ended the course as the battlegroup commander on a twenty-four-hour exercise on Salisbury Plain. The battle-group comprised all the elements I've mentioned above. On this exercise, which involved an advance to contact, a series of small attacks and then a full-scale final attack, I came up with the idea of giving all recognizable features a code letter and number. I then directed the battlegroup, by radio, onto and through these features. As a result the exercise finished six hours earlier than scheduled. I was the only officer on the course to command the complete battlegroup and I received the top grading. Without any doubt the course played a major part in my success as a mechanized company commander in Germany, a post I was to take up in early 1964.

Before finishing this chapter I would like to mention the 'Swinging Sixties'. These didn't really take off until after we moved to Germany in 1964, but the era of the Beatles, Twiggy, and 'Top of the Pops' with their screaming audiences was already beginning during our time in Camberley and would soon see the demise of the swing and dance bands which I loved so much. There were no plastic bottles in 1961 and eating and drinking as you walked along a pavement was unheard of; and there was no spit-ting – indeed, such a thing could lead to a £5 fine (£83 today). On a more serious note, Enoch Powell's 'Rivers of Blood' speech was still a few years away, but mass immigration from the old Empire was already a talking point and a widespread use of the 'Pill' leading to sexual freedom for women and a general loosening of morals had its beginnings during our time in Camberley. However, life for us had been sedate, organized and thoroughly enjoyable. Little did we realize that society as we knew it then was already beginning to disintegrate.

Chapter Thirteen

Company Commander in Germany

I arrived in Oxford Barracks, Münster, in early January 1964. With no quarter immediately available for us, Anne and the girls had to remain in England with our parents and I had to live in the Mess.

The 1st Battalion was commanded by a former Royal West Kent with an MC from the war. I had never met him before, but I knew most of the other officers and the RSM was my old friend Ron Wildgoose of Korea and Iserlohn days. As with many units in Germany at that time the Battalion was short of men and had only two instead of the normal three rifle companies. This meant that I would have to wait for a proper command until one of the rifle company commanders left; in the meantime I was given A Company which comprised the Corps of Drums and the Assault Pioneer and Reconnaissance Platoons.

I only had one officer in A Company, Stewart Anderson. He had been commanding the Company before I arrived and I was more than happy to let him carry on whilst I attended to more important things like getting my quarter sorted out and my girls out to Germany. I chose one of my drummers, Private Cook, as my batman and he served us well for the next two years. Our Putzfrau's name escapes us, but we remember her as a competent, nice person.

As soon as I was allocated the quarter I applied for the family to be flown out and then set about getting our brand new, four-bedroomed house ready for occupation. The fact that it was brand new caused a problem in that, although it was fully furnished, it was full of dust, having never been properly cleaned after the builders left. I therefore asked the entire Corps of Drums if they would volunteer to clean it from top to bottom, assisted by the Putzfrau. For a fee, I can't remember how much, but it wasn't a lot, they all agreed and within a day the place was spotless.

Anne and the girls arrived on 20 January and to my great relief she liked the house. Fortunately, Lincoln School, the Army primary school, was not far from our quarter and Vicky and Gabrielle were enrolled three days later and settled well. As we remember it, it was really quite a good school and the girls' education certainly didn't suffer.

After a few weeks the C Company commander left and I took over. It was a full-strength company of some 120 men; in those days the rifle companies were each allocated a support platoon with two 81mm mortars and two Mobat anti-tank guns. Lieutenant Tony Ward, the first officer to be commissioned directly into the Queen's Surreys, was my Support Platoon commander and, initially, I had a short-service officer, Jim Horan, and two excellent sergeants, Hope and Maume, commanding my rifle platoons; however, before long Mike Goode (his father was a distinguished Queen's officer) and Roddy Mellotte arrived and stayed with me for the rest of my time with C Company. They were all excellent young officers. My third rifle platoon was later commanded by a good Military Police officer doing his infantry attachment and then by Frank le Maitre.

The greatest character in C Company was CSM Jack Chaffer who had joined the Grenadiers in the war and earned an MM as a young lance sergeant at Anzio. After the war he left the Army, but joined the East Surreys' TA Battalion. He spent so much time with it in the evenings and at weekends that someone eventually suggested that he should join the Regiment as a regular. This he did and, by some administrative error, was allowed to sign on for twenty-two years at the age of thirty-plus. He was thus some six years older than me.

Jack was a large, good-looking man with a huge 'presence' and great sense of humour. Fortunately, he and I hit it off at once. I had a couple of days 'handover/takeover' at the end of which I suggested to Jack that everything seemed to be in order and that the Company was therefore mine. 'Oh no, Sir, you haven't got a handover certificate from your predecessor's wife,' said Jack, 'it was *her* Company!' I took his point.

C Company was full of colourful characters. As well as those already mentioned, the Company Quartermaster Sergeant, Colour Sergeant Swift, known as 'Wishbone' after a character in a TV Western series called *Wagon Train*, was barely adequate, but great fun. His biggest problem was trying to keep up with Jack's beer-drinking capability when we were off duty on exercise or on various training areas. After three beers he was usually paralytic. My first personal driver was 'Topper' Brown who came to me under a cloud having been 'busted' from the ranks of sergeant and corporal and unfortunately 'blew' it again after being with me for quite a long time when he appeared drunk on the RSM's Saturday morning drill parade; he ended up telling Wildgoose (the 'Goose') to 'f—- off!' Lance Corporal Hoey replaced him – another great character with a delightful Irish accent. I won't list all the other excellent sergeants and corporals in the Company, or the many very memorable privates, but Sergeants Prior, Campion and Stredwick, Corporals Atkins, Ebbens, Donnelly, Sibley,

Maye, Tickner and Kamil, (a Turkish Cypriot), Bodkin (the Company clerk), Lance Corporals Walker, Soffe, Rodmell, Dingwall, and Privates Hands, Stower, Rice, Cameron and Tiller stand out in my memory – not always for the right reasons! Many went on to higher rank.

Soon after joining the Battalion it became very clear to me that, having spent the last three years in Aden and Hong Kong, no one in the Battalion, even the CO, really knew how to use armoured personnel carriers (APCs) or indeed anything about mechanized tactics. However, having done my All Arms Battlegroup Leaders' course, I did! The CO was quick to realize this and he soon arranged for me and an officer from our affiliated armoured regiment to run an Officers' Day during which we would instruct everyone in armoured tactics and infantry/tank cooperation. Fortunately, the other officer chosen had been with me at Minley and we were old friends. The day was a great success and the Battalion and its affiliated armoured squadron was soon practising what we had taught on the Soltau and Vogelsang training areas.

It wasn't only the Queen's Surreys, however, that had little idea about mechanized tactics. The whole British Army in 1964 was ill-equipped and most of it was still using Second World War tactics. Our main battle tank was the Centurion I had known in Korea, we had no self-propelled artillery and, as already mentioned, the so-called 'mechanized' infantry was still awaiting the issue of a proper tracked APC – the AFV (Armoured Fighting Vehicle) 432. As a stopgap we had been equipped with four-wheeled, one-ton Humber vehicles known to the infantry as 'Pigs'. They were lightly armoured, offered no NBC (nuclear, biological and chemical) protection and were far too heavy for their suspensions when off-road; as a result they were constantly breaking down. Furthermore, they had no fitted radios and, needless to say, the man-pack radios with which we were equipped rarely worked *inside* the beasts; when on the move my poor platoon commanders usually had to give their deployment orders by the use of flags. The final thing that has to be said about the Pig is that it was incredibly uncomfortable for the eight infantrymen in the back who usually arrived on their objective disorientated and feeling sick.

Tactically the infantry was still expected to advance into the attack behind a rolling artillery barrage or to be 'shot in' by supporting tanks, and orders were issued at O Groups with the commander facing his subordinates. These orders were then usually confirmed in written 'Confirmatory Notes'. Radio orders in the infantry, were almost unheard of. We were at last an all-regular Army, but we were still treating our soldiers like National Servicemen. I was determined to change this – at least in C Company. This caused my first disagreement with Jack

Chaffer. Being an ex-Guardsman he was very keen on the daily early morning muster parade where everyone was counted and inspected, but as far as I was concerned this was an anachronism and a waste of time. I therefore gave instructions that my platoons would have their first morning parade with their vehicles and it was up to the platoon commanders to inspect them and carry out 'first parade' maintenance on the vehicles. This was to prepare them for the day we would get our 432s. Jack didn't like this. The next thing I did was to warn everyone that in future there would be no written orders in C Company, only verbal or radio orders. This was put to the test soon after my arrival when we were due to spend two weeks at the All Arms Training Centre at Sennelager. I issued verbal orders for our move there, asked for any questions, answered them and then dismissed the O Group. Afterwards, Jack said he would produce 'Confirmatory Notes' and I told him to forget it. He then announced that this would lead to a major 'f— up!' I told him that Anne would drive me into barracks the next morning, I would get into my Land Rover and drive off, expecting the twenty or so vehicles of my Company to follow me. He smiled. Next morning I set off as I said I would. I'm not sure how many of the Pigs etc followed me out of the barracks, but it certainly wasn't all of them. Anyway they all eventually turned up at Sennelager and I then told Jack he could have a formal muster parade and check the men's clothing and equipment. They were used to having a list put up on the Company noticeboard telling them exactly what they had to have for any event or exercise and this time it hadn't happened. Some of them only had one spare pair of socks, some had skimpy civilian underpants instead of woollen army pants and some had forgotten basic items like razor blades and soap. I then addressed the Company and told them that as professionals they had to grow up and act like responsible soldiers. They were going to set an example to the rest of the Battalion and indeed the rest of the Brigade. And although I say it myself, within six months they had. After one major field training exercise (FTX) in the German countryside, I heard, unbeknown to him, our Second-in-Command, telling an officer in another Regiment that he had never seen an infantry company perform as well as C Company; he went on to say that its reaction time was outstanding and its ability to react to radio orders was unbelievable.

The other things I did in C Company which surprised everyone was to ensure that every soldier was taught to drive and received basic training in at least one other 'skill' as well as his designated job. I interviewed each man and gave him the choice of being trained as a signaller, mortarman, anti-tank gunner or some other speciality. This proved highly popular and ensured that no one was ever bored.

*   *   *

But what was family life like in Münster? It was in fact very domesticated and simple. There were no British nursery schools in the town and so Debbie was at home all day fully occupying Anne's time. There was no one to babysit for us – obviously we couldn't leave Drummer Cook with our three little girls – and so we rarely went out at night, except to our next-door neighbours. Fortunately the Ulster crisis, with its four-month unaccompanied tours, was still in the future and so, apart from a couple of weeks at various training areas like Sennelager, Soltau and Haltern each year and the occasional exercise, I was basically at home every night. Soldiering was also much more relaxed in those days. We started work at 8.30, had an hour and a half for lunch and finished work or sport at 4.30 each day. The weekends were also usually free apart from Saturday morning drill parades and church parades once a month.

Münster was a nice town, and although it had been virtually destroyed in the war, the centre around the cathedral had been beautifully restored in its original style. There was a large market square with a wonderful market a couple of times a week, good restaurants and a large NAAFI and Army cinema. The only minus point was the boringly flat surrounding countryside. Nevertheless, life there was fun, although it has to be said that we led very protected lives. We had no television and the only news of the outside world we received was through day-old British newspapers and the British Forces Broadcasting Service (BFBS) based in Cologne. We were, therefore, only vaguely aware of the major changes taking place in British society during the 'permissive' sixties. We lived in our own little world. The officers got on well together and the relationship between the Officers' and Sergeants' messes was good, as was the Battalion's with the other major units in 6 Infantry Brigade, the 4th/7th Dragoon Guards, the Royal Hampshires and the Cheshires.

Our first major holiday was in May 1964. The Battalion was given 'block leave' so we had no choice of the dates. We took the girls out of school – with the headmaster's permission – and on 3 May set off on a 960-mile journey to the Italian Riviera. We didn't know precisely where we were heading for, but knew we wanted the sun and the Mediterranean and were lucky enough to find a lovely apartment in a wonderful little seaside town called Lerici. We had an idyllic holiday in perfect weather and arrived back in Münster on 31 May, tanned and refreshed and only *just* in time for the Glorious First of June formal dinner in the Mess and other usual celebrations with the visiting officers of HMS *Excellent*.

Following the Glorious First of June celebrations, we moved up to Soltau for infantry/tank training with B Squadron 4th/7th Dragoon Guards. The OC was an excellent young captain who later reached the rank of brigadier. The move of some 170 miles was a good test of our convoy driving (all movement in those days was by road) and on arrival we set up a tented camp in a fir forest on the edge of the training area. We were well away from the CO and Battalion HQ which pleased us greatly. The men slept on the ground in tiny two-man tents known as bivvies, the officers and sergeants slept on camp beds in much larger 160-pounder tents and I had one to myself with a proper iron bedstead and mattress. I had no conscience about this on account of my back problems. Jack and 'Wishbone' played a blinder on this occasion by buying up all the beer in the local NAAFI. As a result C Company was the only company with beer for the first few days. RSM Wildgoose had to come over and beg Jack to sell him some for his Mess.

Fortunately, we were blessed with superb weather for the whole fortnight at Soltau although the dust kicked up by the tanks and our 'pigs' was very unpleasant. At last though, I was able to exercise the Company in proper mechanized tactics with my affiliated tank troop under Lieutenant Tony Mullens. We got along extremely well and I was to serve with him again on more than one occasion. He ended up as a lieutenant general, but sadly died in 2009.

We had a really great and successful time both at work and at play. The latter included a trip with my subalterns to the Reeperbahn in Hamburg. Also on the play side, Jack set up an officers' and sergeants' mess tent where we had very pleasant and boozy evenings, with many games of 'Cardinal Puff'. On the more serious side I made sure all ranks paid a visit to the nearby site of the Belsen Concentration camp. None of the buildings still existed, but the memorials and mass graves were sad reminders of what had happened there.

In August 1964 I took Anne and the girls for a long weekend in Amsterdam. The Dutch border was only forty miles away and we'd already popped over a few times for picnics or for me to play golf at Hengelo. I've no idea where we stayed in Amsterdam, but we took the girls on a cruise round the canals, to the Rijksmuseum to see Rembrandt's 'Night Watch', went to the zoo and did the usual sightseeing. The most memorable incident was in a street called Kanalstrasse. We were all walking along talking happily when, to my utter horror, I saw to our left and right naked women sitting in shop windows! Yes, we were in the red light district. I whispered to Anne, 'Don't look to your left or right and don't say anything but keep walking.' 'What's the matter?' said Anne. A moment later, 'Oh look Mummy, there's a lady in that window knitting, but she's got no clothes on!'

Mention of playing golf in Holland reminds me of an unfortunate episode involving my car. Sometime in late 1964 or early 1965 I enjoyed eighteen holes (and the nineteenth) at the Twentsche course in Hengelo with the Adjutant. Anyway, it was dark by the time we set off for home in our separate cars and, sometime after crossing back into Germany, I switched on the roof light to look at the time. There was no clock on a Morris Traveller dashboard and my old gold watch was not luminous. The next thing I knew I was in a deep ditch! I was unhurt, but there was no way I could reverse out. Fortunately a passing German driver stopped, exclaiming 'Ach, you are kamping?' and gave me a lift, not just to Münster, but all the way home. Anne was furious with me, but at least relieved that I was unhurt. The next day I told Jack Chaffer to organize the Company 3-ton truck and to drive it himself with only 'Wishbone' to assist him. I then set off in my Land Rover to show them the way. We soon found my poor Morris Traveller with its rear end sticking up out of the ditch and Jack reversed up to winch it out. It was at that moment that the tarpaulin at the back of the truck opened up and standing there were about a dozen of my APC drivers, all roaring with laughter. I had always been hard on bad driving and Jack had decided that it would be good for my drivers' morale if they could see that their commander was capable of making mistakes too. Anyway the car was towed to the local Morris agent and the damage found to be only superficial. I was lucky to get off so lightly – my pride was in fact more dented than the car.

The 1964 training year ended for us with a major field training exercise (FTX) against a Canadian Brigade – in those days the Canadians contributed a complete division to I British Corps. It went well and I was delighted with my Company's performance and so, fortunately for me, were the CO and Brigade commander. Amazingly, the Army could designate huge areas of the German countryside, including villages, for such exercises and we were then allowed to drive anywhere we liked in the interests of 'tactical manoeuvre'. This included cultivated land and, even more amazingly, we were allowed to requisition barns and other buildings. Every September when the harvests were in, one would see long military columns blocking the roads, and even the autobahns, and tank and APC tracks covering the fields. Naturally, the farmers and owners were compensated for any damage done.

The year ended for me with a surprising appointment to be the President of a court martial. The accused was a corporal in the Royal Hampshires. I can't remember his alleged offence. I had a civilian judge advocate (JAG) to advise me and two other officers to complete the Board. At one stage when the corporal's Irish wife was giving evidence in his favour, the JAG whispered to me that I should perhaps ask her if the accused was drunk at the time of the offence. 'Of *course* he was drunk,

Your Honour – he was always drunk!' came the reply. We found him guilty, but I have no idea what we gave him as a sentence.

Every three months throughout its time in BAOR the Battalion spent one month on Operation SPEARHEAD. There was still trouble in Cyprus and Malaysia and SPEARHEAD was designed to provide rapid reinforcements for any one of these trouble spots. This meant that we had to practise anti-terrorist (internal security as we called it in those days) as well as mechanized tactics. Sure enough, in early 1965 we were alerted for an imminent move to Borneo. I was horrified. With the large amount of scar tissue on my right leg I knew that there still was no way I could possibly go into swamps or deep jungle. My fiddled medical grading of 'fit for everywhere' was about to be exposed. I went to the CO and told him that I would be unable to command C Company on active operations in Borneo. To my great relief he told me that he was already aware of that and that if we went I would assume the appointment of Battle Adjutant. There was no such thing as an Operations Officer in those days and this was the equivalent. I told him I was very grateful. In the event the alert was cancelled and we never went.

My first big adventure in 1965 was being sent with Jack Chaffer to observe an American FTX called MARNE MIGHT in the Würtzburg area of Bavaria. We spent the first couple of nights in splendid rooms in the US Officers' Club at Kitzingen (Jack on the grounds that he was a Warrant *Officer*), but when the American unit we were observing moved out, we were expected to 'move out' too. The trouble was that we hadn't been told to bring tents with us. The weather was quite appalling with rain, snow and freezing temperatures at night. Needless to say, Jack managed to persuade an American top sergeant to let him share his tent and was most amused when I said I had nowhere to sleep. In the end I decided to take our Land Rover and go back to my very comfortable room at the Club for the rest of the night and then rejoin early the next morning. To Jack's irritation, I did this for the rest of the exercise, enjoying a good dinner each night, whilst he suffered in a tent and ate C rations. Incidentally, one of the most surprising things we discovered during our time with the Americans was that all their combat vehicles, including tanks, carried their full load of wartime ammuntion *all* the time, both inside and outside barracks.

I always worked on the principle that, whenever possible, soldiering should be fun and to this end, and because my boys' barrack rooms were very basic and the woodwork very shabby, I bought with Company funds lots of tins of coloured paint and told them they could paint their doors and inside window frames any colour they liked. I mentioned that if they agreed to have a different colour for each door they would know their way 'home' after a few beers. Everyone was very happy except my old friend Jimmy Kemp, the Quartermaster, who threatened me with astronomical 'barrack damages'. I told him that if he didn't like it he should get the Property Services Agency (PSA) to get the woodwork painted properly; after all, it was *their* job and *his*, to look after the barracks, not mine. That was the end of it. It may be of interest to know that in those days no *single* officers or soldiers in the Army paid for their food or accommodation.

In March 1965 my Company spent three weeks at another training area at Haltern, about thirty miles west of Münster. The boys slept in barns and the officers and senior NCOs in proper bedrooms in a large pub and farm house, the Gasthof Wilins. I was in my element because I, and I alone, would decide the training we would carry out with no interference from Battalion HQ. Apart from the normal field training like recce and ambush patrols, platoon and company attacks and defence exercises, I therefore instituted more exciting events – some of them well remembered by former members of C Company. As well as night patrols to some extremely difficult objectives, like small bridges over a swollen and frozen river which all corporals had to do, the most memorable exercise was 'The Great Train Robbery'. This was modelled on a real-life event which had happened in August 1963 when £2.3 million was stolen from a night train at Bridego railway bridge, near Ledburn in Buckinghamshire. In my version Tony Ward with his Support Platoon was placed in charge of the 'bullion', an ammunition box with bricks in it, which had to be taken every evening at the same time in a 15-cwt truck driven by Jack Chaffer, from a point about five miles from our base at the farm house, back to the farmhouse. Mike Goode, Roddy Mellotte and Jim Horan with their platoons had to steal the 'bullion'. There were no rules. I would follow the 'bullion' truck each evening in my Land Rover to see what happened. I knew the three subalterns would argue about how to carry out their task but I had not anticipated how dangerous it would get. For the first three or four nights nothing happened. Then, on the next night, I was horrified to see a 3-ton truck emerge from a track in a wood and attempt to overtake Jack, who incidentally had chained himself into the driving seat, and force him off the road and to stop. The 'bullion' was also chained to the floor of the 15-cwt and protected by some of Tony's toughest men. The 3-tonner was full of 'robbers' from the other subalterns' platoons. Jack decided at once that he was *not* going to stop and for a good mile or two we had the two trucks side by side roaring along a quiet country road. I was very relieved when the 'chase' truck gave up a short distance from the farm. The final night was even worse. In desperation the 'robbers' decided to attack the truck as it turned into the farm itself. We ended up with a major fight in the farmyard involving most of my Company and with very few holds barred. Fists flew and pickhelves were used and it was a miracle that no one was seriously hurt. The 'robbers' never got the 'bullion' though, and only by throwing a thunder-flash did I attract everyone's attention and stop the fight. The night ended with a lot of beer being consumed and a lot of laughter. Company morale had never been higher.

Our second Italian holiday, again in May, was memorable for two reasons. Firstly my parents were with us which allowed Anne and me to take a short break on our own to see Pisa, Florence, Siena and Rome and, secondly, because we were able to visit Pontremoli, a small mountain town about twenty-five miles north of Lerici. I was keen to visit it because I had heard of it from a former wartime East Surrey officer named Gordon Lett. He had appeared in Münster as a civilian lecturer helping officers prepare for the Staff College exam. We had met him at a party and when I mentioned that we were off in a couple of days time to Lerici, his eyes lit up and he told me an amazing story that he had commanded a small battalion of partisans in the mountains quite near there in 1943–44. The battalion had comprised Italian partisans, mainly communists, and British and Australian former prisoners of war who had been freed when the Italians had surrendered in September 1943. The camps in central Italy had been thrown open and the prisoners had the choice of either staying put and waiting for the British or Americans to arrive, or of setting off north into the mountains. He had chosen the latter course and had ended up near Pontremoli and had taken command of those he found around him. These included a youngster called Elio Fantoni who had acted as a runner and a local priest who looked after the partisans. Elio was now the proprietor of a trattoria called the Grotto Verde and the priest was now Bishop of Pontremoli. He was sure they would both be delighted to see us, so after a few days back with the children we set off and found Elio who welcomed us warmly. The bishop was a different matter. We had no appointment and unfortunately we had chosen a Sunday; as far as the bishop was concerned Sunday afternoon was a time of rest. When we were eventually allowed into his study he fixed me with a stare and made me feel uncomfortable. However, we soon discovered that the reason for this was that he had misunderstood the letter Gordon had written introducing me and had been expecting someone much older – a Second World War veteran in fact. Once this was sorted out he became very friendly and, after calling for drinks, suggested that Elio should take us farther into the mountains to the area where the battalion had been based for its partisan operations. This was some miles away and I asked if I could use the toilet before we set off. My need satisfied, I pulled the chain and nothing happened, so I pulled it again – much harder. To my horror a huge lump of lead flew out of the cistern above my head, missed me by an inch and hit the lavatory pan, smashing it into a dozen pieces and flooding the floor. This made a loud bang of course and Elio rushed in to find me staring at the damage. I had broken the bishop's loo but, to my great relief when I explained, through Elio, what had happened, the bishop simply roared with laughter. All was well and we parted friends. But more surprises were to come. When we reached the tiny village which had been the partisan base we found two very drunken Australian veterans in the local bar. For the first time since the war they had returned for a two-day visit and were still there a week later! After a hilarious half hour with them we returned to Elio's trattorio for a lovely supper.

In 1965 we went twice to the Vogelsang training area twenty miles south of Aachen and near the Belgian border. I always enjoyed it there. The countryside is magnificent, the training area excellent and there was a charming town nearby, Monschau, where we could go for a good meal. Also its connections with the Nazis always fascinated me. The huge barrack blocks where we were accommodated had been built by them and there were many German eagles and 'strength through joy' mosaics adorning the outside of some of the buildings. The first time we went there we did the usual field firing and I put everyone through the battle in-doctrination course. This involved crawling under barbed-wire fences and other obstacles whilst live rounds were fired just above your head. It was perfectly safe, but it still put the wind up a number of the soldiers.

The second time we went to Vogelsang was in August when my Company was designated to run the cross-country section of the BAOR road rally, Roadmaster II. Most units entered this competition which involved teams driving 3-tonners, 15-cwts and Land Rovers over a consid-erable distance around the British sector of West Germany, including the cross-country section at Vogelsang. We all enjoyed this task particularly as it allowed us quite a bit of time for other activities. One of these was a small battlefield tour I ran for my officers and NCOs covering part of the Battle of the Bulge. At the time I had no idea that this particular battle would play a large part in my future life and that I would end up writing three books about it.

I also ran an escape and evasion exercise whilst we were at Vogelsang. I made my young officers the escapees and gave my sergeants and soldiers the job of hunting them down as they tried to reach one end of the training area from the other, a distance of a good six or seven miles. Most of them were caught, but I remember one young officer, an artilleryman attached to me for infantry training, made it, although he arrived totally naked. He had swum across a lake to evade capture and rather than be slowed down by wet clothes he had stripped off! Needless to say the soldiers loved hunting down their own officers.

I mentioned good places to eat in Monschau. The best was probably the Alte Herrlichkeit. I remember one hilarious evening there with all my officers and sergeants. Jack Chaffer expected the officers to pay (or maybe he just pretended that), but anyway he put on a great show of grievance when I passed the hat round at the end of the meal.

The highlight of 1965 was Exercise POND JUMP EAST. The whole Battalion flew to Canada in mid June and set up a temporary tented camp in the 427-square-mile training area known as Camp Gagetown in New Brunswick. Located about halfway between Fredericton and St John, it was a beautiful, but isolated area, ideal for military training with thick woods, lakes, rivers and a small mountain range. We were to be there for six weeks. The RAF flight out was memorable in that my plane, a Bristol Britannia, 'lost an engine' over the Atlantic and we had to divert to Gander in Newfoundland. We were there, restricted to the airport, for many hours whilst the engine was replaced and, believe it or not, one of our soldiers not only chatted up a Canadian girl passing through the terminal but actually married her in the airport chapel! This meant that, as a British Army wife, she was entitled to come back to Münster with us at the end of our training – which she did.

We carried out every type of training at Gagetown from shooting, to operating with Canadian armour, to counter-revolutionary operations in which we used Canadian Vertol troop-carrying helicopters, to route marching and assault river crossings. There were many highlights, many unconnected with military training. On one occasion Mike Goode's platoon had set up camp on a small island on a lake and during the night Frank Le Maitre, who had replaced Jim Horan, swam out and pinched all their boats, leaving them stranded. Not all Mike's soldiers could swim, so he had to beg us to send the boats back to rescue his men and all their equipment. This taught me a lesson and so I insisted that everyone was taught to swim soon after we returned to Münster. Another memorable event was Jack Chaffer making sure the subalterns got up early one Sunday by backing his jeep up to their tents and spraying them with DDT. We were greatly troubled by mosquitoes and cans of DDT were fitted to the rear of a jeep and the chemical then made to drip onto the exhaust pipe thus vaporizing it. It certainly worked on my subalterns and Tim Rogerson who was by now my excellent second-in-command.

On the off-duty side there were also several great highlights. As well as visits to Fredericton, which we christened 'Fredsville' bcause it was so dull, I played golf on the local course and the Battalion threw a big cocktail party for the local military and civilian bigwigs. We had been plagued by bears searching for food and had called in a forest ranger. He shot one and as a deterrent to the others propped it up against the Regimental flag-pole in the centre of the camp. Anyway, during the party a couple of my subalterns, Mellotte and Goode, carried it down to the tented gentlemen's loo and set it up in the half light on one of the multiple 'thunderboxes'. It didn't take long for someone to come screaming out of the loo.

On 1 July, Canada Day, a number of sporting events were organized with and against the local Canadian unit. The History claims we won 'convincingly'; certainly the Canadians were pretty shattered when 'Topper' Brown and I won the cross-country jeep rally and my future RSM, Sid Lea, with our REME sergeant came second.

Shortly after this everyone was given five days' R & R leave. Most went to Montreal or Quebec City, but I hired a large limousine and set off with Mike Goode, Roddy Mellotte, one of the B Company officers and the Battalion Medical Officer. Our destinations were the US Military Academy at West Point and New York City. Peter Field was by now the first British exchange officer at West Point and he and Wha had a very nice quarter in the grounds. My 'boys' dropped me off there and took off for the bright lights of NYC. I spent my first day exploring the Academy with Peter and the following day, as Peter was sadly on duty, Wha drove me down to see the sights of New York. The boys returned the following day and after a BBQ lunch in the garden we set off on our 500-mile overnight return journey. My scrapbook shows that when passing through Maine I was caught for speeding, but let off with a warning: 'The Officer's copy of this warning will be sent to the Secretary of State of Augusta and made part of your driving record.'

In September the Battalion was made part of a Tripartite force (American, British and French) designed to break through to Berlin in the event that the Russians decided to close the 'corridor' through East Germany. Berlin was still garrisoned in those days by British, American, French and Russian troops, each with their own sector. In readiness for this, in my view, ill-conceived and crazy operation, we carried out several days' training at Sennelager using American M113 APCs instead of our 'Pigs' and with American tanks and French artillery in support. My own vehicle commanders had a lot of fun trying to make the American APC drivers understand which way and at what speed they wanted to go, but the most memorable incident for me occurred when I tried to call for fire from the French artillery battery to support a quick attack I was required to launch against a mock Russian 'blocking position' in the 'corridor'. I could see the French battery commander's vehicle about 100 yards behind my Ferret scout car, but he wouldn't answer my calls on the radio.

Eventually, in desperation, I got out of my vehicle, ran back to his and hammered on the rear door. It opened slowly to reveal the battery commander and his crew with cheese, baguettes and a couple of wine bottles on the map table in front of them. They were having lunch! He could see I was not best pleased and after a 'pardon monsieur', he offered me a glass of wine. I replied that I would love one, but that maybe it would be better to wait until *after* the attack.

The climax to our training was an exercise that involved confronting 'enemy' border guards and then moving down the mock 'corridor', over-coming token and minor (platoon-sized) resistance on the way and then launching a full-scale attack, with RAF aircraft carrying out mock sorties in support, against a strong dug-in 'enemy'. This final phase was to take place in front of an international audience of fairly senior officers. The advance went well and I was pleased that my Company had been desig-nated to carry out the big final attack. For this I had the company of American tanks and the French battery of self-propelled artillery under command. We arrived on time in the forming-up place (FUP) for the attack with the US tanks in the lead. I was travelling directly behind them and I soon realized that there wasn't sufficient room for all our M113s to form up behind the tanks and out of sight of the enemy. I therefore radioed the American commander and said, 'You'll have to move up as we can't all get into the FUP'. He thought I had said 'Move out', not 'Move up' and to my horror I saw his tanks set off at top speed for the objective – five minutes before H Hour. I could hardly let the tanks arrive on the objective on their own and, as the exercise was a demonstration in front of an audience, I had no option other than to order my Company to follow. We therefore all arrived on the objective together and in good order, but just as the 'friendly' aircraft carried out a simulated attack with bombs and rockets. We would undoubtedly have suffered heavy casual-ties from 'friendly fire', let alone our 'enemy'. After about fifteen minutes and some sharp words from me to the American tank commander, we were all assembled on foot in front of the audience. Our Brigade commander then proceeded to sum up the exercise and castigate me for attacking before the designated H Hour. There was nothing I could do but to just stand there and take it. I felt about two feet tall. I certainly couldn't start arguing or trying to explain what had happened in front of the audience and I subsequently decided not to bother to try to explain when we got back to Münster. However, about a month later I found the Brigade commander standing, unannounced, in my office in Oxford Barracks. He had come to apologize and to congratulate me for not 'rocking the international boat'. I never found out who had told him what had really happened.

On my return to Münster from Gagetown I had made no secret of the fact that I thought Canada was a bit of a 'dump' and certainly not a place I would ever wish to visit again. It was, therefore, a terrible shock for me when in November, shortly after Toby Sewell took over as CO, I received a Warning Order that my next appointment would be as a junior staff officer at HQ Eastern Command, Halifax, Nova Scotia, commencing 1 February 1966. It was not only a 'bum' job but it was in the worst part of Canada I could think of. In fact, it turned out to be a joke concocted by the Adjutant, Tim Trotman! One can understand my shock therefore when, a few weeks later, I received a genuine posting order sending me to be GSO2 Directorate Land Forces Operational Requirements at Canadian Forces HQ (CFHQ) in Ottawa, Canada. Yes, I was to be an exchange officer with the Canadian Army for two years starting in March 1966. I was shattered. Inevitably the story of the joke warning order had spread rapidly throughout the Brigade and even the Division and a short time later when I was on the range at Sennelager, the Divisional commander came up to me and asked, with a smile, if I would like him to try to get the posting changed. I had about fifteen seconds to decide and, goodness knows why, I said 'No, leave it as it is Sir.' As it turned out, I had made the right decision both for me and for the family.

My happy days in Münster ended with a party given for me by the whole Company; it involving a lot of drinking and a remarkable present. It was a tape-recording organized by Tim Rogerson on which all my officers, Jack Chaffer, 'Wishbone' Swift, all the sergeants and all the *real* characters in the Company sent me a farewell message. Tim announced that everyone was happy about the present as it hadn't cost them anything. The messages themselves were all amusing, some quiet rude and all nostalgic – for me anyway. I still have it. I also received a number of thank-you letters. Jack, who had been posted shortly before me, had written in response to my thank you to him, 'Yes Sir, I too enjoyed serving under you and with C Company. I only hope we may be able to serve together again some day. Odd as it may seem one misses all those scruffy buggers! It is like leaving your family behind'. Mike Goode wrote:

> I have thoroughly enjoyed myself whilst you commanded C Company and at the same time I have learned a lot. For both of these I am extremely grateful to you. Thank you for all that you have done for me and for the help and advice you have either given (or delivered!) to me. I am extremely grateful for all of it. I must also thank you and Anne for all the times you have had me round for meals and drinks and for being so good to us, the subalterns.

I too had learned a lot during my time in Münster – things that would stand me in good stead in my later commands – not least that if you don't keep soldiers busy they soon get into trouble.

Tim Rogerson took over the Company on 11 January 1966, pending the arrival of its new commander and a day later I handed over our quarter and drove home to my parents in Felpham. Anne and the girls had flown home a couple of days before. On 1 March my parents drove us to Southampton and we sailed for Canada the following day.

Chapter Fourteen

Staff Officer in Canada

Fortunately for the Reynolds family we were given the choice of travelling to Canada by sea or air. Naturally, we chose sea and were delighted to find that, as first-class passengers, we were allocated two luxury cabins on the 22,000-ton Cunarder RMS *Carenthia*.

We sailed from Southampton on the night of 2 March 1966 and called at le Havre in France and Cobh in Cork Harbour in Ireland before setting off across the Atlantic for Halifax, Nova Scotia. The crossing was reasonably smooth and we all enjoyed ourselves immensely. Having our personal steward and stewardess was great fun and the girls soon discovered that if they rang their cabin bell they could ask for anything they wanted in the way of sandwiches and soft drinks. This meant they could avoid some of the meals in the first-class dining room where they had to behave. We didn't really mind as we knew the stewardess would keep an eye on them and it gave us some unexpected freedom.

We only remember a few of the passengers. The most memorable was Peter Finch, the actor and film star. Anne was thrilled to recognize him, but less impressed when, on her way to breakfast on the second morning, she saw him emerge from the cabin next to ours which we knew was occupied by a good-looking single lady. The only other two we recall clearly are Herr Doktor Danzer, a single man, who during one of the usual 'tea dances', came up to me and after clicking his heels asked, 'Please, may I dance with your vife?' I agreed, and he and Anne, to her intense embarrassment, did a turn or two to Reg Bowler and his quartet! And the third was a rather portly chap who usually wore a blazer and called himself a brigadier. After some deep questioning, however, he turned out to be a major quartermaster.

The War Office had issued me with a printed guide showing how much to tip our steward and stewardess, the head waiter, our personal waiter and the girl who cleaned our cabins. When I mentioned this to one of the other passengers I became very popular – everyone wanted a look. I can't remember how much each of them got, but the total was quite a significant figure.

137

We arrived in a snow-covered Halifax on the 9th and, whilst I went straight through immigration, poor Anne had to endure a full medical examination. I was furious, but to no avail and when we arrived in Ottawa I made a big fuss about it with the British Defence Liaison Staff (BDLS). As a result, no wives of British military personnel were ever put through this humiliating experience again.

In Halifax we boarded an overnight train bound for Montreal and then Ottawa. Again we were first-class passengers and had our own very comfortable sleeping compartments. We all loved the journey as it gave us a chance to see eastern Canada from grandstand seats. Goodness only knows what the whole trip from Southampton to our final destination cost for the five of us.

We were met in Ottawa, also covered by at least a foot of snow, by the British officer I was taking over from. He took us to the Lord Elgin Hotel in downtown Ottawa and told us that our rooms would be paid for by the British Government for up to twenty-eight days whilst we found somewhere to live. The Lord Elgin was very comfortable, but not really suitable for three little girls and so we decided to forgo the luxury and find a house as quickly as possible; however, a nasty surprise came next morning when I received a message saying that I was to report for work at the Canadian Forces Headquarters (CFHQ) the following day.

I duly reported to a colonel in the Canadian Black Watch, my Divisional Colonel. Fortunately he had taught at our Staff College and was very pro-British and gave me a warm welcome. My immediate boss was a very pleasant gunner lieutenant colonel and I was to share an office with two really nice Canadian officers, Major Al MacIssac, another gunner, and Captain Clare Donnelly of the Queen's Own Rifles of Canada.

So what exactly was my job in Canada? It was well described in my final Confidential Report:

> He has been responsible for the preparation, coordination and staffing of direct fire weapon requirements and policy for the Canadian Forces; in addition, because of his sound regimental background he has been consulted on general infantry problems outside his own specific field.

My predecessor had lined up a couple of houses for us to look at and so, whilst I went to work on day two, his wife drove Anne to see them. She didn't like either, but spotted one with a 'For Rent' board and that evening announced that she had found the place where she wanted to live. When I saw it I was not surprised: 255 Harmer Avenue looked like an

English Georgian house. Situated on the corner of two quiet roads with attractive, well-spaced houses and open-plan gardens, it had two small patios, a large garage, brown marble columns on either side of the front door, a circular marble hall with a beautiful hanging crystal chandelier and four marble busts of Roman senators – soon to be christened after the Beatles as John, George, Paul and Ringo. There was a large drawing room with a huge marble fireplace and two superb chandeliers, a dining room with beautiful swags on the walls and another chandelier, a large kitchen, a breakfast room, four bedrooms, two bathrooms, one en-suite to the master bedroom which also had two separate dressing rooms, and large warm and dry cellars including a huge one under the drawing room complete with fireplace and built-in bar; this was known in Canadian parlance as the 'rumpus room', i.e. a place in which to let your hair down and have fun. Another major plus was that, as well as double-glazing, the whole house had an under-floor, blown-air, gas-operated heating system rather than radiators. The only snags were the price and the fact that, apart from the master bedroom which was beautifully furnished, all the other rooms were empty except for 'broadlooms and drapes' – Canadian for carpets and curtains. I have no idea how much the rent was, but we eventually came to the conclusion that we could *just* about afford it, but would have little left over for holidays. In the event we found that we had been over-cautious and were able to have wonderful holidays.

So how did we furnish it? Simply by buying everything second-hand and hiring a truck to move it. Fortunately for us in the late 1960s the Canadians had gone off traditional English and French furniture and were going 'modern'. This meant that a lot of beautiful furniture, particularly just over the Ottawa river in Quebec Province, was going for a song. Within a week or two, to the amazement of our friends, we had the whole house beautifully furnished and, when our MFO boxes caught up with us, it soon looked like home. I must add that Clare Donnelly helped me every night with collecting and arranging the furniture; he could not have been more generous with his time. Our furniture caused much comment from everyone who came to the house. We knew we couldn't possibly afford to ship it back to the UK and would have to sell it, so whenever someone admired a particular item or indeed something important like the dining-room table and chairs, I always said, 'Well, if you want to buy it when we leave, you can.' As a result virtually everything was reserved at least six months before we left and we doubled or even trebled our money on most items.

Al MacIsaac and his wife also became true friends. Until our new car arrived, Al lent me his. It was an old Ford, but it went well and was a Godsend during our settling-in period. Little did I know it at the time, but it was his only car and he and his wife used buses until I bought a Chrysler Valiant 66. It seemed huge to us but was in fact what the Canadians called a 'compact'. It arrived on 28 March and cost me £882 (£11,900 in today's money).

Our next, or rather concurrent, problem was finding a school for the girls. We soon found a really nice one only a couple of miles from our house – Maison Jeanne d'Arc in the Westboro suburb of Ottawa. It was run by nuns and it was the only bilingual girls' school in the city.

Ottawa in 1966 was a very pleasant, quite small city; in many ways it reminded us more of a county town in England than the capital of a huge country. There were no traffic problems and no slums. The downtown shopping area was quite elegant and the Parliament Buildings, Cathedral, Supreme Court Building and Governor General's Residence were impressive in the Victorian tradition.

Our house was well placed, less than four miles from the city centre and CFHQ, and very near to the main east/west thoroughfares. The Civic Hospital was within half a mile and close by was a lovely park-like area with two lakes, connected by the Rideau canal.

Soon after moving into Harmer Avenue we had a visit from the 'Welcome Wagon'. This was in the tradition of the old pioneering days and we were given tea, coffee, sugar, butter and a cake; also tokens for the local drug store and hair salon. Our neighbours were all very friendly and welcoming, particularly a retired Minister of National Revenue; he was years older than me but we soon became good friends. On returning home from work, and providing the weather was nice, I would usually find him sitting on his veranda sipping a dry martini. I often joined him. One day during our second summer I mentioned that I liked Canada to such an extent that I could see myself transferring to the Canadian Army. 'Don't do it!' he exclaimed. 'You've only had one winter here. Why do you think all the Canadians who can afford it retire to Florida?'

One slight cloud on the horizon during our time in Canada was the movement for an independent Quebec. This led at times to ugly demonstrations and minor terrorist acts like the blowing up of postboxes – fortunately only in the province of Quebec. Things came to a head in July 1967 when President de Gaulle, speaking to a large crowd from a balcony at Montreal's City Hall, uttered the words 'Vive le Québec!' (Long live Quebec!), then added, 'Vive le Québec libre!' (Long live free Québec!). He left Canada of his own accord the next day without going on to Ottawa as scheduled, but the speech caused outrage in English Canada and led to a serious diplomatic rift between the two countries.

Our first month in Canada had been very busy – finding and moving into 255 Harmer, getting the girls into Maison Jeanne d'Arc, taking over a new job and so on. April proved equally busy. It started with a shock. On ringing the Fields at West Point to let them know our new address etc, we learned that Peter had suffered a serious accident whilst parachuting at Fort Benning. His main chute had failed to open and, although his reserve had functioned alright, he had landed badly and seriously injured his back. After being hospitalized, initially in Georgia, he was now in the West Point hospital. I could hardly ask for leave so soon after arriving in Canada, and we decided, despite a 700-mile round trip, to go down for the weekend to see him. It was a great relief to find him being well looked after and recovering well.

Our greatest Canadian friends were Alex and Diana Hughes. They had both been married before and had five children – two of his, two of hers and one of theirs. Alex made himself known to me very quickly as we were in the same Division at CFHQ and had similar jobs. He was a great cook and, once he discovered that I could buy duty-free alcohol through BDLS, he suggested that we should have monthly dinner parties with him providing and cooking the food and me providing the wine. My scrapbook has labels showing that, amongst other fine wines, we drank Chateau Mouton Rothschild 62.

Between 2 and 6 May, Canada hosted the first meeting of the Quadripartite (America, Britain, Canada and Australia) Ad Hoc Working Group on Infantry Anti-tank Weapons. I was heavily involved and it was interesting and enjoyable.

On 9 August we set off on a most memorable holiday. Alex Hughes's mother and father lived on Nantucket Island, Massachusetts, and Alex had invited us to join them there for a two-week holiday. We all got on well, so we accepted with pleasure. We set off in convoy and after a 300-mile trip arrived at Woods Hole, Cape Cod, where we caught the SS *Nantucket* ferry to the Island, sailing past Martha's Vineyard on the way. The Hughes' house, 1 Goose Pond Road, Poverty Point, was located in an idyllic setting on the northern coast and there was certainly no sign of poverty. We were immediately enchanted by Alex's parents, Gordon and Norah, and Anne was thrilled when Alex announced that he would do all the cooking. By the end of the two weeks we were all sporting beautiful tans and our final night was very memorable for the giant lobster Gordon cooked for us. The Hughes were a lovely family.

November 1966 brought bad news about my Regiment. Apparently the Colonels of the Queen's Surreys, Queen's Own Buffs, Royal Sussex and Middlesex Regiments had agreed to voluntarily amalgamate into a single Regiment to be called The Queen's Regiment. I was shocked, but there was nothing to do but transfer my allegiance. This meant yet another new cap badge, buttons and collar badges. I wrote to Dick Craddock, a former

Buff and now the Colonel of the new Regiment, to express my loyalty. I had come to know him well when I had acted as his Chief of Staff at West Byfleet.

In January 1967 I was sent home to the UK and then on to Paris to represent Canada on two infantry weapons 'panels' at an ABCA meeting. I flew to Gatwick with the Royal Canadian Air Force (RCAF) and caught the train to London where the meeting was being held. It caused quite a sensation when the British delegate discovered that the chap sitting behind the Maple Leaf flag on the table was not a Canadian at all, but a Brit.

One person I contacted whilst in London was Peter Mason whom I had hardly seen since our Camberley days. He invited me to dinner at the world-famous Boulestin restaurant in Covent Garden. I was very impressed when the maitre d' greeted him as 'Mister Peter'. We had a fabulous dinner and afterwards I took him to the rooftop cocktail bar in the Hilton, Park Lane. It was quite a night. My final meeting on that trip was in Paris where I attended a two-day meeting of the NATO Infantry Weapons Panel.

The following April I was sent down to the Aberdeen Proving Grounds near Baltimore on Chesapeake Bay for a three-day ABCA visit to look at some of the latest American equipment. I well remember sitting in the brand new Huey Cobra – a very heavily-armed helicopter. It was still experimental at that time.

In May I received a surprise message from the Colonel of the Regiment asking me to go out to Calgary to represent him at a parade at which Princess Alexandra would present new Colours to one of our affiliated Regiments, The South Alberta Light Horse, as well as to the Calgary Highlanders. I flew to Toronto and then on to Calgary where I had a most enjoyable time, staying with the Queen's Own Rifles. It was sunny but bitterly cold for the parade and I had no greatcoat with me, but it didn't matter. I was presented to the Princess after the parade and attended a Ball that evening given by both Regiments at which, to my horror, I had to make a speech. My own RHQ later received a letter from the South Alberta's which read, 'The officers and men of the S.A.L.H. were pleased to welcome Major Reynolds of the 1st Bn The Queen's Regiment at the Presentation in Calgary. The fact that he was able to make the 2,000-mile round trip was much appreciated by all.'

On 26 June, as a member of a Canadian delegation, I attended a briefing and demonstration in Huntsville, Alabama of a new US heavy anti-tank weapon which fired guided missiles. It was known as TOW, proved to be a very impressive weapon and was bought by numerous nations, including the UK.

For our second summer holiday we rented a beautiful house on a lake over in Quebec Province and had an idyllic holiday, swimming, boating and fishing. In mid-September it was time for me to go to Paris again for another four-day NATO weapons meeting. I flew RCAF to Gatwick and Air France to Paris where I was booked in at a super hotel, the West End, in rue Clément Marot, just off the Champs Elysées.

Our final three-week holiday was in West Palm Beach, Florida. The weather was perfect and the beach where we swam every day was beautifully quiet and peaceful. It was a fascinating 4,000-mile round trip and included a visit to the John F. Kennedy Space Centre at Cape Canaveral and a $20 fine for speeding in South Carolina.

In late January 1968 I flew to Vancouver for my final ABCA conference and was delighted by the venue as it gave me a chance to see Vancouver and Victoria Island. I travelled back by train through the Rockies to Edmonton and flew home from there.

As a family we were 'having a ball' in Canada and, instead of returning home at the end of March as planned, I asked the War Office if I could have a six months' extension to my posting. My Canadian bosses were delighted to hear that I wanted to stay longer in my job and backed my application. I was thrilled when London agreed and we looked forward to another spring and summer in Canada. However, when the CO of the 1st Battalion heard about this he put a stop to it and demanded that I return home and join his Battalion in the Persian Gulf as his second-in-command (2IC). He told me in a letter that 'he could think of no better shoulder to lean on!'

On 26 March we said a sad farewell to Ottawa and caught the train to Montreal where we spent a happy night. We had supper served to the girls in their room and after making them promise that they would stay there and behave, we went down for a quiet dinner on our own in the restaurant le Reine Elizabeth. No sooner had we sat down than the waiter brought over a bottle of Château Mouton Rothschild with a note that read, 'This is for your last dinner in Canada. We quietly toast you all and wish you well on your journey. Take with you all our love and we hope fond memories of Canada.' It was signed Alex and Diana Hughes. The following morning we caught another train to New York, where we arrived in Pennsylvania Station in the late afternoon and went on to the Hotel New Yorker. Next morning we took the girls sightseeing and, in the afternoon, boarded the *Queen Elizabeth* for our journey home. It was her penultimate voyage before being taken out of service and replaced a year later by the *QE II*.

The voyage home to Southampton was very exciting. This time we were Cabin Class, but again we had two large, luxury cabins. The bill for the five of us, which I still have, came to £516-7-0 (£6,680 today). I think one of the most memorable things for me about the *Queen Elizabeth* was the car showroom in the middle of the liner – it had a Jaguar and a Rolls Royce on display. We disembarked in Southampton on 2 April. Anne's parents met us and we drove to their new home in Eastbourne where we were to spend the next few days.

My performance in Canada was described in my final Confidential Report dated December 1967:

> The success which Major Reynolds has been able to achieve in these fields [the preparation, coordination and staffing of direct-fire weapon requirements and policy for the Canadian Forces] is a tribute to his ability . . . He can always be depended upon to render sound advice. He works well under pressure and manages to maintain complete equanimity under the most trying of circumstances. If Reynolds has any faults, they don't show. Major Reynolds was an excellent choice to fill an exchange appointment. He is held in the highest regard by all those with whom he has come into contact during his tour of duty in Canada and he and his wife represent their country very well indeed.

I was graded 'Outstanding' and the Director General of Operations at CFHQ not only agreed that grading but added, 'From close observation of Major Reynolds, both on and off duty, over the past two years, I am convinced that he has the potential to reach the rank of major general.'

Our two years in North America had been a wonderful experience for the whole family. As well as seeing another continent our girls had learned to swim, skate, ski and speak reasonable French – albeit with a French-Canadian accent. We would look back on it as one of the highlights of our lives. Sadly the next two years were to be very different – full of turbulence.

Chapter Fifteen

Company Commander in Bahrain

It was nice to be back in England again but we had a nasty shock when we discovered that the house we were expecting to move into, a new army quarter in Sharpthorne, near East Grinstead, was still in the hands of the builders and would not be ready until the middle of May. We could have stayed with my parents or Anne's, but we wanted to be on our own and I arranged to take over a flat in Preston Barracks (since demolished) in Brighton. There was only one snag – the Lewes to Brighton railway line ran directly behind it and everything rattled whenever a train passed. Fortunately there were none during the night and, apart from this slight annoyance, we greatly enjoyed our stay in the town.

The short time I had in England before flying out to Bahrain was fraught with problems. Apart from the fact that we couldn't move into our new quarter until a few days before I was due to leave, we had the problem of once again finding a school for the girls. It was time for Vicky and Gabrielle to go to boarding school but that couldn't happen until the start of the school year in September and in the meantime I had to persuade the headmaster of the local C of E Primary School in Sharpthorne to take all three girls. I went to see him and was delighted when he told me that he would be pleased to take three pupils whose 'feet were not stuck in Sussex clay' and who had actually lived not just in another town, but in another country. Soon after that we paid a successful visit to St Mary's Convent in Shaftesbury, Dorset, and enrolled Vicky and Gabrielle for the September term. The only problem was that Anne would have to put the girls into St Mary's, 120 miles away, without my help.

Our move into 2 The Home Platt, Sharpthorne in late May was not easy. The rear garden was still virtually a builders' yard and we had a mad rush to receive and arrange a houseful of G-Plan furniture and unpack and sort out our own things before I left, on 27 May, for Bahrain. I had, therefore, only a few nights in the house and was extremely disappointed, in fact angry, that I had not been allowed a longer period to settle in the family.

Fortunately for Anne, there were six other 1st Battalion officers' wives, some with children, already living unaccompanied in the Home Platt so she was not alone. But why were these families living miles from anywhere in deepest Sussex anyway? Simply because there were no quarters for either officers or soldiers anywhere near Hobbs Barracks in Lingfield into which the Battalion had been moved after its withdrawal from Münster. The MoD therefore had had to purchase houses wherever they could find them – Sharpthorne for the officers and, to the dismay of the other residents, Uckfield for the other ranks.

Anne was in fact relatively lucky – her parents and sister were within easy reach. During the five months I was away, she was able to see a lot of them and the girls kept her very busy.

I arrived in Bahrain on 27 May and was greeted warmly by the CO. We had come to know each other quite well as brother officers in the Regiment, but had not served together for the last eighteen years. He had been the assistant adjutant and senior subaltern when I joined the Queen's Royal Regiment in Iserlohn in 1950. Everyone in the Battalion knew that I was likely to take over from him as CO, but he made no mention of this and told me I would have to wait to be his 2IC until the present incumbent left at the end of the Bahrain tour; in the meantime I was to take command of B Company. I was far from pleased. I already had two outstanding reports as a company commander from my time with C Company in Münster, and certainly didn't need yet another report as a company commander. No, I had been ordered back from Canada under false pretences. The real reason I had been brought back early was because he wanted the strongest team he could possibly muster, i.e. one in which all his company commanders were Staff College graduates – a very rare thing in any arm or unit.

The Battalion's tour in Bahrain was 'unaccompanied', i.e. no wives and families, which meant the CO had the every officer and soldier under his thumb twenty-four hours a day, seven days a week. As a bachelor this suited him down to the ground. He did, however, allow those serving the full ten-month tour to have their wives out for a two-week period, provided they arranged private accommodation. This scheme was open to all ranks but only three wives came out to Bahrain and they were all officers' wives.

What were we doing in Bahrain anyway? In 1968 the island was still a British Protectorate, but the Government had already announced that the British bases there were to close in the near future. Hence we were the first post-war infantry battalion to serve there 'unaccompanied'. The island later, in 1971, became an independent emirate. The ruler in our time was an autocrat, His Highness Sultan Isa Sulman al Khalifa. As well as the RAF airfield and maintenance base at RAF Muharraq, there was a large naval base, HMS *Jufair*, which was home to a minesweeper squadron and saw visits from RN and American cruisers and destroyers. In addition to our Battalion, there was another infantry battalion in the Gulf at this time – 1st Battalion Royal Fusiliers, stationed in Sharjah in what is now the United Arab Emirates. Both Battalions were under the command of the brigadier commanding HQ Land Forces Gulf, also based in Bahrain. Our mission was to act as a contingency force for any emergency that might occur in Arabia or the Persian Gulf.

Bahrain is about thirty miles long and only ten miles wide and in those days the causeway to Saudi Arabia had yet to be built and the modern international airport did not exist. Oil had been discovered in 1932, but the wealth it brought remained in the hands of the ruling family and the vast majority of the inhabitants remained poor. There was no other industry apart from fishing, and agriculture hardly existed. The Bahrain of those days was a far cry from that seen today and certainly not the financial hub of the Middle East as it later became. Manama, the only town, was ugly and dirty and there were no tourist attractions of any sort. Although the climate can, I'm told, be quite cool and rainy in the winter, by the time I arrived it was desperately hot and humid.

Life in Bahrain was incredibly boring. Based in a hutted camp, Hamala, located in open desert twelve miles from Manama, we worked from 6 o'clock in the morning until midday and then rested or swam in the camp pool or at the 'Ruler's Beach' during the afternoon. Then, as it became a little cooler, we engaged in sport and 'Platoon Projects', designed by the CO to keep the soldiers busy and out of trouble. These ranged from building a catamaran to making a miniature model town in the sand. I really can't remember any of my three Platoon Projects so they can't have been very exciting; they were already in progress when I arrived. In my own case, the only sport I played was golf. It was bit like playing in one huge bunker as there wasn't a single blade of grass anywhere; even so it was no less enjoyable. The 'greens' were just oiled sand tended by an Arab who rolled them flat again after each pair or four moved off.

I have to say that the CO came up with lots of good ideas to keep us busy. Adventurous training was carried out by small groups in Kenya, Iran and Cyprus and as far away as Malaya and Madagascar. One of his most imaginative ideas was a series of 'casino nights' in the Officers' Mess. We all wore white DJs and the majors and captains acted, after some detailed training, as croupiers at the roulette tables. Guests from the three services were invited and, after supper, for which they had to pay, they were free to have a 'little flutter'. These nights were great fun and largely successful, although I personally was never comfortable as a croupier. The

CO used to cruise round the tables looking very like the American film star George Raft!

My short time in Bahrain started with the usual Glorious First of June celebrations. HMS *Jufair* provided the naval element. The celebrations began with a tattoo for which a mock castle had been built on the Battalion square: 2,500 guests were invited to watch the show which traced the history of the Regiment from 1661 to 1968. It was quite a spectacular affair and included a re-enactment of the first muster of the Tangier Regiment on Putney Heath in 1661, drill as performed in the reign of Queen Anne, a naval engagement circa-1794 with Land Rovers made to look like ships of the line, and a very realistic Great War attack on Hill 60 in France. The Band and Corps of Drums Beat Retreat and the fun and games with HMS *Jufair* lasted two full days. I well remember the donkey polo match with both the Naval Commodore on the island, and our CO mounted. The most amusing part of the match was when the Commodore's donkey tried to mount the one being ridden by our CO.

On 12 June all the officers were invited by the Ruler to a dinner in his Palace. The instructions issued to us make amusing reading.

> Officers should arrive at 1950 hrs. The CO will arrive at 2000 hrs. Officers will be presented . . . in the Main Chamber. Here we will be invited to a couple of cups of coffee and maybe a lemonade or even a pineapple juice! As we go into dinner we will go through the hand washing procedure. Don't use too much of the 'perfume' as it is evil smelling and lasts for ages. It is unlikely that there will be any place names except for the CO – it will be a question of just piling in. Officers should try and mix with other guests. Servants will continue piling food on plates – officers need not be frightened of leaving some or refusing any more. Do not worry if various Arab guests just get up and go. The signal to go will be the offer of rose water and incense. Officers should then immediately make their farewell.

I have only three memories of that dinner. First, the Main Chamber looked like the inside of a British Odeon cinema with similar lighting and a throne that looked exactly like the theatre organ that used to rise up in such cinemas during the intervals; second, the ugliness of the boss-eyed Ruler; and thirdly the Army Catering Corps officer attached to our Battalion who mistook the welcoming bowl of burning incense for an ashtray and stubbed out his cigarette in it.

In early July I persuaded the CO to let me spend a few days with the Trucial Oman Scouts (TOS) in what is now the United Arab Emirates.

Their CO was a friend of mine from West Byfleet days, and I arranged, to the annoyance of my CO, for him to send me an invitation to visit his command. On 12 July I flew, care of the RAF, to Sharjah.

The TOS was an amazing outfit. The Trucial Oman Levies, as they were originally titled, had been formed at Sharjah in 1950 under British Foreign Office control. They were originally designed to serve as a bodyguard and small army for the British Political Resident in the Persian Gulf, but they could also be used to protect oil exploration teams and suppress tribal raiding; they were recruited chiefly from the Bedouin of Abu Dhabi, as well as some Somalis, Omanis, Indians and Pakistanis resident in the Trucial States. By 1968 there were five squadrons, each with two British officers.

I had a fascinating first day seeing Sharjah and Dubai before enjoying dinner and staying the night with the CO and his wife in their nice quarter in the former. Dubai was little more than a large trading post in those days; oil had been discovered only two years before my visit and had yet to make an impact on the economy. There wasn't a single skyscraper.

The next day I was driven to Ham Ham (now Ras al Khaima) where I spent twenty-four hours with one of the squadrons. The Squadron commander greeted me from a small swimming pool with a thatched roof. He was friendly, but drunk. Fortunately his 2IC was a young Queen's captain I knew well, Nigel Harris, who looked after me beautifully, showing me all round the camp and village. We had an excellent dinner that night with his commander and some other TOS officers who joined us.

The next morning, at 0630, Nigel drove me to the Buraimi oasis on the border between Abu Dhabi and the Oman. On the way he gave me a very exciting drive up and down vast sand dunes and demonstrated how the shade of just a few branches of a desert bush could provide a drop in temperature of some 10 degrees. The HQ of the Buraimi squadron was located in a large mud fort and there Nigel introduced me to the 'Desert Intelligence Officer', Major Ted Taylor, who was to be our host for the next twenty-four hours. An ex-Buff who would later serve for a short time in my Battalion in Germany, Ted was a remarkable man; an eccentric, but charming and fluent in both Russian and Arabic. Again I had a wonderful day, culminating in a formal dinner of roast beef, roast potatoes and Yorkshire pudding – all this with temperatures in the high nineties! I flew back to Sharjah the next morning and then on to Bahrain on a scheduled flight, arriving back exhilarated and very happy.

Now I must turn to my military activities during my time in the Persian Gulf. I was lucky in B Company, having good and reasonably competent officers. Graham White was the most outstanding and would later serve on my Brigade staff in Germany. Mentioning subalterns reminds me that Mike Goode, of C Company Münster days, was also in the Battalion in Bahrain, but now he was a pilot in the Air Platoon, flying Sioux helicopters. It was great to see him again and, of course, he gave me numerous trips round the island. The only weakness in my Company was my CSM, who was competent but had little personality and was a mere shadow of men like Jack Chaffer and Ron Wildgoose.

The training we carried out on the island was rather repetitive and boring. The CO was quite keen on TEWTS (tactical exercises without troops) and we had one, as far as I remember, every month. The tactics taught were once again those of the Second World War.

In August I took my Company over to Bithnah in the Trucial States for ten days' training. It was good to get away from Bahrain and, as the Battalion Journal says:

> Despite many misgivings about the heat on one hand and floods on the other [one Company camp had been washed away in a wadi during a flash flood which saw the loss of a lot of kit and a helicopter, but fortunately no men], most people thoroughly enjoyed themselves. The training was climaxed by a 36 hour test exercise in which the CO, 2IC, RSM and Corps of Drums carried out both verbal and physical attacks on our impregnable positions. Despite their ambush of the company commander's recce group, the latter kept his cool and we reckon the result was game, set and match to shiny B.

Towards the end of August I received, to my CO's intense irritation, an invitation from David Lloyd Owen, who was by then General Officer Commanding Near East Land Forces (these included those in the Persian Gulf), to come and stay with him for a week in Flagstaff House in Episkopi, Cyprus. The reason for my CO's irritation was because he and David, having served together in Iserlohn in 1950, disliked each other and this dislike sadly increased in 1958 when David asked me rather than him, to be his adjutant in Germany.

David had already written to me in Canada saying, 'I must confess I find being a General very agreeable' and on arrival I could see why. Flagstaff House, standing on its own small peninsula with its own private beach, was large and elegant. It was staffed by Sudanese servants; in addition David had an ADC, house sergeant, a British cook and a British driver for his Jaguar personal staff car. In those days I never even dreamed that one day I would enjoy all these same privileges myself.

By 1968 Cyprus was no longer a Crown Colony; it was an independent

Republic. However, the British had retained two Sovereign Bases – one in Dhekelia in the south-east of the island and the other in Akrotiri and Episkopi. The Turkish invasion was still six years in the future.

David gave me a wonderful time. I enjoyed swimming and sunbathing on the private beach, usually with a thermos of Pimms. As well as visiting the Kato Paphos mosaics and other antiquities in the area, David usually took me to lunch in one of the local villages – Greek and Turkish alternatively. I well remember drinking Arsinoe wine in one Greek restaurant. 'Nice isn't it?' asked David, 'much better than the one you don't knowie!' There was a dinner party for important Greeks and British civilians virtually every night I was at Flagstaff House and by the time I flew back to Bahrain on 31 August I was totally refreshed. The same day David wrote to Anne, 'Just a line to say how simply lovely it has been for me to have Mike here for a bit. We have had a lot of time together. He is looking fitter than I have ever seen him. My only sorrow is that you were not here too.'

Mid-September saw a major Battalion exercise in Dibbah in the Trucial States. It was the climax to our year in the Gulf and we were given the mission of rescuing 'British nationals who were being held by dissidents in the Tayyibah oil field complex'. The dissidents were provided by members of the TOS. The exercise would involve flying one company to Dibbah to seize the airfield, after which the rest of the Battalion would arrive and we would then, with A Squadron 3 RTR under command, advance some twenty miles, basically on foot, to rescue the hostages. Most of the RAF aircraft in the Gulf, including ground attack fighters, helicopters and transport planes were in support. The exercise began with my B Company being flown to Sharjah in Argosy aircraft. There we transferred into Andovers and landed on time at Dibbah and successfully seized the airfield. The CO arrived next with his HQ, followed by C and A Companies. Having led the way so far, I expected another Company to take the lead in the subsequent advance, but no, I was ordered to lead again. As the Company Notes in the Battalion Journal record:

By the evening of the second day we were wondering if anyone except us and the enemy were on the exercise at all. Mention must be made of 7 Platoon's gallant eight-hour climb of Pt 323 [under Graham White] and of 5 Platoon's spirited sortie to rescue the remains of C Company on the third day.'

Graham White's epic climb was necessary, so the CO told me, in order to 'piquet the heights' as per the campaigns in Afghanistan in the nineteenth century. Anyway, having secured the gap leading into the Wadis Shimal and Uyaynah down which the Battalion was to advance, the other Companies took over and A Company in helicopters finally rescued the 'beleaguered oil men'. Next came the withdrawal phase back to Dibbah. This was carried out at night. Once again my Company was ordered to lead the way and, after some spirited actions and with help from A Squadron 3 RTR, finally arrived safely back at the airfield. The Journal concludes: 'The Battalion proved its fitness by not having one casualty evacuated because of heat exhaustion – and it was very hot indeed during those four days.' Needless to say morale in B Company was sky high when we got back to Bahrain. Everyone was well aware that we had done more than our fair share to ensure the success of the exercise – seizing the airfield, leading the initial advance, 'piqueting the heights' and leading the withdrawal. Yes, A Company under Mike Doyle had done a great job in the helicopter 'coup de main', but the really tough tasks had been carried out by 'shiny B'.

We were to be relieved in the Gulf in mid-November 1968 by the 1st Battalion the Cheshire Regiment and, as 2IC designate, I was put in charge of an Advance Party tasked with taking over all the Cheshires' vehicles, weapons, radios etc and moving them from their camp at Weeton near Blackpool to our base camp in Hobbs Barracks near Lingfield. They in turn would take over ours in Bahrain. Accordingly I flew home on 16 October with a large group of officers and NCOs. A problem arose, however, with a demand by the officer commanding our Rear Party in Hobbs Barracks that my group should report to him on arrival in the UK and then, after a few days' leave, report again before moving as a group to Blackpool. I told the CO that the idea of us reporting in at Hobbs Barracks twice was ludicrous and that I was not prepared to do so. On arrival in the UK we would all go straight on leave and then everyone would report to me at Weeton Camp on the designated day. I won the day and briefed my party on what had happened; I then went on to tell them that I was relying on them not to let me down. They didn't!

Chapter Sixteen

Second-in-Command in England and Ulster

We were at Weeton Camp, near Blackpool, for three days taking over the Cheshires' equipment and, although the state of cleanliness of some of it was well below Queen's standards, the takeover went well. Weapons and heavy equipment were loaded into railway wagons which were secured tightly before driving the vehicles in convoy back to Lingfield where everything was again secured and left in the care of the Rear Party. Then we went on Christmas leave.

The CO, being a bachelor and having no family or friends in the East Grinstead area, threw himself into his work and, by the time we returned from leave on 2 January 1969, had already planned the next few months training in the greatest detail. In fact, I began to wonder if there would be anything left for me to do as 2IC, but I needn't have worried.

My first action was to recommend to him that we should change the location of Battalion HQ. Hobbs Barracks (now a light industrial park) was a spacious hutted camp with reasonable accommodation and adequate messes, but the CO's office, my office, the Adjutant's office and the orderly room were all crammed into a small bungalow-type building. We were all on top of each other and you could easily hear what people we saying in the next office. However, behind the main garages at the camp entrance was a very large building with nothing in it except for the Pay Office; the CO soon agreed that we should change things round.

There was only one quarter in Hobbs Barracks which was split into two flats with the CO on the top floor and the Paymaster and his wife below him. Most other officers were out at Sharpthorne and most other ranks were twenty miles away in Uckfield in a very nice, mock-Georgian estate on the edge of the town. However, it wasn't long before this caused trouble with the local civilians who complained that our families were misbehaving, with wives, children and dogs out of control. The end result was that the CO asked me and the Adjutant to meet the leaders of the protest group. I arranged a meeting in a hotel at Wych Cross, not far from Sharpthorne and, after a frosty start, I agreed that the behaviour of some of our families left a lot to be desired, but that only the Uckfield police, not the army, could 'police' the estate. They should therefore complain to their local MP and county councillors and ask for the families to be found more suitable accommodation nearer Hobbs Barracks. Furthermore, I pointed out that as a Surrey regiment, with most of our soldiers coming from the south London area, we were not happy to be dumped in the Sussex countryside anyway and would all welcome a change of location. This, after a few drinks, seemed to do the trick and we parted friends and heard no more of the problem. I must say that I had much sympathy for their point of view; they had paid a lot of money for their houses and to have army families scattered throughout the estate was no laughing matter.

In early February I had to recce and arrange accommodation for an exercise the CO had planned at Otterburn in Northumberland. I stayed at the Percy Arms and enjoyed exploring the moors. However, the exercise itself was a disaster. We had four days of blizzards and were unable to leave the hutted base camp. Reluctantly we had to call it off, but quickly laid on another exercise in Pippingford Park on the edge of Ashdown Forest. We had no winter clothing and no one enjoyed it – least of all me who was stuck in a freezing tent at Battalion HQ as opposed to being active on the ground. I was reminded very much of Korea!

In April the Battalion Band played at the Duke of Norfolk's cricket ground on his estate at Arundel for the match between his XI and the West Indies test team. As Band President, I was the Duke's guest for lunch and tea in the pavilion and was able to enjoy a first class day's cricket. Being Band President was the most enjoyable of my duties as 2IC. The Bandmaster was a hard drinking ex-Argyll and from the outset we got on extremely well. I soon discovered that the Band fund was bursting with money from the many civil engagements they undertook in places like Eastbourne and Brighton, and when I further discovered that most of the bandsmen had bought their instruments with their own money, I was determined to do something about it. The Bandmaster and I went up to Boosey & Hawkes, the famous instrument makers in London, several times over the next few months and, as well as being lavishly entertained to lunch each time, we completely re-equipped the Band with new instruments. Needless to say, I was a very popular Band President. I was less popular with the CO when, at my suggestion, the Battalion marched past on the usual Saturday morning drill parade to the Band playing the Beatles' song 'Michelle'. It was only after I pointed out that the soldiers had loved it and therefore marched better that he saw the point.

Another position I held as 2IC was President of the Warrant Officers' and Sergeants' Mess. Sometime, I think in the spring of 1969, we had a crisis. Les Wilson, the RSM, came to me in quite a distressed state and told me that his Mess had been burgled and all the silver stolen. This silver had only just been re-valued and, although we suspected that someone on the valuer's staff had probably had a hand in the burglary, it at least meant that the insurance company would have to pay up in full. Despite his distress, I pointed out to him that apart from a couple of very special pieces like the 'Pink Column', given by a Colonel Pink and competed for each year by the officers and sergeants in a shooting match, and a silver foot-ball, representing the ball kicked across no man's land by the East Surreys on the first day of the Somme in 1916, the rest of it was mainly sporting trophies and of little real interest. I went on to say that this was a marvel-lous opportunity not only to replace the special items, but also to buy some really nice silver in the form of candelabra and cutlery. It took some time for this to sink in, but eventually the idea was accepted by the whole Mess and in a relatively short time it was one of the best equipped Warrant Officers' and Sergeants' Messes in the Army.

May was a busy month. On the 17th there was a Battalion 'At Home' for some 3,000 guests. It was on the same lines as the one in Bahrain and was again highly successful and well received. Then, on the 30th, a group of officers and warrant officers, including me, went down to HMS *Excellent* in Portsmouth for another enjoyable Glorious First of June. It was at this time that Les Wilson retired as RSM. I had known him since Iserlohn when I was Adjutant. He did really well after being commis-sioned, becoming a lieutenant colonel QM. In retirement, he worked for many years at RHQ and played a major part in establishing the Queen's Surreys' Museum at Clandon Park. We still see each other on Regimental occasions.

In late June or early July I had to carry out a recce for another of the CO's exercises – this time on the Stanford training area in East Anglia. I booked in for one night at the Bell Inn in Thetford and, to my delight, found the cast of the TV series *Dad's Army* also staying there. They used the training area for filming outdoor sequences as it was devoid of build-ings, electric pylons and TV aerials. After dinner, which I had on my own, I adjourned to the bar and ended up chatting to Corporal Jones (Clive Dunn) and Private Walker (James Beck). I asked them why Captain Mainwaring (Arthur Lowe) had dined at a separate table from the rest of them and on his own. 'Well he's an *or*fficer, in't ee?' replied Corporal Jones with a grin. It was a great evening.

On 18 July the Battalion went on block leave. However, we were facing the beginning of the 'troubles' in Ulster, and law and order in the Province, and particularly in Londonderry (Derry as nationalists call it), was deteriorating rapidly. The 1st Battalion Prince of Wales's Own Regiment of Yorkshire (PWO) had already been deployed there to guard key points and the CO had been warned that, although it was thought unlikely, we might be required to take over from them at short notice.

On 1 August, whilst still on block leave, I received a phone call from the CO. We were to take over from the PWO as soon as practicable and I was to fly out to RAF Ballykelly, fifteen miles north-east of Derry, with a recce party on the 6th. He was recalling the Battalion from leave. Apart from this very unwelcome news, I had a major personal problem for my back had given out and I was not only in considerable pain but also finding it very difficult to walk. However, I knew my father had used an excellent chiropractor in Petersfield whom I arranged to see as a matter of urgency. He did a great job and, although I was wearing a corset and still in some pain, I set out from Hobbs Barracks as ordered on the 6th with a party of eleven, including two young officers. Naturally Anne and the girls were very upset at the prospect of another long separation, particularly so soon after Bahrain.

My task on arrival in Ulster was to organize accommodation for Battalion HQ and one company on the RAF base at Ballykelly, another company in a barracks in Omagh and the third company and administrative echelon in the TA Camp at Magilligan. This we did successfully, although after serious rioting in Derry on 12 August, we switched the proposed Omagh company to Ballykelly. With one exception, the RAF was very cooperative and I set up a splendid HQ in a large empty wooden structure, previously used as a Toc H canteen with recreation rooms. By the time the CO and his HQ were due to arrive it was fully furnished with desks, chairs, lockers, filing cabinets and telephones. The only problem I had with the RAF, in whose Messes we were living, was when the PMC of the Officers' Mess refused to allow us into the dining room in our combat kit; we were banished to the bar and bar snacks like aircrew in their flying kit. However, after appealing to the Station commander on the grounds that we had no service dress into which to change, the ban was lifted.

I don't propose to describe the background to the 'troubles' in Ulster in 1969 in any detail, other than to say that ever since the Partition of Ireland in 1922 the Unionists (Protestants) in Ulster had felt themselves threatened, not only by the Republic of Ireland, but also by the substantial Catholic minority in their midst. In order to continue the status quo and control the Catholics, the Northern Ireland Government, independent and devolved from Westminster, maintained an armed police force, the Royal Ulster Constabulary (RUC), and an armed police reserve, the B Specials. Both bodies were looked on with fear and loathing by some Catholics, with the B Specials being considered nothing more than

Protestant thugs. Furthermore, discrimination against Catholics in jobs, housing and even the electoral system had created an atmosphere of distrust between the two communities. Serious trouble in October 1968 and January 1969, during which both the RUC and Protestant mobs attacked civil rights marches organized by the Northern Ireland Civil Rights Association (NICRA), was followed in July and early August by a surge of violence across Northern Ireland. By the end of the second week of August, despite the use of baton charges, CS gas and even gunfire, the overstretched RUC had been forced out of most Catholic districts in Belfast and Derry which became 'No-Go' areas. The crisis came to a head with the annual Apprentice Boys' March in Derry on 12 August. As it passed the Catholic ghetto of the Bogside it was attacked by stone-throwing mobs. The subsequent savage fighting between members of the RUC and nationalist mobs lasted three days, by which time the RUC was an exhausted force. The IRA played little part in what happened; rioters had no rifles or machine guns and used instead bricks, bottles and petrol bombs. It also has to be said that a collection of foreign students and anarchists, known as the 'Foreign Legion', and numerous young hooligans operating behind the Catholic barricades took advantage of this chaotic situation, thereby adding to the problem.

The PWO deployed on to the streets of Derry at about 4 p.m. on the afternoon of 14 August – I went with it in the back of their CO's Land Rover. Its task was to restore law and order, keep the peace and protect Catholics from attacks by extremist Protestants. I was very impressed with their performance and professionalism. Our CO had arrived with his Advance Party on the same day and it became obvious that we would be relieving the PWO on the streets rather than peacefully in various barracks. Shortly after this, the Brigadier commanding 24 Brigade arrived with his staff and took over the HQ I had prepared for us at RAF Ballykelly. We were to come under his command. The CO and I obviously had to make a new plan for the arrival of the Battalion, due in by sea on the 18th, and the Royal Navy agreed that we could base ourselves in HMS *Sea Eagle*, an anti-submarine warfare school, located within Ebrington Barracks. We then spent the next forty-eight hours recceing, arranging when and how we would relieve the PWO and so on. It was a very hectic time. By an incredible coincidence, the CO had also arrived with a bad back and so we both found ourselves attending Altnagelvin Hospital when time allowed. Fortunately the orthopaedic staff soon put us to rights, but it was probably the first time that both the CO and 2IC of an infantry battalion wore corsets on operations! Fortunately, no one in the Battalion knew about this.

When the soldiers of the PWO deployed on the 14th a heavy pall of smoke hung over the city, part of William Street was ablaze, the area below the Rossville Flats in the Bogside looked like a battlefield and a strong smell of CS gas pervaded the area. They were, however, received with general relief by both communities. To most people it meant that bloodshed had been averted and peace of a kind restored, but while the Catholics regarded the troops as protectors, the Protestants looked upon them as the means by which the Catholics would be subjugated for good. The omens were not good.

Most of the Catholics in Derry lived in the Bogside, Creggan, Brandywell and Rosemount areas, west of the Foyle, called by the residents 'Free Derry'. The main Protestant areas were Fountain Street, next to the Diamond, and Cloughglass, both on the west side of the river, and the Waterside district, on the east side. The members of the Londonderry RUC were a sorry sight after the rioting, having suffered many casualties from bricks, bottles and fire bombs. They were totally exhausted and morale had also been shaken.

When we relieved the PWO, starting at 4 a.m. on the 20th, we were understrength, having only three instead of four companies. We set up a Tac (small, forward) HQ with the RUC in Victoria RUC Station and deployed the companies, commanded respectively by Mike Hare, John Francis and Brian Faris, across the main parts of the city, but not in the Catholic areas. A Echelon were based in *Sea Eagle* and B Echelon in Caw Camp, a small TA centre on the way out of Derry on the east side. My future RSM, Sid Lea, was the RQMS there. Company locations included shops, shirt factories, a disused gymnasium, an old jail, a deserted police station, the public lavatories in Waterloo Place and the city walls. At first there was little in the way of proper shelter for the soldiers who lived and slept on the pavements. However, by the end of the first week all the street locations had some form of shelter, toilets and heating. The men were fed using containers of food prepared in *Sea Eagle* and, to our surprise, the soldiers were served cups of tea and given cakes and biscuits by the local population, including residents of the Bogside.

Our manpower problem was alleviated to some extent by the CO's request for reinforcements being met by C Company of the Duke of Edinburgh's Royal Regiment (DERR) being flown in on the 26th and put under his command. It was based in the Duncreggan Camp TA Centre. Furthermore, a company of the 2nd Battalion Grenadier Guards also came under command and was based in Agnes Weston's Royal Sailors' Rest in Foyle Street. We also had an immediate reserve in a submarine depot ship moored on the river – HMS *Stalker*, a Second World War LST (Landing Ship, Tank). These reinforcements allowed us to develop a system for our companies of nine days on the streets and three at rest in

Sea Eagle; however, the 'resting' company was always at three hours' notice to move for riot duties. For those off duty or resting, welfare services were quickly established, including films, good canteen services and even dances with the local girls. As a result of the latter a number of Derry girls became regimental wives after the tour. I should also mention that, subsequently, when we learned that we were to stay in Derry for four months, we gained approval for every officer and man to have one period of five days R & R back in Britain, with free return flights.

Apart from our normal duties the CO and I organized a system whereby he would be 'Duty CO' between the hours of 6 p.m. and midnight on one night and I would do the same the next. This was the period when most of the trouble occurred. We based ourselves at Tac HQ, but spent a lot of time touring the city in our Land Rovers, checking on what was going on and visiting our Companies.

Relations with the Navy in *Sea Eagle* started well, but deteriorated rapidly. We used their Wardroom bar and ate in their dining room and our senior NCOs did the same in their Petty Officers' Mess. However, the CO's unfortunate decision to bring the Colours with the Main Body was the first cause of trouble. He asked for them to be displayed in the Dining Room as in an Army Mess and the Commander of *Sea Eagle* saw this as the first step in a takeover by the Army. He and the CO took an instant dislike to each other. The other bone of contention was that, while our soldiers were living and often sleeping on the streets, the sailors were in warm 'cabins' and were continuing life as if nothing had happened, or was happening, just down the road. Our demand for more accommodation fell on deaf ears. Relationships became so bad that one night after dinner I decided something had to be done about it. Fortunately, above the Commander of *Sea Eagle*, was the Captain, Tony Morton. He lived in a spacious house within the 'barracks' and, without an appointment, I knocked on his door and asked his steward if I could speak to the Captain urgently. Tony Morton welcomed me at once and over several drinks we talked for over an hour. At the end of it the problems were solved. We were given much more accommodation and although the CO and the Commander avoided each other as much as possible the rest of us got on well. Fifteen years later, when I next met Tony Morton in Brussels, he would be a full admiral and I would be a major general.

Our relationship with the commander of 24 Brigade had its ups and downs. The main trouble was that he established an advanced HQ on the top floor of Victoria RUC Station, directly above our HQ. This was much too close for comfort. Indeed on one occasion when there was some minor rioting very close to Victoria, he was found telling John Francis how to deal with the situation. The CO told him he had no business interfering in this way which soured his relationship with both the CO and the Battalion.

Following our initial deployment, we entered into a negotiation phase with those behind the barricades – firstly with the Derry Citizens' Defence Association (DCDA), the body which was effectively ruling the Bogside and Creggan, and later with the Bogside Citizens Defence Association (BCDA). The CO, quite understandably, used me, as a Catholic, to be his main negotiator with the representatives of these two groups. Between us we spent, according to the Regimental History, some fifty hours in talks with people like John Hume and Ivan Cooper, both Stormont MPs, Eamonn McCann, Eddie McAteer and Paddy Doherty. The first and last of these became very well known to me. None of our soldiers entered 'Free Derry' during these talks but, while we tried to persuade the BCDA to take down the barricades and accept some sort of interim police force, we hinted that, if necessary, force would be used to achieve this. However, at that time neither the CO nor I, being Englishmen, really understood the 'Irish problem'. A good example of my ignorance and naivety showed when I told a Catholic priest that as long as there were separate Catholic and Protestant schools in Northern Ireland the problem would never be solved. 'What do you expect me to do?' he asked, 'bus my kids across the Foyle to a Protestant school or vice versa?'

'Internal Security' as practised by the British Army in the late 1960s was basically designed to put down riots in British possessions in Africa and the Middle and Far East. The 'enemy' was expected to be non-white and certainly not UK citizens. Hence, when the Battalion arrived in Derry, it brought with it banners that read 'Disperse or we fire' and every soldier carried a bayonet which he expected to 'fix' before deploying against a mob. It soon became very clear that we were *not* going to be able to fire on a Derry crowd that did not disperse and a newspaper campaign, led by the *Daily Mirror*, demanded that bayonets should not be seen on the streets of the UK. It didn't take long for the order to come through that they were to be handed in and shipped back to Hobbs Barracks. No, we were going to have to find other methods of controlling the mobs. Accordingly, we established rooftop observation points throughout the city in places like the old city walls and the Rossville Flats, and a barrier and barbed-wire cut-off system at the entrances to the walled city from the Bogside and other strategic points; these were aimed at blocking off potential flashpoints and lines of advance. These barriers were permanently manned to effect rapid closure. If trouble did start, as soon as more than one company was deployed, command and control was to be exercised by the CO or me directly on the streets. The idea was to quickly seal off any crowd or riot from further reinforcement and get troops and wire barriers between the rival factions. We had CS gas, but never used it although our soldiers always had respirators and steel helmets to hand and carried their personal weapons firmly attached to their person.

The first real trouble occurred on 11 September when some members of the 'Foreign Legion' fomented a small riot in Waterloo Place – this was the occasion when the Brigadier interfered. It was fairly easily contained by John Francis's B Company and not long after this, on the 24th, following visits by a delegation of Labour MPs and Denis Healey, the Minister of Defence, the barricades came down. Against my better judgement, however, the CO agreed that a white line should be painted on the road to replace them. This line, to be guarded by our soldiers, separated the Nationalist sector from the commercial area of the city. Nevertheless, it was some sort of achievement. Another plus was the setting up of a telephone link between the BCDA and our HQ which led to another success when we negotiated the recovery of a brand new bus which was being used as a barricade in the Rosemount area.

The negotiation phase came to an abrupt end the same day that the barricades came down. I was 'Duty CO' and in my Land Rover when, at about 2230 hours, I received a message saying that there was trouble in the Diamond in the heart of the city. I drove there immediately and placed my Land Rover between a large crowd of about 300 Catholics who had come up from the Bogside, a couple of them carrying Republican flags, and an equally large crowd of Protestants. For the next half hour I helped men of C Company DERR keep the two crowds apart, often by the use of physical force. When John Hume, the MP, suddenly appeared on the scene I invited him to address the Catholics, appeal for calm and invite them to go back down into the Bogside. He did so from my Land Rover, but said quietly to me: 'I think this could turn nasty. You're going to need some more soldiers.' I immediately radioed for another company to reinforce us. John Francis's Company arrived very quickly, but not before a group of 'Prods' emerged from a pub, jeered at the 'Cats' who responded with bottles and, by rushing forward, some of them broke through the DERR cordon. In the ensuing mêlée, a Protestant, William King, was kicked to death and I was hit by a Catholic bottle on the head, knocking me to the ground, and a Protestant brick on my right hand, cutting it badly. I thus became the Battalion's first casualty! Whilst I was moved to the steps of the Court House for emergency treatment, our Companies managed to separate the opposing factions and send the Catholics packing.

On 29 September I flew home for my R & R leave. It was wonderful to see Anne and Debs again. And there was good news to come. There was a letter waiting for me from the Military Secretary (MS), dated the 29th, which said, 'I am directed to inform you that you have been provisionally selected for promotion to the substantive rank of lieutenant colonel in the promotion year 1970.'

Things remained reasonably quiet in Derry for the next four weeks, but we were inundated with visits – the CGS, General Sir Geoffrey Baker, the Vice Chief, Lieutenant General Sir Fitz-George Balfour, Jim Callaghan, the Home Secretary, the new Chief Constable of the RUC, Sir Arthur Young, and a large number of MPs. The local Unionist MP, Robin Chichester-Clark, a junior minister at Westminster, wrote to me in September saying, 'Now that the spate of Conservative MPs has some-what abated, I would like to . . . thank you for all your help in looking after them and for your patience and kindness in doing so.'

One popular visitor who came at about this time was the Colonel of the Regiment, General Dick Craddock. However, one evening when he, the CO and I were having a drink in the Wardroom of *Sea Eagle*, he dropped a bombshell. The CO mentioned that, with my forthcoming promotion now in the open, he expected me to take over from him the following June. We already knew that the 4th Battalion of the Regiment, the old Middlesex, was to be disbanded at about that time, but neither of us realized that the officer who had already been selected to command that Battalion, was now to be given the 1st Battalion. Dick looked me straight in the eye and said, 'Mike, you can either wait three years for the 1st Battalion, or you can have the 2nd in twenty months time – as far as I'm concerned it's your choice, but of course MS will have to agree.' He clearly wanted an answer there and then. I knew that the 1st Battalion was due to move to Berlin and the 2nd to Werl in West Germany in 1971. I also knew that soldiering in Berlin was largely ceremonial, whereas the 2nd Battalion would be a fully fledged mechanized Battalion in an armoured division. I didn't hesitate, 'I'd be honoured to be given command of the 2nd Battalion, Sir.' Dick confirmed me as his nomina-tion for that Battalion in writing a few days later. Although I didn't know it then, once again I'd been very lucky. Command of 2nd Queen's would lead me on to command a mechanized brigade and to become a general. Had I gone to Berlin I doubt if either would have happened.

The next step in trying to achieve some sort of normality in Derry was the introduction of joint, unarmed, Royal Military Police (RMP) and Battalion foot patrols into 'Free Derry'. This happened on 12 October. The soldiers had powers of arrest, although to my knowledge they never actually arrested anyone. However, this achievement had taken a lot of negotiating and I personally spent hours in Paddy Doherty's small home, 10 Westland Street, deep in the Bogside. Despite our differences we became quite good friends – at least so I thought until I said goodbye at the end of our tour, of which more shortly. One example of his friendship was an offer to take me over the border into the Republic for a 'surprise'. Murdering British soldiers was not yet on the agenda, so I had no hesitation in accepting and one Sunday we drove to a lake thirty miles inside Donegal, where we found a rowing boat waiting for us. Once out in the middle of the lake, Paddy brought out a bottle of poteen which we enjoyed as he showed me the beauty of the 'Emerald Isle'. I should add that poteen was, and probably still is, illegal, and even banned by the Catholic Church.

On 15 October the Government announced the introduction of Northern Ireland Pay – 3/6 a day for a private (17.5p today) and 7/- a day for a major. This caused trouble as well as satisfaction though, since the RAF and Navy also received it even though they were not involved in any way with the 'troubles', but merely carried on with their normal peace-time duties.

October also saw the beginning of a new problem. The publication of the Hunt Report on the future of the RUC caused a Protestant backlash. It included the disbandment of the B Specials and various constitutional reforms. These measures were seen as a sell-out to the rebellious Catholics and the Army, as an instrument of Westminster, was suddenly identified with that sell-out. The first demonstrations in Londonderry came on 18 and 26 October with sit-downs that temporally blocked the Craigavon bridge over the river Foyle. This was followed by more trouble in the Diamond which the RUC was unable to deal with and only after we flooded the area with troops was order restored. We did the same at the bridge and in the city centre the following week and that finally persuaded the organizers that further attempts to cause trouble would be futile. On 14 November the *Times* reported, 'The first hundred days . . . of the Ulster 1969 campaign are over with an almost bloodless victory for the military.'

Mention of the Hunt Report and B Specials reminds me of two things. The first was a visit to the B Specials in the Whitehall Armoury. I did this one night when I was Duty CO. My repeated knocking on the door finally led to it being opened and, after some difficult negotiations, I was finally invited into a canteen for a drink. They were a sinister-looking lot, but eventually relaxed and invited me to a 'shoot' on their 25-yard indoor range. The idea was to put out lighted candles. I had to fire first and after putting out four of my five candles I was accepted as a 'good bloke'. Goodness knows what their reaction would have been if they had known I was a Roman Catholic!

The Hunt Report incident was much more serious. It was decided to give the RUC in Derry new uniforms. The trouble was that they were not *new* uniforms. They were second-hand, some with high-collars, and City of London Police buttons. One evening in Victoria, I was invited by the

District Inspector to see what some of his men looked like. They were almost in tears – few of the uniforms could be made to fit and they looked like 'Bow Street runners' in an old film. Not surprisingly the uniforms were quickly withdrawn and the whole idea dropped.

The final phase of our tour was a relatively peaceful one. The Nationalists were quiet, waiting for the promised reforms, and the Loyalists were disillusioned and disorganized. In mid-November we launched a 'Hearts and Minds' campaign, masterminded by the CO but with lots of ideas from his senior ranks, designed to foster community relations and keep the hooligan elements off the streets. One of our officers ran a Sports Club in *Sea Eagle* with swimming, football, hockey and gymnastic facilities for up to 250. Another club was opened next to a recently established RMP post in the Bogside.

The peaceful phase also gave us much more of a chance to relax. On 13 November I and several others attended a formal dinner in *Sea Eagle* to commemorate the raid on Taranto and sometime later that month a few of us nipped over the border one Sunday to enjoy a Guinness or two in the Red Castle Hotel in Redcastle, County Donegal – the sale of alcohol was banned on Sundays in Ulster. I should also mention that a number of the *Sea Eagle* officers and their wives often entertained us to tea and meals during our time in Derry.

As Christmas approached there was an exchange of presents between our soldiers and the local people and we even arranged for a helicopter-borne Santa Claus to land in the centre of the city, following which he toured the Bogside in a decorated Ferret scout car. In return, over a thousand presents, mainly of cigarettes, and Christmas cards were received by the Battalion.

Before our departure the CO received numerous letters of congratulation on the performance of the Battalion; they included ones from the GOC Northern Ireland, the Deputy Army Commander, the Captain of *Sea Eagle*, the Resident Magistrate in Londonderry and the Catholic Bishop of Derry. The latter wrote, 'Over and above the generous cheque conveyed to me by Major Reynolds . . . I value what you have done in restoring order and confidence to our community.' The cheque was part of the money raised by our soldiers for the benefit of the children of the whole city.

I said goodbye to Paddy Doherty just before we ended our tour on 12 December. He smiled as we shook hands, but then, looking me straight in the eyes, he said, 'Michel (sic), it's been good to know you, but I have to tell you that if you and your soldiers come back again and I have a gun, I'll shoot yer!' I was shocked. Little did we know that, within two and a half years, we would meet again.

The CO wrote his last report on me shortly before we left Ulster:

Whilst in Londonderry he has proved his capacity for hard work and decision taking. Likewise he has been a most admirable fellow to have at one's side in all the negotiations that have taken place at all hours of the day and night. . . . He is ambitious and knows where he is going. Whilst I admire him for this I believe he must remember that it is only the Wellingtons who can defeat the system [I don't think he knew that I'd been told I looked like Wellington and had played his part in the film *Proud Heritage*]. . . . His grading is based on his performance in Londonderry which I consider to have been outstanding in every respect.

He duly graded me Outstanding. The Brigade commander wrote:

I have only known Major Reynolds for a short time. He has done very well indeed and has shown that he can take decisions, is calm under stress, writes and expresses himself legibly and clearly, and is an obvious future commanding officer. However, when I compare him with the officers of seven major units which have passed through this Headquarters in the past year, I would grade him a high A.

I should have queried the 'seven major units'. There were no other major units under his command that were facing the sort of situation we were up against in Derry and so this sort of comparison was invalid. Unfortunately, I was destined to serve under this officer again within three years.

The CO was appointed OBE for his performance, and that of the Battalion, in Derry. He told me he had put me in for an MBE. I didn't get it.

As I flew out of RAF Ballykelly on 13 December, I looked down on Derry and the river Foyle and thought, 'Thank God I'll never see that place again.' Little did I know what was in store for me or that over one thousand soldiers and policemen would die in Ulster before the end of the 'Troubles'.

Christmas 1969 with Anne and the girls in Sharpthorne was wonderful and it was lovely to see my parents and Anne's again during our three weeks' block leave. I got a bit of a surprise though, sometime soon after returning from leave, when I received a signal from MS warning me that I might be required at short notice to assume the appointment of Chief Instructor of the NCOs' Wing at the School of Infantry in Warminster. In the end nothing came of it and I was left wondering where I would go after leaving the Battalion.

In February the commander of our parent 2 Infantry Brigade paid a visit to the Battalion and, over a drink in the Sergeants' Mess before lunch, turned to the CO and told him that he thought it a pity that no one from the Battalion was coming on a forthcoming battlefield tour of Tunisia, particularly as the Queen's had played such an outstanding part in the fighting there. Although it was *my* responsibility as 2IC to decide who should go on which courses and attend events like battlefield tours, the CO had put in a 'Nil Return' during our Christmas leave without even consulting me. 'I'm afraid we're all much too busy,' he said. 'I'm not,' I said. To the CO's horror the Brigadier said, 'Marvellous Mike, see you in Tunisia!'

On 24 February I joined about fifty other officers of 5th Infantry Division to fly from RAF Lyneham to the Tunisian island of Djerba. Exercise LIVELY LADY had been organized by the Divisional commander, Sandy Thomas, a New Zealander with a DSO and an MC, who had fought as a company commander in the New Zealand Brigade in Tunisia. Also with us as Directing Staff were eight British and three German officers who had taken part in the fighting, including Major Generals Darling DSO and Gordon DSO, CO 7th Bn The Rifle Brigade and Brigade Major (BM) 131 Queen's Brigade respectively, Colonel Watson, CO 6 DLI, Wing Commander Garton DSO DFC RAF, and Major Sandys MC, Anti-Tank Platoon commander 1/7th Queen's. The Germans were Major General Freiherr von Liebenstein, commander 164th Light Division and two officers from the famous 21st Panzer Division.

We stayed in two very nice hotels during the tour in Djerba and Gabès, both with beautiful swimming pools, good restaurants and interesting food. All this was paid for by the MoD. The battles we studied in detail were Medenine, where 1/7th Queen's Anti-Tank Platoon had played a key role and knocked out twenty-seven German tanks, and the Battles of the Mareth Line and Tebaga Gap. It was all utterly fascinating and whetted my appetite for battlefield tours. The only downside was nearly freezing to death in open trucks as we were driven considerable distances to the various 'stands' early each morning. It was fine once the sun came up, but paralyzingly cold before that.

Having thoroughly enjoyed the tour we waited at Djerba airport on Sunday 1 March for the RAF to collect us for our return journey. There should have been two aircraft, but only one turned up, the other having apparently broken down in Malta on the way out. All the senior officers piled into the one that had arrived, leaving the rest of us to wait for the other. After about two hours we received a message saying it was beyond immediate repair and they had no idea when we would be picked up. To my surprise I found that I was the senior officer left behind and therefore expected to do something about this. I remember one chap who seemed to think it was so important for him to get back to the UK that he bought a ticket for the next commercial flight home, but the rest of us were in no such hurry. We returned to our hotel and, although it was a Sunday, I then rang the British Embassy in Tunis and asked the Duty Officer for instructions. He wasn't pleased to be disturbed but, after conferring with the Military Attaché, told us to stay where we were and await recovery. The Embassy would pay our hotel bills. As a result we enjoyed a further three days, swimming and sunbathing and enjoying excellent food. Not only that, but we were paid a generous local overseas allowance for those three extra days. Needless to say, my CO was not pleased about my late return.

From 1 March to 14 April the Battalion performed Public Duties at Buckingham and St James's Palaces, the Tower of London and the Bank of England. I had no responsibilities for any of this and was able to relax and enjoy the fun which took the form of dining at St James's with one of the Guard commanders, enjoying dinner and the Ceremony of the Keys at the Tower and having dinner at the Bank's expense with the officer commanding the Bank of England picquet. Sadly the picquet no longer exists.

In March I received my posting order – I was to be GSOI, Land Operations Division of HQ Allied Forces Central Europe (AFCENT) in Brunssum in Holland; I was to report to there on 20 April and take over the job on the 29th.

Shortly before leaving the Battalion I was given a very nice formal 'Dining Out' in the Officers' Mess and went on to enjoy a wonderful day with the Band in London. It started with a farewell lunch in Wellington Barracks during which I was presented with a small silver drum mounted on a plinth, 'From the Bandmaster and Band'; the card with it read, 'We would like you to accept this gift as a token of our appreciation for all you have done for us. We wish you every success in your next appointment. We feel that our loss is their gain.' After the lunch the Bandmaster and Band Sergeant Major took me on a tour of some of their favourite London pubs. I slept on the train on the way home and failed to get off at Crawley where Anne was expecting to pick me up. I rang her again and told her that I was at Balcombe and would start walking. She said 'don't', but I did and she found me, complete with bowler hat and umbrella, walking along with one leg on the grass verge and one in the road. She was *not* pleased.

In a farewell letter the CO wrote to me:

> I am sorry things have not worked out as we had hoped since there is nobody I would rather have handed over to. I'm sure you will hit

2 Queen's like a breath of fresh air. I believe ours has been a rewarding partnership over a very difficult period. Certainly I have greatly valued your backing and none more so than in Derry where I'm afraid you did not get the credit you deserved. We may not always have seen eye to eye, that is the prerogative of friends, but I can assure you that I have always valued your advice and experience.

On the 18th I left the Battalion for a month's leave, at the end of which we delivered the girls to school and, after bidding them a sad farewell, caught the Dover-Zeebrugge ferry on 20 April and drove to Holland. A new adventure was about to start.

Chapter Seventeen
Staff Officer in Holland

We arrived in Brunssum in south-east Holland on 23 April 1970 and booked into the NATO Officers' Club where the officer I was replacing had reserved a room for us. He had written to me a couple of weeks earlier:

> You are getting the best British occupied house in AFCENT [Allied Forces Central Europe]. It's in a delightful village called Gulpen where the neighbours, Dutch, are great friends of ours. The house has a huge drawing room and separate dining room, with a beautiful fireplace surrounded by blue Dutch tiles, seven bedrooms and not a bad kitchen. It has oil-fired central heating and a fitted washing machine. The cellar can take four cars and is a ready-made night club.

It was a good description and we were indeed very lucky to get such a large and attractive house. I discovered later that, during the battle for Aachen in October 1944, the cellar had been used by the Americans as an operating theatre for soldiers wounded in the fighting. We found only one snag to our new house – my predecessor was still living in it. This only lasted for a couple of weeks though and the Officers' Club was reasonably comfortable.

Our new home was owned by an extremely nice Dutch couple. He was a former mayor of the town and she had been a lady-in-waiting to Queen Juliana. As well as the Army G-Plan furniture, the house had quite a lot of their furniture which they kindly agreed we could continue to use.

Gulpen was a very pleasant small town located exactly halfway between Maastricht in the west and Aachen in Germany in the east – ten miles to either of them. The town had a well-known brewery and immediately behind our house was the highest point in Holland – a hill (1,000 feet!) with a statue of the Virgin Mary on its summit. We could see it from our drawing room, standing well above our pleasant rear garden. Our dining room and our bedroom overlooked the very centre of Gulpen with its market place, nice shops and a superb bakery.

The part of Holland in which we lived was the Limburg province, a very pleasant area with rolling hills and attractive villages and small towns. Gulpen was about twelve miles from the HQ at Brunssum and the drive to get there, through a heavily industrialized area, was far from pleasant and took about half an hour. It was well worth it though and those of us who lived away from the HQ felt very sorry for those who lived much closer. Fortunately, I soon made friends with other British officers living in the area and was able to join a car pool, thus freeing our car for Anne for three weeks out of every four.

HQ AFCENT was located, to my surprise, in the offices of an old coal mine and was headed, also to my surprise, by a German general – Jürgen Bennecke. He had fought in the Second World War and was the first German to command a senior NATO headquarters. His deputy was British Air Chief Marshal Sir Frederick Rosier.

The Land Operations Division in which I worked was headed by an American brigadier general and there were about twenty other lieutenant colonels in the Division – American, British, Canadian, Belgian, Dutch and German. My branch, the Combat Readiness Branch, was headed by a German Colonel. He was a charming man who immediately endeared himself to me by telling me that 'I want to make it clear that in my Branch we make *no* decisions. If we do, we will upset the Brits or the Americans or the Germans or someone, so it's better we just smile and agree with them all!' When I reported to him on my first day and called him 'Sir', he immediately replied, 'Ja, Sir, I like that – we don't have it in the German language – that's a pity!' Like most of the senior German officers in the HQ he wore an Iron Cross.

I shared an office with an amusing American infantry lieutenant colonel, Jack Sheldon. He had just returned from Vietnam and we soon became good friends. Our job in Combat Readiness Branch was 'the coordination of the operational aspects of multinational, air mobile and nuclear land forces'. Jack covered the nuclear side whilst I did the rest. However, I have to say that I was usually looking for something to keep me busy.

The eight other British lieutenant colonels and their wives and two cavalry bachelors of the same rank in the HQ soon became very good friends and we enjoyed many good parties with them. According to Anne's 'Entertaining' diary she put on nineteen lunch and dinner parties in our thirteen months there. Amazingly, long after we all retired, the majority of us continued to meet annually for a reunion lunch, but sickness has sadly taken its toll and the last one was a couple of years ago. We were also invited to all the various national day celebrations – Queen Juliana's birthday, the 'fete de la Dynastie Belge', Canada Day, 'the 4th of July' and so on.

My American brigadier general and Jack Sheldon are memorable for two particular incidents. In the case of the former it was a lunch party his wife threw for the Divisional wives. The Brits turned up, in usual fashion, in tweed skirts, low-heeled shoes, jumpers and pearl necklaces. The Brigadier's Japanese-American driver (who was to receive a medal in front of us all for driving his general to work successfully for a year!) greeted them all in the large hallway of the house and there they awaited the arrival of their hostess. To their amazement and great amusement, she appeared at the head of the staircase wearing a full length, green evening gown.

In the case of Jack, he asked Anne and me to accompany him and his wife to a dinner at a wealthy German's house near Eschweiler. Jack was a little unsure of himself and needed, as he put it, 'an English gentleman's support'. I can't remember how on earth he'd met this German who lived in a vast turreted house, complete with farm buildings surrounding a cobbled square. The dinner was delicious and afterwards the German invited the ladies, but not Jack and me, to see his private collection which was housed in a small cellar with a door like that on a bank vault. To Anne's horror, once they were inside, he closed the door and showed them his wartime memorabilia – including his Knight's Cross with Oakleaves and his Nazi officer's dagger complete with Swastika.

The Dutch are infamous in western Europe for their meanness. After living in Holland for a short time we soon understood the reason behind expressions like 'Dutch treat' and 'going Dutch'! The Italians say NL on Dutch cars means 'no lira', the Germans say the Dutch flag has horizontal lines so that you can still see that it's the Dutch flag even when it's been worn down by the wind to a width of just a couple of inches, and the Belgians say that if you get stuck in a traffic jam it will usually be caused by a Dutchman in a mobile home or towing a caravan as they rarely stay in hotels. Certainly we were never invited into a Dutch officer's house, even for a drink, whereas the Dutch officers in the HQ always accepted invitations into ours. The final crunch for us came when our landlords, knowing that we were only using four of our seven bedrooms, asked us if we would have their daughter and her husband to sleep in our house over Christmas. Knowing they didn't have room themselves, we could hardly say no and they duly arrived on Christmas Eve. All was well until they returned from midnight Mass and proceeded to take baths, waking up our little girls who were waiting for Father Christmas. We were furious at their arrogance and I was determined that their behaviour should be punished. When leaving on Boxing Day, he came out with the usual 'Oh, you must come and stay with us in Amsterdam!' I had my diary ready and said 'yes, that would be lovely – when?' With that we fixed a weekend in

February but, to our amazement, when we arrived at their apartment they just handed over the key and disappeared, telling us to post the key back to them. It was a nice apartment though and we had a lovely time in the Dutch capital.

One of our first expeditions was to Brussels. I had discovered that we could stay very cheaply in the Belgian Officers' Club there – the Club Prince Albert. The rooms were good and the food excellent and we soon fell in love with the Belgian capital. Little did we dream that thirteen years later we would live there.

Golf was back on the menu in Holland and I was able to play two of the best courses. Tony White, of Camberley days, also got in touch and he and Joy invited us down to stay in their 'residence' in Cologne. He was by then a major general working in Bonn with responsibility for Anglo-German service relations. His letter of invitation reads: 'Very glad to know it won't be long before you can have my balls – or mine yours! There is a course right next to the house so all we have to arrange is for you to come down and spend a weekend.' We had a lovely couple of days there, the golf being particularly memorable for Tony, instead of shouting 'Fore' at a foursome of Japanese in front of us, bellowing 'Get out of the way you bloody nips!' They duly did so, bowing politely as we passed through.

In mid-June I took a week's leave and we decided to see Vienna and Salzburg. Our most vivid memory of our stay in Vienna is not the famous Woods but the Lipizzaner stallions at the Spanish Riding School. We arrived at the entrance to find a notice on the door saying the School was closed and were standing there obviously looking dejected when a man came up and asked us what was the matter? I told him we had driven hundreds of kilometres to see the horses and the School, which had some truth in it even if it was a bit of an exaggeration. At this he announced that he was the Director and we would be his guests. He ushered us inside and, for the next hour or so, we had a private viewing of the stallions and their riders rehearsing their amazing performances. It was a truly memorable experience. We also took in the Hofburg, the Prater and the Vienna Woods, not to mention a Sachertorte or two. On the way back we spent two lovely days in Salzburg.

On our return home I received the news that I was to be promoted to the substantive rank of lieutenant colonel with effect from 30 June and shortly after that came the wonderful news that I was to take command of the 2nd Battalion, The Queen's Regiment on 1 July.

The big event of that first summer was our holiday in Austria. We headed for Salzburg and, knowing that we couldn't afford a hotel in the city for the five of us, decided to look for a '*zimmer frei*' in a nearby village. With our usual good luck we stumbled upon Koppl, only five miles from the centre of Salzburg and set in the beautiful rolling country of the Salzkammergut. There we found a delightful apartment in a farmhouse. With *The Sound of Music* still fresh in all our memories, it wasn't long before we had to pay a visit to the nearby church where Maria and Captain Von Trapp had been married and I had to walk down the aisle with Vicky on one arm and Gabrielle on the other, and then do it again with Debs. Another highlight of the holiday was an evening visit to the Hohensalzburg where we were entertained to Austrian folk dancing, complete with yodelling and thigh slapping. We could not have had a more successful family holiday.

The military highlight of my time in AFCENT was a visit to part of the Allied Command Europe Mobile Force (Land) which was exercising in Turkey. This multinational force was the NATO 'fire brigade': in the event of any serious threat by the Soviets to the flanks of NATO its mission was to deploy rapidly to the threatened area and demonstrate NATO solidarity. Fortunately for me, I had responsibilities for multinational formations so I demanded to see the ACE Mobile Force in action. Accordingly, in mid-October, I attended Exercise DEEP EXPRESS as an official observer. I flew to Istanbul where I was able to spend a full day exploring the city, including St Sophia, the Blue Mosque, Topkapi Palace, and the incredible Grand Bazaar. Next morning I took off in one of about half a dozen helicopters heading for the area of Corlu in Turkish Thrace where the AMF(L) was exercising with elements of the Turkish First Army. The lead helicopter carried General William Westmoreland who had commanded US operations in Vietnam during the height of the war there in 1964–68 and was now Chief of Staff of the US Army. The two Turkish pilots in the Huey in which I was flying had no maps and it soon became obvious that we were merely following the aircraft in front of us. This became even more obvious when I noticed that we were following the coastline and making no attempt to turn inland towards Corlu. We all eventually landed at Gelibolu, the HQ of the Turkish First Army, where we were greeted by its commander. We were told that the weather was too bad to fly upcountry and that we could either go by road in coaches or have a conducted tour of the Gallipoli (Gelibolu) battlefields. Westmoreland, to my surprise, chose the battlefield tour and we had a superb day being shown the battlefields and hearing about the fighting as seen from the Turkish point of view. It was a unique experience. However, the result of this was that we never saw a single AMF(L) soldier that day. The second attempt the following day was only partly successful; maybe General Westmoreland saw some action, but all I saw was a few British armoured cars of the Life Guards and a logistical base camp. It didn't matter though – ten years later I would be *commanding* the whole AMF(L).

Sometime in April 1971 Anne brought home a book for me from the American Library in AFCENT – there wasn't a British one! It was called *The Damned Engineers* and was about the 1944 German Ardennes offensive, better known as the Battle of the Bulge, and specifically about the role played in that battle by an American engineer battalion. I read it and decided that I wanted to see the ground where the fighting had taken place. It was after all less than forty miles from where we were living. We drove down one sunny weekend with a picnic and whilst Anne read her book or picked wild flowers, I would get very excited and tell her that a Tiger tank had been knocked out 'just over there' or that 'this bridge was blown up by the Yanks just before the Germans could cross it!' She wasn't very interested, but I soon decided that the lessons of this battle were as valid in 1971 as they had been in 1944 and that I was going to use parts of the Battle of the Bulge as a training vehicle for the officers and sergeants of my upcoming command by means of a battlefield tour. The book that Anne had brought home for me was in fact to change my life and lead not only to a very happy retirement after I left the Army, but also to me becoming a recognized military historian and author.

On 2 June, in order to celebrate my birthday on the 3rd and our sixteenth wedding anniversary on the 4th, we set off for another ten-day holiday in Lerici. We found it as pleasant as ever and were again blessed with lovely weather. Immediately after our Italian holiday I decided that it was time to prepare myself physically for command of 2nd Queen's. I gave up booze, went on the Scarsdale diet and swam an increasing number of lengths in the AFCENT swimming pool every lunchtime. A month later I was slim and pretty fit.

My final Confidential Report for AFCENT ended: 'Lieutenant Colonel Reynolds' work has won him the esteem of his NATO colleagues and senior officers. Together with his wife he has played a full part in the life of the Headquarters.'

On 19 June we handed over our lovely Dutch house and, on the 23rd, after five nights in the Officers' Club and several farewell parties, left Holland and drove to Unna in West Germany. One of the most important periods in my military career was about to begin.

Chapter Eighteen
Commanding Officer in Germany and Ulster

The Battalion I was to command was based in Albuhera Barracks near Werl, Nord Rhine-Westphalia. The barracks were located on the edge of a forest, a couple of miles south of the small and pleasant town and had been built in 1953 by the Canadians and occupied until 1970 by a battalion of the Royal 22nd Regiment – the 'Vandoos'. When the Canadian Brigade Group assigned to NATO moved south to the Lahr area of Baden-Württemberg in the late 1960s, the barracks was offered to the British and 2nd Queen's, 600-plus strong and fresh from nearly three years as a resident battalion in Belfast, was complete there by January 1971.

Albuhera Barracks was considered one of the best in 4th Armoured Division because of its location and excellent facilities which included its own cinema, with films changing every second day, two bowling alleys, separate brick-built Protestant and Catholic churches, complete with steeples, an eighteen-hole golf course, and a separate annex with first-class garages where all the APCs and heavy equipment could be stored under cover.

Werl, population 29,000, was a friendly place and we had inherited from the Canadians a club, the Queen's Club, right in the middle of the town where our soldiers could drink and eat at duty-free NAAFI prices. It had two bars, a restaurant, a dance floor and discotheque. It proved very popular and was an excellent source of income for the Battalion. The larger towns of Dortmund and Soest were within easy reach and there was an excellent road and rail network making trips to the UK or other parts of Europe very easy. Married quarters, again near the middle of the town, were plentiful and good and there was a large British Forces primary school complete with medical and dental clinics, and a NAAFI and Salvation Army Red Shield Club in the quarters' area. Furthermore, in contrast to most of the flat North German Plain, the countryside surrounding Werl was very attractive.

My predecessor was Jack Fletcher, a popular and excellent CO who had been awarded an OBE for Ulster – many thought it should have been a

DSO. After a staff appointment Jack went on to command the Dhofar Brigade in Oman and had been selected to be a major general when he tragically died of cancer in 1976.

Jack and his wife had lived in an unattractive four-bedroomed house right on the edge of the quarters patch in Werl and he recommended that, as CO, I would be much better off in an apartment, twelve miles away in Unna. Anne and I duly arrived there on 23 June and moved into a large ground-floor apartment in an ugly two-storey building put up in the 1960s and looking very like a barrack block. Above us was the Battalion Paymaster and two of my company commanders lived in a similar block next door. These two blocks were the only British quarters in the town. Our apartment had a large drawing room with a balcony overlooking the garden which we shared with the Paymaster and his wife, a good-sized dining room, good kitchen, master bedroom with en suite bathroom, and three other bedrooms and a bathroom. We were far from thrilled but had no choice other than to make the best of it. At least Unna itself was a pleasant town with a regular market and reasonable shops and restaurants. There was no NAAFI shop, though, so we had to drive twelve miles to our old stamping ground in Iserlohn or a similar distance to Dortmund for that. However, as I now had a personal staff car and I made it available to Anne, this was no great hardship. My driver, Private Greenfield, a small, cheeky boy from Eastbourne, served us well and was popular with our girls who called him 'Greenfly'!

I took command of the 2nd Battalion on 1 July 1971. I had agreed Jack's suggestion as to who should be my Adjutant during the week before I took over but was a little surprised that I had to go across to him, Patrick Gwilliam, in the Mess and introduce myself, rather than the other way round. It was typical of Pat though – very laidback. Nevertheless, he was a charming person, the son of a former brigadier in the Royal West Kent (RWK) Regiment, and turned out to be an excellent Adjutant. Sadly he died in late 2011.

I inherited George Brown MBE BEM as my RSM. He had been in the appointment for over two years and was a powerful figure. I liked him and we got on well but I knew that, in less than two months, he would be succeeded by my old comrade Sid Lea from the days of Stoughton Barracks, Iserlohn, Münster, Bahrein and Lingfield.

I was given a choice of batmen and chose the excellent Lance Corporal Hodges. A former anti-tank gunner, he proved to be a first class batman and valuable driver when we were 'in the field'. We also had an excellent full time Putzfrau – the wife of one of my soldiers.

By the time I took command I had very clear ideas about the sort of

Tokyo

China 1977 – on the Great Wall

Sailing with the Masons, May 1980

My acceptance speech on being appointed to command the AMF (L)

Briefing at HQ 1st Hellenic Army in Larissa, Greece – August 1980

Exercise Anvil Express in Turkey, September 1980. I introduce SACEUR to my staff

General Evran, military ruler of Turkey (on right) visits my command,
September 1980

One of my Turkish friends – General Oka

Signing autographs in Udine, NE Italy

Visiting my Alpini in Turin

With my Norwegian comrades in Bodo, North Norway

Queen Margrethe visits the AMF (L) in Denmark, September 1981

Commander's Ball Heidelburg Castle, November 1981 – with Air Chief
Marshal Sir Peter and Lady Terry

King Olaf of Norway visits my command, March 1982

Visiting US Camp Derby near Pisa October 1982

AFSOUTH Conference Naples, January 1983 – with Sir Peter Terry & US
General Lawson Chief of Staff SHAPE

US General Bernie Rogers, Supreme Allied Commander Europe,
meets a senior NCO of the British contingent

Turkish heads of services and Interior Minister in farewell toast to me –
Sarakamis

Inspecting my Belgian paras and Canadian infantry, Sarakamis – June 1983

British Signal Sqn, US Paras, British Recce Sqn and Joint Helicopter Force say
farewell in Sarakamis, June 1983

As Colonel Commandant of the Queen's Division I escort Maggie Thatcher on
Horse Guards, June 1985

Aboard US nuclear sub *Phoenix*, November 1985

Colonel The Queen's Regt, January 1989 – September 1992

The march on 10 Downing St in an attempt to save the Regiment, 13 August 1992

Pied Peiper Tour, October 1993 – with my dear friends Marie-Berthe and
Edouard de Harenne

With Jamie Wilson, my publisher, at the launch of my first book at the RCDS,
June 1995

Signing copies of my first book for Belgian friends

Sid Lea, my old RSM, visits, 1997

With our daughters on our Golden Wedding Anniverary

Battalion I wanted and, within a few days, addressed all my officers and senior NCOs. The address was subsequently put on paper so that it could be read by all newly-joined officers, warrant officers and sergeants and all newly promoted sergeants.

> I believe we are luckier than most men in that we are in a profession which is respected and rewarding and at the same time well paid. However, the military life is rewarding only if we are prepared to contribute something towards it, and in this way it is a demanding profession.
>
> It is probably harder to be a leader at this time than ever before. We live in a permissive, godless, self-indulgent age – the age of those who want something for nothing. I believe though, that the men we lead, by the very fact that they have joined the Army, have shown (perhaps subconsciously) that they do not believe in permissiveness and self-indulgence. They have joined an organization from which they expect discipline, a challenge, a tough life and comradeship. In a word, they expect to be treated like men. And that is the way they will be treated in this Battalion. They deserve our respect and they shall have it. You and I have chosen to be leaders. No one has forced us into our present positions. Remember though, that leadership is a way of life; the only reason we have privileges is because we carry responsibilities. If you are not prepared to accept responsibility, don't expect any privileges from me. Remember too, that our responsibilities do not end at 1630 hrs or on Fridays.
>
> I believe that a battalion should be thoroughly professional. However, I do not think it will be professional unless it is happy. Happiness stems partly from confidence and confidence can only come from knowing your job. The amiable fool has no place in this Battalion. My aim therefore, is to have an efficient and happy Battalion with a reputation for being 100 per cent professional. Everyone must know and understand his job and do it to the satisfaction of himself and me.
>
> A word about tradition. Traditional methods and ideas are usually good because they are well tried and proven. However, tradition must not restrict us. If a new idea is demonstrated as being better than an old one, we must adopt it.
>
> Two further points. Physical fitness is of paramount importance. This is a personal responsibility for officers and senior NCOs. And secondly, everyone must train himself to act on verbal orders. This Directive is *written* only to ensure that you *all* know my views.

Readers may be surprised that I said we were in a profession that was well paid. However, an article written by a visiting journalist says a married lance corporal with two children living in a quarter in Werl in 1971 was being paid over £50 a week gross and £30 a week after tax and quartering charges. This is the equivalent today of £16,400 a year *after* tax and with *free* housing.

I had also decided to make some significant changes in the way the Battalion lived and functioned in barracks. However, the BAOR training cycle and events in Ulster would mean that many of these changes would have to wait a while. One that did not wait was more or less forced on me by our Brigade commander, John Roberts. An ardent Catholic, at our very first meeting he told me that he thought it was disgraceful that my predecessor had changed the large Catholic church within Albuhera Barracks into a Protestant church and the Protestant church in the barracks next door, occupied by a Military Police Company, into a Catholic church. Our predecessors, the Vandoos, being mainly French Canadian Catholics had used the bigger church for themselves and Jack Fletcher, with a mainly Protestant Battalion, had reversed this. The Brigadier demanded that, as a Catholic, I should change things back again. I told him I did not think this was a reasonable thing to demand. However, it made me think about the whole business of church attendance and, after discussion with Paul Mears, my Methodist padre who later became Chaplain General to the Army, I decided to leave the Albuhera church to the Protestants and close the RC church in the Military Police barracks. It was much too far away from the Werl quarters and few attended it. I therefore went to the headmaster of our primary school in the quarters patch and asked him if he had a large classroom I could turn into an RC chapel. He said this would be no problem and within a few weeks we had a flourishing RC chapel within walking distance of most of our families. Since we had many Irish Catholic wives as a result of the Ulster tour, this proved very popular. Whilst on the subject of wives I should mention that, as the Battalion had served in Hong Kong before Ulster, we also had quite a number of Chinese wives. In 1971 every major unit in Germany had a Families' Warrant Officer. Ours was George Gordon, a WOII with a DCM and a BEM. He was a well-liked tower of strength to our wives and, of course, to Anne.

My 2IC was Mike Hare, a company commander in Lingfield days and our next door neighbour in Sharpthorne so we were already good friends.

On 19 July, less than three weeks after taking command, my Battalion moved up to the Soltau training area in readiness for combined arms training with the 4th/7th Dragoon Guards. I had been looking forward to this as it would give me a chance to assess the capabilities of the Battalion and my company and platoon commanders. However, my hopes were soon dashed. Within twenty-four hours I received a warning order for an emergency tour of unknown duration in Londonderry in Northern Ireland beginning in less than three weeks' time, on 8 August. We therefore returned quickly to Werl, handed over our vehicles to the care of our excellent REME Light Aid Detachment (LAD) under Captain Pat Burke and began Internal Security (IS) refresher training.

Just before we left for Northern Ireland, John Davidson, my Assistant Adjutant in Iserlohn and a fellow company commander in Bahrain, joined the Battalion. He was a fairly senior major and naturally expected to be given a rifle company but, to his great surprise, I told him he was to remain behind as Rear Party commander. I needed a strong character for this job and knew he would do it well. John had just completed two years in Norway and was an excellent skier and I also told him that as well as running the Rear Party whilst we were away I wanted him to set up a Battalion Ski Hut in Bavaria for our use during the forthcoming winter. I wanted as many soldiers as possible to learn to ski and for families to use the facility as well; that soon put a smile on his face.

On Thursday 5 August, I led the Advance Party to Ulster. I took all my company commanders and flew from RAF Gutersloh to RAF Aldergrove. We were met by typical Ulster weather – cold, wet and miserable – and then had to endure a two-hour drive to Shackleton Barracks where 2nd Royal Green Jackets (RGJ) were our hosts. Shackleton Barracks was the old RAF Ballykelly – the airfield I had last seen in December 1969 and had hoped never to see again. The following day, while the QM, Peter Collman, and his staff started improving our accommodation and drawing up our IS equipment and ammunition, I took my commanders on a detailed recce of Londonderry. It had changed in that the Republicans were now armed and the atmosphere in the city was tense. Two days later, on the 8th, I was briefed privately that Operation DEMETRIUS (internment) would commence the following day, but I was not allowed to tell anyone until 9 a.m. on the 9th. However, they heard it on the radio as they got up and we also learned that the numerous arrests and raids on the homes of suspected members of the Provisional IRA (Provos) had provoked riots in Belfast, Londonderry and Newry. At 9 a.m. I told the Advance Party that we had been designated as Province Reserve Battalion and were to move at once to the old Torpedo Factory in Antrim. This naturally caused many problems for the QM and his staff. Anyway I set off with the Advance Party, first to the Torpedo Factory and then into Belfast. Most of my party knew the city well, having been based there for a couple of years before coming to Germany, but I didn't.

I don't remember much about the recce but I got a very nasty shock when I got back to Antrim at about 8.30 p.m. My Battalion had been placed under the command of Brigadier Frank Kitson's 39 Brigade and was being deployed into Belfast. I was not consulted about this deployment and, by the time I knew about it, it was already underway. My own Tac HQ was to set up in Mountpottinger RUC Station, with Maurice Dewar's B Company and Support Company of the Duke of Wellington's under command. They were to be located in the Short Strand bus depot which had been the target of hijacking and bus burning all day. Andy Cowing's A Company was in Ballymurphy under command 2 Para and George Goring's Support Company was in the Lower Falls under 1 RGJ. Ewan Christian's C Company was still in transit from Germany and, although to be located with me in Mountpottinger, was to be held in Brigade reserve. My Echelon, having nowhere else to go, stayed in Antrim. I was furious and spent the following few days desperately trying to get my missing companies back under command. I eventually achieved this and by the 26th we were responsible for most of East Belfast. The intervening period had seen many successful searches with incendiary devices, blast and nail-bombs, hundreds of petrol-bombs and other bomb-making equipment being found. These finds often resulted in outbreaks of mob violence which were sometimes met with CS gas and baton rounds.

I remember being frustrated at this time by the constant redeployment of my men. For example, on the 26th, just after I had regained command of my Battalion, 39 Brigade told me to provide guards for a large number of RUC stations, an ordnance depot and two power stations, as well as the Royal Victoria Hospital (RVH) where one of my subalterns, Merrick Willis, had already been shot and seriously wounded by gunmen in a passing car. I should also mention that our living conditions during this period were quite appalling, with many soldiers having to sleep on the floors of the numerous buildings we occupied, including filthy places like the Short Strand bus depot.

Rather than try to give a detailed description of our time in Belfast with its riots, shootings and bombings, I will restrict myself to a few distinct memories of my time in Mountpottinger. One was the hijacking of an Ulsterbus right outside the RUC station. It was surrounded by screaming women, some carrying babies, and I was sure that if we tried to retrieve the bus they would set it on fire. I therefore gave orders to stand back and not intervene. It was a very tense time but in the end the ugly crowd dispersed and we recovered the bus. In the middle of all this Anne rang up with the girls to say goodbye before going back to school – very distracting but I was able to pretend nothing much was happening!

The most memorable incident was when the Reverend Ian Paisley demanded to see 'the officer in charge of East Belfast'. He was ushered into my office and immediately started bellowing at me that I was not doing enough to protect *his* Protestants in East Belfast. He was a huge man and very intimidating. However, after he had let off steam a bit, I told him that if he sat down and let me speak I was prepared to discuss matters with him. When he did so I immediately threw a map onto the desk in front of him and said, 'I have five hundred and fifty men. That's how they are deployed. If you know a better way to do it, please tell me!' He was clearly nonplussed and shut up. We then had a long discussion on the 'Troubles' at the end of which he said, 'You must understand that everything I do and say is for the rights of a Protestant minority in a United Ireland.' I asked him if he thought this was inevitable and he said 'yes'. I then said that he could never say this outside the room in which we were sitting and he agreed. The only other person to hear this conversation was the Chief Superintendent of Mountpottinger. Looking back, I'm sure I would have had a much more difficult time with Paisley had he known I was a Roman Catholic.

A more amusing incident occurred when I received an invitation from the owner of the *Belfast Telegraph* to come to a reception at his home in East Belfast following his daughter's wedding. I could bring two of my officers if I wished. I took Pat Gwilliam and Raymond Low, my IO, and we arrived at about 8.30 p.m. to find a large party going on in the house and in marquees in the garden. After a while he suggested that I should join some of his more important friends in his study. We were in uniform, of course, and it wasn't long before an important looking gentleman began to quiz me about the 'Troubles'. After a couple of whiskies I suggested that one of the problems was the segregation of the Ulster population and that it was unlikely that there were any Catholics at the party. 'Of course not!' he replied. 'Well I've news for you.' I said, 'There are three – me and the two officers I've brought with me!' I shall never forget the look on his face as he walked away.

On 25 August Sid Lea arrived at Mountpottinger and took over as RSM. Although like me he was an ex-1st Battalion man, he soon became popular and highly respected. In retirement he has remained a close friend.

We were extremely lucky in that we suffered only one other casualty during our six weeks in Belfast. On 14 September, twenty-one-year-old Private Paul Carter was shot dead by three gunmen whilst on guard outside the RVH. A hostile crowd tried to make off with his body but were prevented from doing so by Private Thorn. Carter was the first fatal casualty suffered by the Regiment in Northern Ireland. His father later laid on a full military funeral for his son in his home town of Brighton, complete with gun carriage. Wreaths were sent by the Prime Minister and the Government of Northern Ireland.

On 17 September we returned to Germany and I was met at Gutersloh by my Brigade commander. He congratulated me on a good tour in Ulster and then, to my amazement, told me that the Brigade was about to take part in the annual 4th Armoured Division Field Training Exercise (FTX) and that he wanted my Battalion to participate. 'But Brigadier,' I stammered, 'we're due three weeks' block leave and the Battalion hasn't even taken part in a brigade exercise, let alone a divisional one and apart from all that we've had no chance to prepare for it.' 'Exactly,' he replied, 'everyone will sympathize with you and say it's grossly unfair – you can't go wrong! And you can all have your block leave after it's over!' And so it was to be – three days later we drove out of barracks in our APCs (AFV432s) and four days after that were part of the 'Red' (Soviet) aggressor force on Exercise FOREFRONT VI, advancing west through the Sibbesse gap with a squadron of Chieftain tanks of 4th/7th Dragoon Guards under command.

My Battle Group (BG) HQ staff were surprised to discover that, although I based myself with them, I commanded directly from my own APC – codenamed ØC. ØC was driven by a splendid Lance Corporal signalman, 'Prof' (Professor) Boden, who later became an RSM and, apart from another signaller, the only other occupant was a Canadian exchange officer, Ed Peterson, whom I had appointed as my Operations Officer. As well as running my Tac HQ, he commanded the vehicle so that I could concentrate on the tactical situation and give the necessary radio orders.

I should now perhaps put in a word here about the wartime role of 2nd Queen's. Readers may recall that when I was Adjutant in Iserlohn back in 1958 our emergency battle positions had been way back on the Rhine. As a company commander in Münster in 1964 they had been on the river Weser and now, as a Battalion commander in 1971, I was recceing positions on the river Leine, only some fifty kilometres from the inner German border (IGB). We still trained for nuclear war, but it was felt in the higher echelons that, if we could hold the Soviets conventionally for a reasonable period, commonsense would prevail and they would draw back rather than risk a nuclear exchange.

I don't remember many details of FOREFRONT VI, but I certainly recall that my Advance Guard moved so fast in the dark that, within hours of the exercise starting, Tony Mullens (later Lieutenant General Sir Anthony Mullens) with his Chieftain tanks and Simon Boucher's A Company reported that they were well behind the 'Blue' front line. This was completely unforeseen in the exercise scenario and caused great problems for the Directing Staff and umpires. Everyone was also surprised by the way I had grouped my BG. The normal way in the British Army in the 1960s and 1970s was to attach a troop of tanks to a company of infantry and a platoon of infantry (four APCs) to a squadron of tanks. I was convinced that, whilst a troop of tanks could certainly help a company of infantry, there was little a platoon of infantry could do for a squadron of tanks. For the advance I had therefore formed a squadron/company group as my Advance Guard, directing that in open country Tony would be in command and in close country or built-up areas Simon would take over. I was directly behind them in ØC! Thanks to their professionalism, and that of their men, the results were dramatic to say the least.

I have to admit that I drove the Battlegroup (BG) hard throughout the whole exercise, but it paid off. Before the post-exercise debrief the Divisional commander, Major General (later General Sir) David Fraser, took me to one side and told me that he never singled out any particular unit for praise on such occasions, but he wanted me to know that he had watched our performance closely, including by helicopter, and had been most impressed by all he had seen and heard over the radio; he described our advance, final positions and overall performance as outstanding. On 4 October my Brigade commander wrote to me:

> I must write at once to congratulate you on your battalion's perfor-
> mance on FOREFRONT VI. I was never in doubt that you would get
> by – but like everyone else who had a look at you, I was amazed and
> delighted with the whole thing. I don't think any brigade in BAOR
> has ever had a more 'exercising' time and you can be thoroughly
> proud and pleased with yourself.

I published this letter on Battalion Part I Orders, but left out the last two words. I added:

> I wish to congratulate all ranks on their fine performance on this
> exercise. I knew you *could* do it – thank you for *doing* it. The skill
> and professionalism of this Battalion was admired by all who saw
> us.

Immediately after the FTX we all took three weeks' leave; Anne and I spent ten days following the Weinstrasse in Alsace and then touring part of the Black Forest and Switzerland, before heading for Paris through Burgundy and Champagne. We enjoyed glorious weather, good hotels, delicious food and excellent wine.

On return from leave I issued my first CO's Directive in which I gave a forecast of events, warned all companies and departments that I would be carrying out detailed inspections before Christmas after which, provided they were up to scratch, I would leave them alone. Basically my

Directive told them that they should be 'fit, able to use their weapons accurately' and be 'properly trained in their role as infantrymen'. It included a word on sport: 'The more we do, the happier I will be. Better to enter and lose, at any level, than not to enter. GO TO IT.' The Directive ended, 'Enjoy your soldiering.'

I then turned my attention to a number of matters with which I was unhappy. The first was my Technical Quartermaster (Tech QM), someone I knew well because he had been a Queen's Bandmaster – hardly the right background for a Tech QM. I interviewed him and he admitted that the job was beyond him and that he was on tranquillizers. I therefore arranged for him to be sent to a much quieter job with the TA and be replaced by a more suitable officer. The fact that the replacement was a Fusilier didn't go down too well with the Battalion hierarchy but they soon came to recognize his ability.

The next problem was food and the Dining Hall, both of which were below the standard I wanted. While in the UK in the November I visited the ACC Records Office where I told the OC that I wanted a new dynamic head cook, but that I wanted the old one to get a nice job. He seemed to appreciate that I had taken the trouble to put my case personally and met both requests. The soldiers soon had excellent food – better and with a far better choice than the officers or sergeants in fact. I then turned my attention to the Dining Hall. I told Peter Collman that I was fed up with the soldiers having to carry their own mugs, knives, forks and spoons (KFS) to the Dining Hall and that I wanted these items, together with glasses and paper napkins to be made available as in a civilian restaurant. He told me he didn't think the idea would work and, sure enough, at the end of the first week he was able to tell me that all the KFS had been pinched. I wasn't prepared to give up though and told Sid Lea to get the whole Battalion on parade. I then told them that they could pinch as many sets of KFS as they liked, but I was going to go on providing them until they each had as many as they wanted. After the laughter subsided, I added that this didn't worry me and that they would end up paying for them anyway through 'barrack damages'. They took the point.

I also decided to provide music in the Dining Hall and ordered the Battalion Band under Bandmaster Danny Game to play there at least once a month at lunchtime. He wasn't keen, but it proved a popular event and this led me to go further and provide piped music. We purchased a tape recorder which we positioned in the Catering Sergeant Major's office so that the 'boys' couldn't interfere with it, and two large speakers on the walls of the Dining Hall. I then had a ceremonial opening, turning on the music myself to loud cheers. All was well until about 3 p.m. when Sid Lea came into my office and told me someone had pinched the speakers! I was furious and ordered him to get the whole Battalion on the Square at once. By now I had a small green box to stand on when I addressed my soldiers and, using it, I told them that until I got my speakers back the cookhouse would remain closed and that the only hot food available would be from field cookers which would be set up in the woods adjacent to the camp. The threat soon worked and within an hour the culprit appeared in Sid's office. He said he didn't really know why he'd done it; he then took Sid to the place where he'd hidden the speakers. I told Sid to take no action against him.

I also turned my attention to the corporals. They had their own bar, but it was in the NAAFI which I thought was inappropriate, so Sid and I decided to give them a building in the barracks to turn into a proper Mess. We then commissioned the Dormunder Ritter Brauerei (brewery) to provide attractive bars and lounges which it would furnish at its own expense. The brewery found this idea very attractive and we soon had a flourishing proper Corporals' Mess – the first in the British Army I believe.

I had also come to the conclusion that the Officers' Mess was a little antiquated in its approach to ladies and their entertainment. Unlike messes in the UK and many parts of Germany, we already had, thanks to the Canadians, a bar. I called a Mess meeting and suggested that the 'ladies room', which was virtually unused, should be closed and that officers' wives should be allowed to use the bar and have lunch, but not dinner, in the dining room; also that single and unaccompanied officers should be allowed to host mixed supper parties at their own expense in what had been the Ladies' Room which would be re-christened the Supper Room. The only place that would be out of bounds to ladies would be the ante-room, except on formal mixed Dinner Nights. These ideas met with unanimous approval.

My next target was the Paymaster, known to the officers as 'Caspar, The Friendly Ghost'. It was soon clear to me that he was doing nothing more than his basic job and was failing to offer any advice to the senior ranks or to the Sergeants' or Officers' messes. I therefore told the BAOR Chief Paymaster that I wasn't prepared to put up with him any longer and wanted him replaced. This was done very quickly and his successor was an instant success who went on to a most successful career and ended up as a brigadier. He and I made great changes to the way the individual Battalion accounts were organized – we centralized all the balances, invested the proceeds in gilt-edged stocks and distributed the profits proportionally.

At the end of the year we had two important changes of command in the Division. In late October Major General (later General Sir Anthony) Tony

Farrar-Hockley took over as Divisional commander. An extrovert, flamboyant paratrooper who had been a prisoner in the Korean War, he was a complete contrast to David Fraser. I had known him briefly during our Ulster tour as he had been the Commander Land Forces (CLF) Northern Ireland at that time. In December our Brigadier completed his appointment as Commander 6 Infantry Brigade and, on leaving, wrote my first report as a CO:

> Reynolds has brought something new to 2nd Queen's. He is completely in command of affairs – is not weighted down by the problems which invade a Regiment daily in BAOR . . . I believe he is certainly the outstanding Commanding Officer of those I have commanded during the past two years . . . I have no doubts that he has the presence, skill and natural qualities of leadership to command a brigade.

To this Farrar-Hockley added:

> Although I have only had Lt Col Reynolds in my divisional command for two months, he was formerly under me in Northern Ireland. There, as in BAOR, I found him a first-rate commanding officer. I agree that he is a potential brigade commander.

The New Year saw the opening of our own ski hut at Unterjoch in Bavaria. John Davidson had done a great job, ably supported by another good skier, David Gardiner, an attached Royal Signals officer. Over the coming weeks 170 members of the Battalion spent a fortnight there learning to ski – one week *Langlauf* and one week downhill.

As well as ski instruction, I decided to do something to encourage my single soldiers to get away from barracks at weekends. Few single soldiers had cars in those days and so I purchased a dozen bicycles, together with tents and camping equipment for them to rent at a very modest fee. They were soon in constant use.

Individual training started in late February, followed by three weeks at Sennelager for field firing. This went well except for a visit by our new Brigade Commander, David Alexander-Sinclair. Somehow, we ended up at different gates to the camp and his visit started more than an hour late. Then, to compound the problem, I took him to see my mortar platoon, only to discover on closer inspection that we watching the Royal Anglians' mortars. David was not pleased and disappeared saying he would return that night to watch some night firing. Fortunately, all went well with that and he went away happy. In fact, he became very fond of my soldiers, finding them less 'stiff' than most 'heavy' infantrymen and similar in attitude to the ones he'd known in the Rifle Brigade.

Sennelager was followed in April by two weeks at Soltau for mechanized training with the Queen's Royal Irish Hussars. We lived in base camps under canvas and again there was time for parties and no doubt the inevitable visits to the out of bounds areas of Hamburg. Although the temperatures were in the mid-80s and the dust made it more like North Africa than northern Europe, we had a great time and by the end of the training period the CO of the Irish Husssars and I were both happy with the performance of our officers and men.

The other exciting event of the early summer was my first Battlefield Tour. Readers may recall that I had decided to run one of these after reading a book, *The Damned Engineers*, about the Battle of the Bulge during my time in Holland. I selected four captains and two lieutenants and gave three of them *The Damned Engineers* and the other three another book – *The Battle of the Hürtgen Forest*. I allowed them eight weeks to prepare their tours and, on 8 May, forty of us set off in a luxury coach for Monschau – all my company commanders, nine other officers, two warrant officers and thirteen sergeants. After arriving in the beautiful little town of Monschau and a light lunch, we spent the first afternoon being led through the battle of the Hürtgen Forest. It was a fascinating story and it finished with a small reception given by the Bürgermeister of Schmidt. That evening people dined with whom they liked in the various restaurants in the town and, with subalterns like David Wake, John Stirling and John Pratten, there were inevitably high jinks afterwards – including Wake being thrown into the river that runs through the middle of the town!

The whole of the following day was spent following the actions of *Kampfgruppe* Peiper, a leading Waffen-SS Battlegroup, in the Battle of the Bulge. It was a huge success. The Regimental Journal described the two days as follows:

> The satisfying thing with the tour was that, as opposed to a TEWT, it is more conclusive. We did not break up at the end with many questions begged or unanswered and a vague feeling of irritation with one's brother officers in general and with the DS in particular. We had two days away from barracks, seeing a new and lovely part of our host country and a little of Belgium. The officers and senior ranks had a chance to talk to each other in conditions more relaxed and unhurried than obtains at mess functions and everyone had learned something and enjoyed themselves. We look forward to many more Battlefield Tours.

One of my responsibilities at this time was to foster Anglo/German relations. Accordingly I got to know the Bürgermeister of Werl, Frau Doktor Röhrer, and her Stadt Direktor and, as well as attending and providing support for many local events like the annual Werl carnival, I agreed that my Assault Pioneers should build a 'Trimm Dich Fahrt' (fitness course) in the woods surrounding the barracks. It was excellent training for them. Frau Röhrer and I opened it formally and it proved a great attraction for the local civilians. Probably my most popular action, however, was to open the golf course in the barracks to the Germans. Although it had proved popular with many of the senior ranks, I simply couldn't bring myself to put soldiers to work maintaining the course and running the clubhouse, particularly with another Ulster tour on the horizon. So I suggested to Frau Röhrer that, whilst we would still use the course whenever and as often as we wished, the town would provide the groundsmen and clubhouse staff and the number of playing German members would be restricted to sixty. She agreed and this arrangement worked perfectly. When I left Werl I received the following letter from the German Club President:

> I wish to say that your invitation for us to come into the Golf Club has made sixty serious men and women into sixty crazy but happy golfers. Sir, whatever may happen with Golf Club Werl, your name will be mentioned whenever golfers in Werl meet and talk about golf!

I should add at this point that the person I appointed to be my German liaison officer was none other than Captain Nigel Harris, my host and guide during my visit to the Trucial Oman States in 1968. As well as speaking Arabic, he was a fluent German speaker and a tremendous help in establishing good relations with the town and my affiliated German unit, the 441st Jäger Battalion based near Hamm. The CO and I became good friends and we arranged and enjoyed several exchange visits for our officers, NCOs and soldiers. The same thing happened with my affiliated Belgian unit, the 1st Grenadier Regiment in Soest.

I'm not sure exactly when it happened, but it was probably in early 1972 that I had to court martial one of our wives. Few of them realized that they were subject to military, not civil, law when living in Germany. Consequently when the German authorities informed us that one of our corporal's wives, a German, had brought her child into the local German hospital with what appeared to be cigarette burns on his body and several severe bruises, I called in the SIB. It transpired that the child was her stepson and, as a result of the SIB investigation, I remanded her for trial by court martial; this led to her being sentenced to eighteen months in Holloway prison. It had a dramatic effect on our wives. The lighter side to this story is that when she was due to appear before me in my office for me to read out the charge and ask her if she had anything to say in mitigation, Sid asked me if he should march her in, as he did with soldiers on disciplinary charges, or ask her to come in and just stand in front of my desk. I asked him how big she was and he replied, 'Bigger than you and me, Colonel!' 'Ask her to come in and sit straight down on the chair near the door,' I replied!

In mid-July 1972 my parents came out for a week's visit and it was during this that I got a very nasty shock. On the afternoon of 24 July I was showing my father some of the Mess silver in the silver room, when I was handed a handwritten note from my Brigade commander. It read, 'I have just been told that 2nd Queen's is to move to Northern Ireland on Friday 28th July with all B vehicles and one company's worth of 432s. *No one is to know but yourself for the moment.* Sorry we know no more. Yours ever, David.'

Not being able to warn anyone or take action to implement this totally unexpected and sudden move made me very frustrated and not a little angry, particularly because the planned Rear Party for our scheduled Ulster tour in October was on leave and we had adventure training parties in Sardinia, Bavaria and the Harz mountains.

The following day, the 25th, David rang and told me the order was cancelled; but then, in the small hours of the 26th, he rang again and said the move to an undisclosed destination in Ulster was now definitely on, but that I was not required to take the 432s. I was to leave the following day, the 27th, with my recce party and the main body would start flying out on the 28th! I rang Pat Gwilliam and told him to assemble an O Group for 8 a.m. The first warning had allowed me to plan for an unexpected move and I gave the necessary orders to a very surprised audience.

I quote now from the September issue of the Regimental Journal:

By lunchtime on Thursday 27th July 1972 the nine strong recce party led by the CO was on its way to Northern Ireland. . . . From late evening on the 28th, the main body was moved from RAF Wildenrath in one lift of five Britannias and twenty-five Hercules to RAF Aldergrove. . . . one aircraft took off every twenty minutes and to add a touch of drama to the already dramatic situation, the Hercules unloaded at Aldergrove with their engines running. . . . By the evening of the 29th the Battalion was 99% complete at the weekend training camp at [Ballykinlar] about one hour's drive south of Belfast, where it was placed at one hour's notice to move from Sunday 30th. Equipment was delivered, issued, fitted and modified all that day and night.

Operation MOTORMAN, the removal of the makeshift barriers defending the Catholic 'no-go' areas in Ulster, for which we had been deployed to the Province, took place early on the 31st, but we were not involved. Instead we listened to it on the radio and watched on the few available TV sets. But then, to my horror, I found myself in much the same situation that I had faced almost exactly the year before – HQ Northern Ireland placed my Battalion under command 3 Brigade at Portadown, which in turn detached my B and Support Companies to under command the Queen's Own Highlanders and Gordon Highlanders respectively. I was left with only half my Companies and an operational area in the south of County Down. Then, on 2 August, everything changed again; I was placed under 8 Brigade in Londonderry and told to move at once to that city in order to operate in the Creggan area. The downside was that A Company was detached to help 24 Brigade in Belfast, leaving me with only C Company. I remonstrated with every senior officer I could contact – two brigade commanders and the CLF himself, Major General (later General Sir Robert) Ford. It worked and by 5 August I had B and Support Companies back under command; A Company followed on 10 August.

Our partners in the Creggan, a post-war housing estate occupied almost entirely by Catholics with a high unemployment rate, were initially the Royal Scots and then our own 3rd Battalion; they looked after the southern half of the estate whilst we had the northern. To our south in the Bogside were, first, the 3rd Fusiliers and then 2nd Scots Guards. Above the Creggan was a hilly area known locally as 'Piggery Ridge'. Amazingly this general area had inspired the hymn 'There is a Green Hill Far Away' and this was where the Army decided to build a battalion-sized camp – Creggan Camp. It dominated Creggan and the Bogside and was hated by the local population who considered it a symbol of British domination. The camp was occupied first by part of our 3rd Battalion, then by part of the Coldstream Guards and finally, halfway through our tour, by my B and Support Companies and Recce Platoon.

Our initial accommodation in Derry left much to be desired. Companies were based in two schools, an RUC station, an old supermarket, a former wartime merchant cargo ship and an old factory. My HQ started in a school but soon moved, along with one of the companies, into Brooke Park, a large, quite elegant 1840s building which had once been an orphanage and still had a public library on the ground floor. This was a major security risk and, to the irritation of the locals, I had it closed.

Sometime after we left, the Provos blew it up! I quote again from part of the December 1972 edition of the Regimental Journal:

> As force levels and deployments of our fellow units west of the Foyle changed, our operational area increased accordingly . . . we reign over the whole Creggan estate, the Rosemount parish and more real estate to the north-east. . . . [also] half the 'enclave' – the country-side between Londonderry and the Eire border. A notice in the Operations Room at Tac HQ reads '2 Queen's Real Estate Co. Ltd.: invest with us and watch your area grow!'

The full story of our four-month deployment in Derry can be read in Jonathan Riley's Regimental History, *Soldiers of the Queen*, which describes in detail the many bombings, shootings, riots and stonings with which the Battalion had to contend. I will make just a few comments about the situation in Derry in August 1972 and then quote from letters I wrote at the time, list some statistics from the Battalion records and record some of the more interesting or unusual happenings during our time there.

Derry in 1972 was a very different place from the one I had left in December 1969. The Provisional IRA was now armed and, mainly as a result of 'Bloody Sunday' in January 1972, the Catholic population hated the British Army and everything to do with the British. There was a ready pool of youths prepared to take on the security forces at any time and they were backed by armed men whose aim was to kill British soldiers. Fortunately for me personally, when I saw Paddy Doherty again soon after my arrival, he did not carry out his 1969 threat to shoot me if I returned to Derry and he had a weapon. He was by then the organizer of the Bogside Community Association and, although his attitude was defi-nitely cool, he was not unfriendly.

Not long after our arrival in Derry we received a visit from General Sir (later Field Marshal Lord) Michael Carver, Chief of the General Staff. I was put in his heavily-escorted Land Rover and we drove round my oper-ational area visiting my soldiers. He had a reputation as a very tough and hard man and most people were quite frightened of him. Towards the end of the tour he asked me if there was anything I wanted to raise with him. I replied.

> Yes sir. We came out here at virtually no notice on an emergency tour and I'm told we will soon return to Germany. However, we're due to come back to Ulster in a little over two months' time on a scheduled four-month tour and before that we're meant to carry out the normal Northern Ireland training package at Sennelager. It just

doesn't make sense to any of us. The Battalion is fully experienced in this type of operation and we've only just had the agony of saying goodbye yet again to our families. Why can't we stay here now and complete a four-month tour?

He thought for a minute, smiled at me and then said to the MoD colonel accompanying him. 'Fix it!'

On 31 August I wrote to Dick Craddock and told him that it was now agreed that we would return to Werl by the end of November and explained how we were deployed. I went on, 'We are ordered to try to win the hearts and minds of the locals which of course militates against firm military action which we would otherwise like to take. The soldiers find this hard to understand and difficult to accept.'

On 7 October I wrote to him again to describe our current situation:

We took over the whole of the Creggan on 28 September when the Coldstream Guards left without relief. Our area now comprises some 4,000 houses, seven schools and 20,000 people of whom 99 per cent are Catholic. Three-quarters of our area was formerly 'No-Go'. There is no change in the attitude of the locals. They dislike the British Army intensely. We patrol in platoon-sized groups, mainly on foot. In addition we man numerous OPs, vehicle check points [VCPs] and defensive posts. All military vehicles are stoned continuously by children, usually under about 12, who are organized by older teenagers under the direction of the IRA. We search houses and arrest only on information provided by Special Branch, except in the case of 'hot pursuit' after a shooting or bombing when we enter anywhere at will. This week has been particularly active. We arrested three wanted persons, raided over twenty houses, found an Armalite rifle and over 200 rounds of ammunition, but had two soldiers shot and wounded. The first was saved by the bullet hitting his rifle butt first and then passing through his side without doing too much damage. He is being evacuated today. The second, Private Davenport, was wounded in his lower stomach and it has damaged the nerve to his left leg. We shall not know for a week whether he will get back the use of his leg. Last week Graham White's Recce Platoon had a great success in finding a 150lb bomb under a culvert. It would have killed the crew of any vehicle passing over it. Also Lance Corporal Moynihan had a lucky escape when a bullet was deflected by his flak jacket [body armour]. Private Bate [who had been struck by a bullet which exploded a baton round in his pocket on 18 August causing serious injuries], is apparently recovering well.

Nine days later I wrote to my Brigade commander in Germany:

> We have just had our most successful week. Last Tuesday we raided a house and 'lifted' an explosives officer and a gunman who admitted shooting three soldiers. On Saturday we raided another three houses and arrested two bombers who have been charged. We also found bomb-making kit. Last night a nail-bomb was command-detonated near a C Company Land Rover, slightly wounding the radio operator. Two other nail-bombs, linked to it, failed to explode. If they had we would probably have lost David Wake, Sergeant Hunt and the operator. As a result we set up snap VCPs and Simon Boucher's A Company got three chaps with a fully-loaded Thompson [machine gun] and a Colt .45 pistol. Then early this morning we raided another house and lifted two more suspected gunmen and some bomb-making kit. As you will have gathered we are at last getting enough intelligence on which to base our operations. It's been an uphill fight as we started from scratch, but our tails are definitely UP!

According to 8 Brigade HQ the Battalion arrested a total of sixty members of the Provisional IRA during our tour. These included two 'Directors of Operations', one 'Company commander', one 'Intelligence Officer', two 'Explosives Officers' and a 'Training Officer'; the remainder were snipers or bombers or in possession of firearms. I should add that Martin McGuinness, second in command of the Provos in Derry at the time, was top of our wanted list (we thought he was the CO), but we never found him. He later became Sinn Féin's chief negotiator in the so-called 'Peace Process' and, in 2007, deputy First Minister in the Northern Ireland Assembly alongside Ian Paisley!

Also during our four months in Derry we discovered a total of 6,720lb of explosives, 473 rounds of ammunition and were involved in forty-two shooting incidents during which forty-nine rounds were fired at us and thirty-two rounds returned. During riots we fired 828 baton rounds, forty-nine CS gas cartridges and threw eleven CS gas grenades. We suffered no fatalities but, as mentioned in my letters, three members of the Battalion and one Sapper attached to us were wounded by sniper fire and one chap was injured by a bomb. Over twenty soldiers received medical treatment as a result of missiles being thrown at us.

I was very worried about snipers and spent long hours at night in Brooke Park trying to think of a way to outwit them. Other battalions in Derry had already suffered a number of fatal casualties as well as having had soldiers wounded by sniper fire. I eventually came up with the answer.

The Regimental History describes it as follows:

> The concept of multiple patrolling was invented by Lt Col Reynolds and was first tried out by the 2nd Battalion in the Creggan in an attempt to defeat snipers. The theory was that a sniper would be deterred by the presence of more than one patrol in the same area, as there would be a serious risk of his escape route being cut off.

I therefore ordered that there would always be a minimum of *two* patrols in the same area. This stretched the Battalion almost to its limits; however, it did the trick and we suffered no more casualties. My concept was later refined by cutting the size of the patrols to as little as five men, thus allowing for many more patrols and this soon became standard practice in the British Army. And a final word on patrols: I remember getting very angry one day when I was returning to Brooke Park in my Land Rover and saw a patrol consisting of my Adjutant, RSM, Intelligence and Signals officers, plus a few other members of my HQ, coming towards me. 'Well, we felt we had to show the boys that we're not just desk wallahs!' explained Pat Gwilliam. 'Never again!' I retorted. 'One of you at a time perhaps, but I don't want to risk losing my entire staff in one go!'

My only direct *personal* contact with the Provos came one night towards the end of our tour. The Regimental History describes it as follows:

> The Commanding Officer, touring the area with his Rover Group, surprised three men bringing an RPG-7 rocket launcher out of a house; the rocket launcher was recovered but the team escaped. No. 1 and No. 2 Platoons of A Company cordoned off the area and carried out a detailed search, but with no result.

We had a change of Brigade commanders in mid-October. Brigadier MacLellan, whose subsequent career was blighted by the 'Bloody Sunday' affair, handed over to David (later General Sir David) Mostyn whom I had known as a fellow CO in Ulster a year previously. He had jumped the rank of full colonel. Brigadier MacLellan wrote:

> Before relinquishing command I wish to thank the Battalion for the loyal support it has given me and for the excellent work it has done towards restoring peace to this troubled land. I also want you to know how much I have admired the courage, restraint and professional skill you have displayed under the most difficult circumstances. You have lived up to the best traditions of your

Regiment and enhanced your already splendid reputation. It has been an honour to serve with you.

The new Brigade commander and I got on very well at first, but towards the end of our tour we differed on policy. When we had about a month to go he got me into his office and told me that I was being too hard on the local population. 'Come on Mike, like me you're a Roman Catholic and you know they're not all bad. We mustn't lose the 'hearts and minds' battle.' 'I'm sorry David,' I replied, 'After "Bloody Sunday" we will *never* win the hearts and minds of these people – they hate us. The only thing these people understand is strength. I haven't lost a man yet and if you think I'm taking my foot off the accelerator at this late stage in our tour you're wrong!'

Of course he didn't like being spoken to like this and this was reflected in his final message to me when we left. I still have it:

Personal for CO from Brigade Commander. On the eve of your departure I send you my grateful thanks for a job very well done. By your efforts in the Creggan you have made an outstanding contribution to keeping the peace in N. Ireland. Please tell all ranks how much I have admired their courage and patience when operating under the most difficult and frustrating conditions. I know that on occasions you have felt that you have been somewhat constrained by my policy of trying to keep unnecessary harassment of the civilian population to a minimum and of only searching on strong evidence. Your magnificent efforts have resulted in 60 hard-core IRA being put out of battle since 1 October. 40 of them have been charged. CLF has told me that this is considerably higher than the equivalent figures for any other area in the Province. I cannot thank you enough.

When the honours list was published a short time after our return to Germany my name was not on it. Everyone in the Battalion had expected me to be awarded an OBE as this was the accepted way of rewarding a *unit*, not just a CO, for excellent service – in Army language, OBE stands for 'Other Buggers' Efforts'! We had, after all, spent six out of the last eighteen months in Ulster. What really hurt was that it was a well-known fact that virtually all COs of units completing successful Op BANNER (Ulster) tours received OBEs, or even DSOs. I was, therefore, bitterly disappointed.

Anne, George Gordon and the other Families' Office personnel had done a marvellous job with our wives whilst we were away. It was no easy job for 'girls will be girls' and 'boys will be boys' and there were plenty of young men, including other British (Irish!) soldiers sniffing around Werl in our absence.

We were complete in Werl by midnight on 29 November and then spent four days sorting out our kit and vehicles before starting six weeks' leave. However, before we went on leave, I told Sid to assemble the whole Battalion in the gym so that I could thank them and congratulate them on their superb performance in Ulster. This I did and then to everyone's surprise I asked our Padre, Paul Mears, to lead us in a few simple prayers of thanksgiving for our safe return. A Christmas card I received that year, which I still treasure, reflected the same theme. It reads, 'Not particularly from an RSM to an officer, but to a man who has taught me much about life. The past four months have been hell for you but you did bring us back, each and every one of us. Sincerely, S Lea, RSM 2nd Bn, The Queen's Regt.'

The beginning of 1973 saw the whole family take a short holiday in Baden Baden where we stayed in the luxurious French Officers' Club. It also produced my Annual Confidential Report. I won't quote it all, but David Alexander-Sinclair wrote:

> In the seven months we have worked together, Lt Col Reynolds has proved himself to be an outstanding Commanding Officer. In barracks and in the field, there is never any doubt who is in command of 2nd Queen's. He exercises command (personally or on the radio) calmly and confidently; his orders are clear and unmistakeable, and all are aware that only the highest standards of performance will be accepted. He reacts very quickly to the unexpected; the battalion's sudden move to Ulster in July, for instance, was carried out efficiently and calmly, with no fuss or complaint whatsoever. He fights hard for his battalion's interest but, if the decision goes against him, accepts the situation without complaint (indeed, he has generally planned for the situation already!). Lt Col Reynolds takes a very great pride and interest in each officer and soldier. This they repay with respect and affection. He has the knack of combining a relaxed attitude and complete lack of pomposity in the Mess with a professional and incisive bearing on duty. His relationship with his RSM and Sergeants' Mess is a model. All this contributes to a happy and highly efficient Battalion. I must mention particularly the special and continuous efforts Lt Col Reynolds has made to establish and foster Anglo-German and Anglo-Belgian

relations in Werl. These have been most successful and are, again, a model to us all. He is an amusing and most likeable companion, who is always ready to help others. He himself offered and provided training help to two non-infantry units going to Ulster. One of the COs told me that the realistic and ruthless training given undoubtedly saved casualties. He can be reluctant to admit when he or his battalion is in the wrong; this doesn't happen often but he must remember we are all fallible. I am delighted (though in no way surprised) at Brigadier Mostyn's glowing account of Lt Col Reynolds' and his Battalion's performance on active service. [In his insert, Mostyn had rated me 'Excellent' and recommended me for command of a brigade 'in due course'.] From my longer knowledge of Lt Col Reynolds I have no doubt whatsoever that he should be graded 'Outstanding'. I strongly recommend him, now, for promotion and command of an armoured, mechanized or infantry brigade.

My Divisional commander, Tony Farrar-Hockley, added in his part, 'Lt Col Reynolds is clearly an outstanding commanding officer, fitted now to command a brigade.' And the Corps commander, Lt Gen Sir Roland Gibbs, wrote:

I agree that Lt Col Reynolds possesses all the qualities of the outstanding commanding officer, and this is clearly seen by the high morale and cool proficiency of his Regiment. He has certainly enjoyed an extremely successful tenure during which his Regiment has given first class service both in Northern Ireland and over here. I strongly support the grading of 'Outstanding' and recommendations.

1973 was another tough year for me, the family and the Battalion. I had spent part of the Christmas planning my last six months in command and the Training Directive my officers and senior ranks received on their return from leave left them in no doubt as to what I expected of them. Its punch line read, 'As a result of our performance in both BAOR and Ulster our reputation stands high. If we are to maintain that reputation we must ensure that we are truly professional and beyond criticism.' I then added a questionnaire designed for commanders to see if their soldiers were properly trained. It covered every aspect from map reading, to use of radios, to driving, to drill, to NBC training and unarmed combat. It certainly gave them plenty to think about.

Thus we began a three-month intensive individual training period, interrupted only by Tony Farrar-Hockley deciding to personally carry out part of our annual Fitness for Role (FFR) inspection on 13 March. It was probably the strangest FFR ever inflicted on a unit, in that various 'teams' descended on us early in the morning and tested every element of the Battalion. For example, some mock casualties, delivered by helicopter, suddenly appeared on the golf course and my Provost staff was required to minister to them; a private soldier in the mortar platoon had to bring our six 81mm mortars into action – a job normally done by at least a sergeant; Sid Lea had to join part of C Company in a Battle Fitness Test; and the Divisional commander himself put members of A Company through weapon and map-reading tests. But strangest of all was the drill parade he ordered. When he warned me about this he said he would personally drill the Battalion. He had discovered that 2nd Queen's had not done a ceremonial parade for six years, yet he still allowed us only two rehearsals. Sid took the first and I commanded the second. After discussing matters with Sid we decided that he was likely to try to get us in a mess by giving us unusual orders like 'form hollow square' and 'present arms' from the 'order'. We, therefore, rehearsed carefully and tried to make it as amusing as possible for the soldiers. On the day itself, it became hilarious. I marched the Battalion onto the parade ground and then Farrar-Hockley took over. Sure enough he told us to 'present' from the 'order' and when, to his surprise, we did so, he yelled out 'Oh no, that's wrong! You can't 'present' from the 'order'.' Sid immediately came out with 'Permission to speak Sir?' 'No, Mr Lea, thank you.' But Sid was, and still is, a little deaf and continued to explain to Farrar-Hockley that the necessary movements were laid out in the drillbook. The soldiers were by now in fits of laughter. But more chaos was to follow. After we had, as expected, formed 'Hollow Square', Tony asked me to produce my most junior, full lieutenant. I thought for a moment and then called for 'Mr Benson', but as soon as he saw a Long Service and Good Conduct ribbon on 'Ivy's' chest, he realized that he was an ex-member of the Sergeants' Mess and demanded a Sandhurst-trained lieutenant instead. I called for poor Raymond Low who was then told to get the Battalion back into 'line'. Raymond did quite well and gave the order 'about turn' but forgot that this meant the centre company was facing the wrong way. His order 'reform line, quick march' ended in more chaos and laughter.

The next day I received the following letter from Farrar-Hockley. It ended:

My inspection showed me that a unit of high quality, such as yours, can contend simultaneously with two demanding roles. I do not fear to send you these words of praise because I have confidence that they will not cause 2nd Queen's to become complacent but, rather, reinforce their determination to seek continually high standards. My congratulations to you and all ranks.

With the FFR over we spent the usual two weeks field firing at Sennelager followed shortly afterwards by mechanized training at Soltau with 9th/12th Lancers and a squadron of the Royal Scots Dragoon Guards (Scots DG). The latter was a newly amalgamated regiment and was new to the armoured role. Little did I realize then that, within three years, the whole of the Scots DG would be under my command in Osnabrück.

As I've already mentioned, I firmly believed that the busier you keep soldiers the less trouble they will get into and the more contented they will be. To this end, on our return to barracks, I told my Rifle Companies to prepare for some unusual training. A Company was to run a flotation camp at Hameln where all their APCs were to 'swim' the river and Crispin Champion's B Company went to Todendorf 'to teach the rest of the Corps how to shoot down enemy aircraft'. The plum assignment, though, was given to Peter Barrow's C Company. It was to move to an Italian barracks in Scandicci, a suburb two kilometres from the centre of Florence, and live for seventeen days with the Italian 78th Infantry Regiment. Needless to say, I flew down to Florence to see how they were getting on. I found the Italians had done all in their power to make the visit a success, although squid for the first meal had not, in general, been well received! Training had begun the first morning with a muster parade watched in awe by the Italian soldiers. When Peter had asked the CO where the local training area was, his host had apparently looked puzzled and asked why he wanted to know – wasn't the barracks good enough? However, Peter, being a very outdoors and adventure training sort of person, insisted and eventually the Italian pointed to the nearby hills and told him to help himself. With that C Company had marched out, watched with incredulity by their hosts and cheered by scores of locals who hadn't seen a British soldier since the Second World War. During the visit most of the Company spent their off-duty hours frequenting discos and pizzerias in Florence and trying, in the main unsuccessfully, to chat up the local girls. All in all it was a very exciting and enjoyable visit, for me as well as them, particularly as I was entertained royally by the CO.

A few months before I left the Battalion, I received a letter from the Divisional Brigadier, 'Your internal recruiting and very small discharge by purchase rate are an example to us all and something to be particularly proud of. I wish I knew how you do it, but it appears that you are too busy to fit in a visit for me to find out!' I replied that it was because we were *all* busy *all* the time that we kept our soldiers. In fact, although that was true, it was also due to some excellent counselling of anyone thinking of leaving the Army, first of all by Sid Lea and then by Roger Jennings, my internal recruiting officer and Motor Transport Officer. When I moved Roger to be 2IC B Company, Brian Morris took over both jobs and played his vital part in our splendid retention rate. Both Roger and Brian went on to be Quartermasters. As already mentioned, poor Brian died of a heart attack whilst playing basketball when he was QM of the 3rd Battalion in Gibraltar, but I am still in touch with Roger.

My time as CO was now drawing rapidly to a close but, before I describe the final events, I must mention some of my officers and senior NCOs who have not yet featured in these memoirs, but who played a vital part in making 2nd Queen's, according to my Divisional and Corps commanders in private discussions with me, the best mechanized Battalion in BAOR at that time and one of the best they had ever seen. Desmond Butler who took over from Mike Hare as 2IC, Gavin Bullock, who took over A Company from Simon Boucher, Roger Pitman (Command Company), Richard Murphy (Support Company), Chris Grove (Admin Company), Mike Jelf (Recce Platoon after Graham White), and subalterns like Peter McLelland, James Myles, John Huskisson and John MacWilliam immediately come to mind, as do CSMs Fred Boyne, Ongley and Barnacle and my Provost Sergeant, Mike Rowney. The latter went on to be a major QM. Many of my officers also had very successful careers. Crispin Champion, Peter Barrow, Peter Cook, who took over from Raymond Low as IO, and David Wake all went on to command 2nd Queen's, John Davidson 1st Queen's, Gavin Bullock 3rd Queen's and Simon Boucher 5th Queen's. Raymond Low, as Chief of Staff Northern Ireland, reached the rank of brigadier; Peter McLelland commanded the London Regiment and Ian Baillie, my Signals Officer, the Queen's Divisional Depot before tragically dying in post. John MacWilliam left the Army and became a White Father in Algeria. Yes, I was very fortunate – I had a very strong team.

At the end of June the half-yearly promotion list showed me selected for the rank of colonel in 1974. However, when I received my posting order my delight turned to disappointment and anger. I had been selected to be GSOI Operations at HQ Northern Ireland – a lieutenant colonel's appointment. Before I could complain though I received a phone call from Farrar-Hockley's ADC telling me that the GOC wished to see me at once and that a helicopter was already on its way to collect me. On the way up I rehearsed what I was going to say, but on arrival I was told to sit down, shut up and listen. Tony then told me that this was merely a mark-time job and that I would soon jump the rank of full colonel and get a brigade. I replied that he couldn't be sure of this and that, if my face didn't fit in

Ulster, I might not get a brigade. He told me not to worry, but little did either of us know how close I was to being right!

David Alexander-Sinclair gave me a brilliant final Confidential Report, again grading me as Outstanding and recommending me for a brigade; so did Farrar-Hockley, Roly Gibbs, the Corps commander, and Harry Tuzo, C-in-C BAOR.

Anne and I were 'dined out' by Sid and seventy-eight members of the Sergeants' Mess and their wives; at the conclusion of the Dinner I was presented with a beautiful silver tray, decanter and glasses. This was followed on the 12th by thirty of my officers and their wives and girl-friends entertaining us to a superb farewell dinner and dance during which I received a magnificent silver salver engraved to 'Lt Col Mike Reynolds from the Officers of the Second Battalion'.

One of my final acts was to tell Sid that I was recommending him for a quartermaster's commission. He wouldn't have it though; he said that having reached the top of one tree he had no intention of starting again at the bottom of another. He would be leaving the Army. I was sad, but I'm pleased to report that his post-Army career has been a happy one.

I handed over 2nd Queen's to Mike Newall on 10 August and, on the 23rd, set off for Lisburn in Northern Ireland to take up my new appointment. I had been told that we would have to wait for a quarter there so once again I had no alternative other than to leave Anne and the girls at my parents' home in Felpham.

Chapter Nineteen
Staff Officer in Northern Ireland

I come now to the unhappiest period in my military career. I suppose it is because I was unhappy that my mind has eliminated many of my memories of that time. I can't even visualize the Officers' Mess in which I lived for nearly a month whilst we waited for a quarter.

As GSOI Operations I worked directly for the Commander Land Forces (CLF) Northern Ireland. I had known him as the brigadier in Londonderry in 1969 and readers may recall that it was he who had downgraded my 'Outstanding' Confidential Report at the end of that tour to a high 'A'. I soon detected that as CLF he was frustrated. He kept talking about 'winning', or rather 'not winning', the war against the Provisional IRA and found it hard to accept that there was little he could do to influence events. Virtually all the soldiers in Ulster were under the command of the three Brigade HQs permanently based in the Province, and nearly all the day-to-day intelligence and the resulting operations were in the hands of, and directed by, the three Brigade commanders. The only unit directly available to him was the Province Reserve, the 1st Battalion, Duke of Edinburgh's Regiment based in Ballykinlar.

The GOC Northern Ireland at that time was Lieutenant General Sir Frank King. A charming former paratrooper who had been captured at Arnhem, he was happy to leave day-to-day operations to his CLF. I didn't see a lot of him, but when I did we got on well.

My own staff officers were Major Willy Rous, Coldstream Guards, as G2 Ops, Captain Edmund Burton, a gunner, as G3 Ops and a member of the Pay Corps who was responsible for keeping the statistics. They all worked in the Ops Room which was also manned on a twenty-four-hour-a-day basis by a series of temporary watchkeepers – all young captains. Willy was a brilliant officer and rose to be a full general. Tragically he died at an early age from cancer. Edmund did extremely well too, becoming a lieutenant general.

Each morning CLF, the GSO Plans, Charles Hince, and I would be briefed by Willy on the previous twenty-four hours' activity. I used to pop back to the Ops Room several times a day, however, and have long talks with Willy and Edmund. Inevitably these were usually about the current situation.

At first my relationship with CLF was friendly, but as time went on it deteriorated until it became clear that he disliked me. Eventually the situation got so bad that I went in to see him and said it was obvious that he had little time for me and asked to be relieved of my appointment. He glared at me and said, 'No one resigns on me. No, I don't like you, but I won't get anyone any better so get out and get on with your job!' Gabrielle wrote in her diary that night, 'Pa got blown by the General. Gosh! Please God help him.'

I won't dwell on the situation in Ulster during my time there. It lurched from bad to worse and back again. However, I will mention one of the more interesting incidents. One morning I switched on the early BBC news to hear that, during the night, troops in Belfast had arrested a number of suspected terrorists. The next minute CLF was on the phone, absolutely furious, because he said they had acted prematurely. He told me to meet him in the Ops Room in half an hour's time. He became even angrier when it transpired that I knew nothing of the operation in question – nor did Willy. The only person who had known about it was the Colonel Intelligence, who controlled the 'Red Files' that contained very sensitive information. I wasn't allowed to see these files and I told the CLF that, in view of this, I accepted no responsibility for what had happened. He didn't like this at all, and when I suggested that it was about time that I *was* made privy to these files, he exploded again and said that was out of the question. As a matter of interest Charles Hince wasn't allowed to see them either.

With day-to-day operations in the hands of the three Brigades, I had little to do myself other than oversee the Ops Room and try, usually unsuccessfully, to pacify CLF. However, having found that the relationship between HQ Northern Ireland and its subordinate HQs left a lot to be desired, I decided to do something to improve matters. I therefore arranged for monthly private lunches to be attended by myself, Willy and the three Brigade Majors (Chiefs of Staff). The first was held in our Mess and subsequent ones in rotation in the Brigade Messes in Lisburn, Portadown and Londonderry. These were highly successful and soon led to a much better atmosphere.

Apart from these lunches I only remember leaving the HQ once and that was to brief members of the Northern Ireland (Political) Executive, led by Brian Faulkner, on the military situation in the Province. It took place in the very impressive Stormont Castle on the outskirts of Belfast.

Enough of the military side though: what about the other aspects of our life in Ulster? HQ Northern Ireland was located in Thiepval Barracks in the quiet town of Lisburn, just outside Belfast. The quarter I was allocated eventually was an unattractive, four-bedroomed, red-brick house, with a small garden within the barracks. It had a tiny study which apparently made it suitable for a lieutenant colonel! Neither Anne nor I can remember much about Lisburn. Anne rarely went there, doing most of her shopping at the local NAAFI. Although we had lots of quarters around us we can recall only a few of our neighbours. The Ryans lived next door to us; he was serving in the HQ of the Ulster Defence Regiment (UDR) and I was to meet him again four years later in, of all places, Toyko. Willy and Judy Rous were within walking distance and, to our surprise and delight, Tony and Pat Baxter took over a nice quarter almost opposite us across a grass-covered square. Tony had joined me in the Mess soon after I arrived whilst he too waited for a quarter.

One very memorable dinner party we went to was down in Ballykinlar with Bill Turner, CO of the Province Reserve Battalion. Since, as already mentioned, this was the only unit directly under the command of HQ Northern Ireland, I had come to know him very well. Their quarter was within the barracks and, on this particular night, after the ladies had withdrawn to leave the gentlemen with their port, we suddenly heard a series of explosions. No one moved and after a few minutes the phone went and Bill learned from his Duty Officer that the Provos had fired half a dozen mortar rounds into the camp. He asked if appropriate action was being taken and, having been assured that it was and that no casualties or damage had been caused, he reassured the ladies that all was well and we continued to pass the port.

At the beginning of May I received a call from someone in the Military Secretary's branch in the MoD telling me that I was to be promoted to the rank of brigadier and given command of 12 Mechanized Brigade in Osnabrück, Germany, at the end of the year. Tony Farrar-Hockley had been proved right – I was indeed to jump the rank of colonel.

Almost immediately after this I went back to England to lecture to the officers of Aldershot Command on the current situation in Ulster. My talk, delivered in the Officers' Club to a large audience, went well, but immediately afterwards I got a terrible pain in my lower back and slumped into a chair just off the stage. The next thing I knew I was in the Cambridge Military Hospital being told I had a kidney stone. I don't really remember much of the next few hours except being told that to avoid losing the troublesome kidney I was to try to flush it out by drinking lots of water and/or orange juice. I managed this quite easily and, as it turned out to be 'gravel' rather than a stone, I kept my kidney. However, I had another kidney attack early one morning shortly after my return to Lisburn. Anne called the doctor who again told me to drink lots of orange juice. It worked and from then on I was alright. He went on to tell me that I should drink at least two litres of water every day. When I asked if it could be *soda* water with some whiskey in it, he said yes – as long as they were 'long' whisky and sodas. I have heeded this advice ever since!

We only had one proper holiday during our time in Ulster and, for obvious reasons, decided to have it well away from the 'Troubles'. Fortunately, Bill and Rosemary Turner came to our rescue and offered their super house, The Holt, a few miles south-west of Newbury. It was a large house, with a lovely garden, tennis court and a regular home-help – Mrs Brin. We had three weeks there in late July/early August with beautiful weather and were able to have many old friends to stay, including Peter and Wha Field and their children, Alex and Di from Ottawa and theirs, and my parents. We all loved it, playing lots of tennis and popping into Newbury to the shops. We were much indebted to the Turners and were very sad to hear a couple of years later that Bill had died of cancer.

In October I flew out to Germany for a four-day recce of my new command. I stayed in our future home, Talavera House, and was thrilled at the thought of living there – it was a magnificent house. The officer I was to take over from was a cavalryman, Rennell Taylor, whom I had known when I was commanding 2nd Queen's. He was a charming person and we got on well. Sadly he also died of cancer at an early age. My visit coincided with a Divisional CPX so I saw my future HQ 'in the field', or rather in a very wet forest, as well as in barracks. In addition, I spent a fascinating day touring the Garrison.

Just before I left the HQ the CLF insisted on writing a totally unnecessary Confidential Report on me – after all I had already been selected for promotion to the rank of brigadier and to command a brigade. Nevertheless, he went ahead and in it he said he doubted that I had the imagination or drive to command a brigade. I learned later that the Military Secretary had torn it up and I always like to think that Frank King may have intervened on my behalf.

My last day in the HQ was 24 October and in my farewell interview with the CLF I told him that I was going out to Germany with the firm intention of getting an 'Outstanding' Confidential Report as a brigade commander and that I would send him a signal when I achieved this. And, as will be seen in the next Chapter, this is exactly what I did.

We left Lisburn finally on 1 November after attending several farewell parties and a big one in the Mess which Willy laid on for my brother officers. I was amazed how many turned up.

I wasn't due to take command in Osnabrück until 6 December and so we had just over a month to 'mark time' in England. We stayed for a few days with my parents in Felpham and during that time I arranged with the Housing Commandant in Brighton to take over a fully-furnished 1930s house in Hove owned by the MoD. It suited us well and we had a very happy time there.

Chapter Twenty

One Star Commander in Germany

Anne and I arrived in Osnabrück on 6 December 1974 and by the time the girls arrived for Christmas we were fully established in a colonel's quarter in the part of Osnabrück known to the British as 'Kleine Mayfair', where most of the garrison's senior officers lived. We were destined to spend a couple of months there whilst alterations and decorations were carried out in Talavera House. Following its purchase from the German authorities, we were allowed to decide on some minor structural alterations, such as incorporating the butler's pantry into the kitchen and modernizing the bathrooms and loos. Most importantly though, and with the help of an expert from the Property Services Agency, Anne was allowed to choose the internal decorations for the whole house. This she greatly enjoyed and, by the time we moved in, a rather old-fashioned, although quite attractive, house had been transformed into a really beautiful one.

Not surprisingly, everyone was very friendly to us and we were soon showered with invitations to drinks and dinner parties. We were surrounded by most of my HQ staff and most of the unit COs. James Percival, Cheshire Regiment, was my first Brigade Major, but he had stayed on only to see me in until his successor, Mike Regan, arrived on 12 January. My DAA & QMG (Chief of Staff Administration) was Brian Harding, a charming and highly efficient Gunner. My Station Staff Officer was a retired Green Howard, Lieutenant Colonel John Bottomley, and his assistant was a retired major, Leo Tanner. Jimmy Knight, ex-SOE in the war, was my Services Liaison Officer (SLO), responsible for relations with the Germans. They had very nice wives, as indeed did all my staff officers. Brian, Jimmy, John and Leo were to be very important to me for I soon discovered that I was not only commanding 12 Mechanized Brigade but also the largest British Garrison in the world with, including wives and children, some 12,000 souls.

Soon after my arrival I paid a courtesy visit to my Divisional commander, Major General Desmond Mangham whom I had known in Cyprus when we were both staff officers in Episkopi. He gave me a very warm welcome during which he mentioned that he knew about my problems with the CLF in Northern Ireland. 'Don't even think about it Mike – that's all in the past and I'm sure your tour in Twelve Brigade and the Second Division will be a very happy and successful one.' Fortunately, he was right.

Our move into Talavera House (41 Lürmannstrasse) went well and it was a joy to be able to spread ourselves out and enjoy its space and luxury. Situated on a small hill, the Westerberg, and within walking distance of the city centre, Die Sonne Haus (the Sun House), had an interesting history. It had been built in 1936 by a wealthy and prominent Nazi – indeed, a foundation stone, complete with Swastika, lay just below our dining-room window. The city had been badly damaged by Allied bombing during the later stages of the war but, after it was captured by 1 British Commando Brigade in April 1945 – fortunately with only thirty-three British and about fifty German casualties – Die Sonne Haus had been repaired quickly and used as an Interrogation Centre, then as a British Officers' Mess and, finally, as the residence for the Brigade and Garrison commander.

Talavera had large drawing and dining rooms, six bedrooms, a garden room/study leading out into a large, walled garden with two lawns, lovely trees, beautiful flowerbeds, surrounded by box hedges, a small swimming pool and even a pergola large enough to take a military band. A full-time former Yugoslavian gardener, Giorg, tended to all of this.

The Regiment had provided me with a splendid house corporal, Lance Corporal King, who set up home in one of our heated cellars, complete with bathroom and loo, but our cook, Lance Corporal Davison, my full-time staff car driver, Corporal Norton, and Agnes, our German full-time housekeeper, all being married, lived out. We were very spoiled.

My HQ, with a total strength of thirty, was located in Quebec Barracks, alongside the 1st Battalion, The Staffordshire Regiment. The officers of the HQ shared a Mess with those of the Brigade Signals Squadron. Mike Regan, my new BM, was a Light Infantryman and we hit it off from the moment we met. His charming wife, Victoria, and Anne also soon became really good friends.

I realized very quickly that I had a good set-up with an excellent staff. On the personal side I had Betty as a PA. She was a formidable lady. My office was at the end of the HQ building and she guarded me like a prisoner: even the BM, who had to pass through her office to get to me, was sometimes asked why he wanted to see me. She was very efficient, though, and we all liked her. Under Mike there were four G staff officers – John Armstrong, Peter Crocker, Andy Styles – all infantrymen – and

Peter Clark (RAF), my Forward Air Controller. Under Brian Harding on the AQ side, were Howard Holroyd, later succeeded by Graham (Blossom) White of Queen's Surreys and Bahrain days, but now Military Police due to knee problems, Murray Wildman REME, later succeeded by Albert Smetham RCT, and my Brigade Electrical and Mechanical Engineer, Hamish Harvey. Brian Harding handed over to Christopher Hammerbeck, Royal Tank Regiment, halfway through my command in January 1976. I also had four Protestant padres and one RC – Hugh Martin. Heading the clerical staff was Conductor (senior to a WOI) George Bartle RAOC, now sadly dead. Then, in my Brigade HQ and Signals Squadron, I had Tony Willcox as OC; he handed over after about a year to Bill Robins, and under them were John Chambers, Mervyn Lee, Craig McColville and Ian Brown, with Jimmy Akehurst as the RSM. All those mentioned were very high quality officers. Regan, Wildman and Robins became major generals while Harding, Hammerbeck, Willcox and Lee reached brigadier rank. And, as far as I am aware, most, if not all, of my HQ staff went on to successful civilian careers. Amazingly, many of us have met and still meet, initially bi-annually and now annually, for a reunion. The only rule is that you must have served under Reynolds in Osnabrück. These reunions were started by George Bartle, who organized two overnight reunions in the UK, continued by Brian Harding in Antwerp, then by me in the Ardennes and Brussels and, finally, today by Mike Regan who currently arranges a splendid lunch in Pimlico. What better indication could there be of the superb camaraderie we enjoyed during those two happy years in Osnabrück? Once again I had a very strong team.

I have to say that my working hours, and indeed those of my staff officers, were very relaxed – except when we were on exercise. I never arrived in the office before 9 a.m., went home for lunch, except when Anne was having an all-ladies lunch party, and always got home by 4.30; indeed I often took the afternoon off.

What units did I have under me in 12 Mechanized Brigade? First of all I should explain that it was the only *mechanized* brigade in I British Corps – the other five brigades were armoured. As such, I had the following combat units: one armoured regiment, the Royal Scots Dragoon Guards (Scots DG); three mechanized infantry battalions, the Staffords, Queen's Own Highlanders (QO Hldrs), later replaced by the Devon and Dorsets (D & D), and the Argyll and Sutherland Highlanders (Argylls), all located in Osnabrück. In support was a self-propelled artillery regiment, 40th Field, located with the RAF fifty kilometres away in Gutersloh, and an engineer regiment, 25th Engineers, located in Osnabrück. Administrative units supporting my Brigade were the 12th Ordnance Field Park, (RAOC),

12th Field Workshops (REME), 659 Squadron Army Air Corps, 15 Squadron RCT, 7th Field Ambulance RAMC and 12 Royal Military Police Company, again all located in Osnabrück. And one of the most satisfying things was that all my units were up to strength. The Brigade was therefore an all-arms force of some 5,000 men – ideally structured for its wartime role.

I've already mentioned that, in 1975, Osnabrück was the largest British Garrison in the world. In addition to my Brigade, the following units were also located within the city: 23rd Engineer Regiment alongside 25th Engineers, 2nd Armoured Division Workshops, 35 Army Education Centre, two Medical Reception Centres, the 2nd Division Postal and Courier Unit, a Pioneer and Civil Labour Unit which administered the civilians employed by the Army within the Garrison, and 629 Mobile Civilian Transport Group (MCTG) which ran all the buses, ambulances and heavy transport vehicles and was manned mainly by Yugoslavs – many of them former prisoners of war.

I cannot remember, and have been unable to find out, exactly how many wives and children we had in the Garrison, but there were a lot! Nor can I be sure how many married quarters there were, but there were certainly eight housing estates, each with its own retired warrant officer warden, with a small staff including a full-time SSAFA sister to help him. Completing the Garrison there were three Primary and one Secondary schools, three NAAFI shops, a Garrison Library and, as well as British (SKC) cinemas in all the larger barracks, a central SKC cinema. There was no British television in Germany at this time, only very boring German programmes, so the SKC cinemas were very popular with all ranks.

It was clear from the beginning that I would have to divide my time more or less equally between the Brigade and the Garrison. I also decided to make a considerable effort in improving Anglo/German relations. Although the local population, especially the shopkeepers, bar and night-club owners, welcomed the money we brought in, it was inevitable that, with so many troops in one town, there would be frequent incidents that could possibly, and sometimes did, damage good relations.

My initial visits to the major units in the Brigade began soon after my arrival. I started with the Scots DG and was a little surprised to discover that virtually all the officers were away skiing – typically cavalry! The CO, Stephen Stopford, was a charming, highly intelligent officer who controlled his Regiment well and went on to become a major general. Angus Fairrie, CO Queen's Own Highlanders, was very different. He was painfully formal and, as his 2IC told me later, 'While you were trying to move the Battalion into the twentieth century, he was dragging it, kicking and screaming, back into the eighteenth!' He loved ceremonial and, when I inspected the Battalion as part of their FFR assessment in April 1975, they put on a spectacular parade in full dress, with band, pipes and drums and all their APCs in perfect condition surrounding the parade ground. And, to be fair to Angus, his Battalion had very high morale. When I handed him his Confidential Report when he and his Battalion left Osnabrück later that year, I told him that I had been unable to recommend him for command of a brigade. He smiled and said, 'That's the last thing I want Brigadier, I'm going to be the Regimental Secretary.'

The Argylls also put on a spectacular parade in the August of my first year but went one better and paraded their regimental mascot, a Shetland pony. Their CO, Alistair Scott-Elliot, was a much more retiring officer but controlled his Battalion well and knew his job. The first time I visited them I was astounded to be asked by their QM whether I recognized him. When I said, 'No, why?' he replied, 'Well Sir, I recognize you – we were together as privates at Fort George in 1948 and so was the QM of the Queen's Own Highlanders!' It was a quite amazing coincidence. I should perhaps add that my Highlanders were a very tough lot and I would have been delighted to have them with me in war.

The Staffords, under Malcolm Maclarney, and then, for my last three months, Mike Hague, were the most highly trained of the three mechanized battalions. Malcolm would certainly have reached one-star rank and probably two, but he left the Army and moved to his wife's home country, Norway.

Graham Owens commanded 25th Engineer Regiment. A strong character and an excellent engineer, he could be a little tactless at times. During a formal visit of the Quartermaster General (QMG) we found, as well as all his regimental transport on the square, piles of engineer equipment surrounding it. When the General asked why, Graham pointed out that he didn't have enough transport to carry it! He went one further. When we went to the Mess for lunch we were offered drinks by a waiter wearing combat kit. The QMG looked surprised and was clearly very irritated when Graham complained that not all his men had Number 2 dress and so the waiter had nothing else to wear.

Readers will recall that I had wanted to become a helicopter pilot way back in the mid-50s, but that David Lloyd-Owen had told me that I should be the VIP and not the driver. Well now I *was* the VIP. There were six Scouts and six Sioux in 659 Squadron and I made it very clear to the OC, John Everitt, that I intended to make use of them myself on a very regular basis. In fact I used them so often – to visit units, other HQs and on recces and on exercises – that he issued me with my own flying helmet and flying gloves.

Another important officer I should mention was Lieutenant Colonel Pat Thoresby who, as well as commanding my Field Ambulance unit, was my Senior Medical Officer; as such his advice was very important to me. He wasn't the smartest officer – beret usually on the back of his head and the first time I inspected his unit he saluted from the roof of an armoured ambulance, jumped down and promptly fell flat on his face!

My priorities with regard to the Brigade were to ensure that it was well trained for its wartime role and that our wartime General Deployment Plans (GDP) were thoroughly sound and understood – at least by all the senior ranks. To this end I quickly issued training directives on how battle-groups and combat teams should be structured for specific tasks and how infantry should, and should not, be used. I learned later that these made a considerable impression on my COs and company commanders. One of the Queen's Own Highlanders' company commanders later became an instructor at the Staff College and wrote to me asking for copies of my directives.

The next thing I did was to tell Mike Regan that I wanted a testing CPX to get us ready for the Divisional CPXs which were due – one in March and two more in June, and a Corps one, SUMMER SALES, in early July. My own CPX involved our Brigade HQ and those of most of my major units. I also made it clear that, unlike the past when the Brigade and unit HQs had always deployed into woods, we would in future deploy, as indeed we would in war, into barns and buildings. This edict was greeted with delight by everyone. Amazingly, although money was available to pay German owners for the use of their buildings and for any damage done, few HQs in BAOR at that time used these facilities. One of my favourite locations was a castle near Bodenburg which I first used during Exercise SUMMER SALES in 1975. It was near our GDP positions and the owner was delighted to have us there and often invited me in for drinks.

The absence of units in Ulster was disruptive to our mechanized training cycle, but the situation demanded that all my major units spend four months there at least once in every two years. Internal security training before deployment meant they spent another two months away from their BAOR role. Fortunately, I was able to visit all of them in Ulster. On the subject of visiting units outside BAOR, I should add that, in September 1975, I had a marvellous eight days with the Scots DG on the Suffield training area in Alberta, Canada. Apart from glorious weather, having a game of golf and enjoying Calgary, I followed them closely on their last major exercise and didn't hold back with my criticisms. Of course, as cavalrymen they didn't like being corrected by an infantryman but they accepted my points gracefully.

One of my biggest innovations during my Osnabrück tour was the introduction of a battlefield tour. I told my staff that the annual Brigade Study Day, as carried out by all brigades in BAOR, was abolished and that in April 1975 Peter Crocker, Andy Styles and Murray Wildman would conduct forty officers of the Brigade on a tour following the exploits of *Kampfgruppe* Peiper – the same battlefield tour I had made my officers and sergeants do when I was commanding 2nd Queen's. Crocker christened it Exercise PIED PEIPER and it was a huge success. The 2nd Divisional Public Relations team carried an account of the tour in the Divisional newspaper. It ended: 'The fact that three weeks later the actions of Battlegroup Peiper are still being hotly debated in the Officers' messes throughout Osnabrück is a powerful indication of the success of the venture. Everyone is asking: "When is the next 12 Mech Bde Study period?"' Indeed it was so enjoyable and instructive that I repeated the tour in May 1976, for another forty officers, with equal success.

My interest in the Battle of the Bulge naturally increased with each PIED PEIPER tour and in June 1976 I was fortunate in being able to join a two-day NORTHAG Terrain Study Period in the Ardennes. It was well organized and I was thrilled, not only to hear about and discuss the events of 1944 with several senior commanders who had taken part in the fighting, but also to have dinner with them. Amongst the most interesting were Hasso von Manteuffel, Commander of Fifth Panzer Army, Brigadier General Bruce Clarke, Commander Combat Command B of the US 7th Armored Division, and Major William Desobry, Commander of one of the US 9th Armored Division's teams defending Bastogne. I still have the menu card with their autographs – not surprisingly, as the tour was organized by a Brit, Major General Mike Walsh, we dined on Boeuf Wellington.

With regard to our GDP, Mike Regan and I recce'd the whole Brigade position east of the Sibbesse Gap, only a few kilometres from the Inner German Border and blocking one of the main routes for an advancing Red Army. Then, with my COs, we sited every minefield, battlegroup, combat team and artillery gun position together with their alternative positions. We pretended we were on TEWTs when doing this, but I have little doubt that Soviet agents were monitoring us. Many years later, after the collapse of the Soviet Union, I was able to visit the former East Germany and drive towards and through what had been my Brigade position. I was delighted to find that we would have presented the Soviets with a major problem, providing that we had reached our positions in time, had been given time to prepare them and had been supplied with sufficient ammunition. Taking into account what happened in the first Iraq war when we had to buy artillery ammunition from the Belgians, the latter point is open to question. I have to say that my time wargaming at West Byfleet came in very useful when siting these positions.

Turning now to Garrison affairs and Anglo/German relations, I was determined to improve both and the introduction of a new-style Garrison magazine proved a major step in achieving this. Brian Harding came up with its title, *Gateway*. In the first edition I wrote:

> When I arrived last December I thought that one of the ways in which life might be improved would be to have a magazine which was more representative of Garrison activities and which might also indicate some of the opportunities open to us while serving in this part of Germany. Why *Gateway*? We have chosen the name because we thought the Waterloo Gate [Heger Tor – main gate into the original town] represents not only the historical link between the British Army and Osnabrück but might also perhaps suggest that there was more to Garrison life than there is within the four walls of your own quarter, barrack block or even your own particular unit.

It was an immediate success and soon had an unofficial name within my staff –*Reynolds News* – after an old UK Sunday newspaper of 1850 to 1967. As well as allowing local shops and businesses to advertise – which paid for the costs of the magazine – units were able to report their achievements and we were able to let everyone know when and where the many Garrison facilities were available and what was happening in the town in the way of sport, exhibitions, concerts, dances and so on. It proved a very useful tool.

I devoted a considerable amount of time to Garrison matters. Without going into all the details, during my time there we saw many of the barracks renovated and with improved heating systems and, during my first year, enough new married quarters were built to end the waiting list – indeed, a soldier could even be allocated a married quarter before going home to get married. And during the second year, Anne opened a superb new Middle school, named Derby, to record the fact that Osnabrück was 'twinned' with that English town; we saw the size of the classes in our junior schools reduced and we opened a new families' medical centre, a new families' dental centre and a large community facility in the largest quarters area.

I was very lucky in having Jimmy Knight as my Liaison Officer with the Germans. He knew all the important people and his enthusiasm was infectious. The fact that I had learned German at Cranleigh and Sandhurst was a great help and, although I was far from fluent, my pronunciation was good which helped, not just in conversations, but also when I had to make speeches. Soon after arrival I visited the Oberbürgermeister and the Oberstadtdirektor and we were soon on excellent terms. I also made a tour of the local area, paying formal calls on the Bürgermeisters of the surrounding towns of Bad Rothenfelde, Melle and Georgsmarienhütte.

Three of the highlights of our Anglo/German relations were our annual Massed Bands' concerts, Queen's Birthday parties and the affiliation of 12 Mechanized Brigade with 32 Panzer Grenadier Brigade. The annual Massed Bands' concerts in the Bremer Brücke Stadium were to celebrate the Queen's Birthday. This was a regular fixture long before I arrived, but I decided to expand it and make a very important change – instead of free entry to the stadium we would make a small charge. I was a firm believer that if you make a German pay for something he will value it more – and so it proved. And my decision to divide the proceeds between the British and German Red Cross and SSAFA inevitably proved very popular. The Germans were particularly fascinated by the bagpipes and kilts and in both years we had capacity audiences.

Also in June each year we put on a large party in the garden of Talavera House to celebrate the Queen's Birthday. There were some 100 guests, including the most important Germans in the area, my COs and my own HQ staff. As well as a Regimental band playing on the pergola, we put on magnificent displays of silver from each of our Regiments on stands around the main lawn. The parties were hugely successful.

Before leaving the subject of Anglo/German relations I should mention one near disaster which fortunately turned out well in the end. British children set fire to the local German church in Belm, an area where we had a lot of married quarters. The damage was considerable and, although the building was insured, I decided to make a voluntary appeal throughout the Garrison to raise money for some of the repairs. It was highly successful, raising DM 14,657 (£3,000 today). In his thank-you letter the Bishop of Osnabrück wrote:

> I would like to assure you that the incident should not be detrimentally ascribed to the children just because they are British children – German children too are no angels. In your endeavour to make good the damage I see a sign of integration with the German Catholics who live in Belm. Thus, out of a tragic incident, something positive has grown.

My efforts at improving relations with the people of our host city were rewarded dramatically by my election to be a 'Schinken Senator' (ham senator!) of the Pumpernickel Garde. *Gateway* described it thus:

The Pumpernickel Garde is dedicated to the cause of a happy Osnabrück. The 'Rats', seated at the High Table and resplendent in crimson dinner jackets, presided over the ceremonies. Red- and white-clad pipers opened the proceedings followed by a procession of musicians and members of the rival Carnival Society, the Green and White Garde. A second procession then formed up behind the Band and Drums of the 1st Battalion, The Staffordshire Regiment, immaculately turned out in No. 1 Dress and spiked helmets. Brigadier Reynolds, escorted by his German sponsors and the SLO, Mr Jimmy Knight, then marched to the rostrum [in front of 650 people] to the sound of 'Colonel Bogey'. There he was welcomed by a former Lord Mayor of Osnabrück, who presented him with the traditional gold-embroidered 'Cap of Fools' in blue, white and scarlet worn by the Ham Senators and with a silver medallion showing the Osnabrück Rathaus. In the speech of welcome it was mentioned that Brigadier Reynolds is the first Englishman to be appointed to the Order. The Brigade Commander responded in fluent German as follows: 'Tonight you bestow on me and my soldiers a great honour . . . I feel particularly honoured to join such an illustrious band of merry gentlemen. A merry Osnabrück is very dear to my heart for the 12,000 British who share your lovely town are indeed Osnabrückers – we share your Gasthauses, theatres, restaurants, shops and TV, your parties and your history – we even share, on a strictly competitive basis, your pretty girls! I trust and hope that you will always think of us, not for our occasional indiscretions, but for our friendliness and cooperation in making Osnabrück a happy place for everyone to live in.' The enthusiastic applause which greeted the Brigadier's speech left no doubt as to the warmth of his welcome and he and Mrs Reynolds clearly found the remainder of the evening, which was enlivened by four bands, a comedian and an attractive girl singer, a riot!

As well as entertaining all my unit commanders, officers from Divisional HQ and my own HQ officers and their wives in Talavera, we had other rather unexpected guests. One was David Steele, Moderator of the Church of Scotland, and his wife; not altogether surprising I suppose, considering that I had three Scottish regiments in my Brigade. Anne was a bit worried when he asked her if she would mind ironing his jabot and lace cuffs for a dinner party we gave for them – especially when she was told by his wife that they were especially made for the Moderator by ladies in India. She also told us that he wore ladies' black tights under his breeches!

Our excellent house staff at Talavera made entertaining reasonably easy. They were all good workers. Agnes was a delightful person and even invited us to her son's wedding and her own wedding anniversary party. Corporal Davison was a first-class cook and one of our German neighbours told us she thought Corporal King was the best waiter she had ever encountered. He was certainly a good House Corporal, but he was a bit of a rogue too. One night when he was off duty the doorbell rang and, despite me telling her not to, Anne opened the front door. Standing there, dripping wet in the rain, was a young English girl. She asked for Corporal King. Again against my advice, Anne invited her in and, to our amazement, she told us she was madly in love with him and, until a couple of nights before, when he had thrown her out, had been spending the nights in his room in our cellar. 'I don't know why I love him,' she went on, 'he's always got a bloody cold!' We advised her to return to England as soon as possible, which she did. Corporal King received the very sharp edge of my tongue.

Amongst our many guests in Talavera were Peter and Wha Field. He was commanding 1 PARA in Berlin during our time in Osnäbruck and they came to stay at the end of 1975. We had five wonderful days with them on a return visit in April 1976. I was most impressed by the fact that Peter seemed to know the name of every one of his soldiers and it was obvious his Battalion had very high morale. Berlin was fascinating as usual and, as well as a boat ride on the Havel, we toured the Soviet, French and American zones and 'did' the shops on the Kurfürstendamm, the city's smartest shopping street. One memorable event was a visit to the Russian ballet in the Soviet zone. Fortunately for me, who likes ballet music but not the dancing, there were not enough tickets for all of us, so I volunteered to stay behind. I didn't really want to dress up in the required Mess Kit anyway. While the rest went off to find it wasn't *Swan Lake* anyway, but something much less exciting, I went to the Berlin Philharmonic Hall and was lucky enough to get a returned ticket to see Herbert von Karajan conduct the Philharmonic in a superb concert. The final highlight of our visit was the Berlin Tattoo with the massed bands of the Parachute Regiment and a Sioux helicopter actually flying into and around the Deutsche Halle.

Other friends we were delighted to see again in Germany were Tony and Pat Baxter. He came out to our Divisional HQ at Lubbecke as Colonel AQ early in our tour and, as well as seeing quite a lot of him on Divisional exercises and at conferences, we entertained each other in our homes two or three times during our more or less concurrent tours.

In May 1975 Anne and I grabbed a quick week's holiday on our own in our old haunt of Lerici and then in the July we had our last holiday with all three girls. My first BM, James Percival, owned a very nice house in Javea, a Spanish coastal resort roughly halfway between Valencia and Alicante and he had offered it to us at a very reasonable rent. It took us two days to drive down there, which was far from pleasant, but once we got there the girls were thrilled with the setting and the weather. Not quite so with us though, because the villa was within noise range of a nightclub – in fact it was on an estate of villas owned mainly by Brits and we had to drive inland for several miles to see any Spaniards at all. Even so, we had a good three weeks and arrived back at Talavera with nice suntans. Talking of driving reminds me that in the November of that year I bought a very smart green Volvo 144. It cost me £2,860 – £17,900 today.

Just a word now about our girls. Vicky had been anxious to leave St Mary's as soon as she could after passing her basic O-levels and didn't want to go on to university. There was no such thing as a 'Gap Year' at that time. Nevertheless, we insisted that she did a year's residential course at a Secretarial College in Sussex called Fryerning. She then joined us in Osnäbruck and, with the help of Brian Harding, I got her a job as secretary to the officer running the 2nd Division Officers' Study Centre. This was located in the town and, as every young officer in the 2nd Division had to attend courses there, she had the pick of the young officers of my Brigade and indeed of 4 Guards Armoured Brigade in nearby Münster. Gabrielle followed her example and, after she graduated from Fryerning in mid-1975, I was able to fix her up with a job as PA to the CO of the Staffords. Thus she, too, was able to join in the fun. It didn't take her long – in October 1975 she spotted Austen Ramsden of the Scots DG and from then on the poor chap was a marked man. We didn't meet Vicky's future husband until June 1976. That summer Anne, Gabrielle and I had enjoyed a marvellous holiday in Porto Ercole in Italy, but Vicky had stayed behind and when I entered the kitchen to get a cold drink after the long, hot drive home I was confronted by a man dressed as Dracula with a beer in his hand. When I said, 'Who the hell are you and what are you doing in my house?' he nearly dropped the beer and stammered, 'Corin Pearce Sir, First Royal Anglian!' It turned out he and Vicky were off to a fancy-dress ball in one of the Messes. Despite the fun she was having in Osnabrück, by the end of the summer of 1976 Vicky wanted the London 'scene' and, with the help of my BM's wife, she got a job with the interior designer Charles Hammond in Chelsea. Poor Debs was still at school during our time in Talavera but she enjoyed all her holidays.

A word now about our financial affairs at that time. My _net_ pay was £8,885 (£55,500 today) and our total cost of living – rent, heat & light, food and drink – was about £425 a week at today's prices. We paid, duty-free, at today's prices: £2 for a gallon of petrol; 80p for 20 Rothmans;

£18 for a bottle of Moet champagne, £8 for whisky, and 65p for a bottle of Amstel beer. We lived well!

I've already mentioned that in June 1976 we had another marvellous holiday in Porto Ercole with Gabrielle. On this occasion we rented a lovely house in a tiny piazza right in the middle of the town. It belonged to a lady we had met on the beach in the same resort three years before. Once again the weather was perfect and our time there led to a major change in Gabrielle's life. Another house in the piazza had a parrot that shouted 'Hullo', or something not so polite, at us every time we came home. After a week of this I shouted back, 'Shut up you damn parrot' and this was answered by a female American voice that exclaimed, 'You shouldn't shout at my parrot – come and have a drink!' The owner of the voice turned out to be a wealthy American lady and we quickly became friends. This led to her recommending Gabrielle to an American couple as a 'companion' to their youngest daughter. They were immensely wealthy, having an apartment in Rome, a house and estate near Florence and another apartment in the smartest part of New York. They also owned the largest yacht in the Lloyd's register; it was based in Porto Ercole. This recommendation led to a fantastic change of life style for Gabrielle; it started on 10 November 1976 when she left us to join the family in Rome. Little did we realize that, within a few years, it would change Debbie's life too.

Another holiday we greatly enjoyed, this time with Debs, was in Oberammergau. I had done a short course at the NATO NBC School (what a place to site a Nuclear, Biological and Chemical School!) there in January 1976 and had discovered that the VIP apartments could be rented very cheaply for short holidays. I didn't hesitate and, in late July, we had a very happy ten days there and were able to show Debs 'Mad' King Ludwig's castles and the glorious Bavarian countryside.

Mention of NBC reminds me that sometime in late 1976 I was asked to give a presentation at the NBC School in Wiltshire on the 'Realities of NBC training in BAOR'. My visit there coincided with a Guest Night and as the CLF from my time in HQ Northern Ireland – now a lieutenant general and the Director of Military Operations (DMO) – was a guest, the Commandant, a Queen's colonel, asked me to 'hold his hand' when the DMO arrived – he knew the latter's reputation and that I had worked for him. By now the DMO knew that I was a very successful Brigade commander and, needless to say, he greeted me with an outstretched hand and 'My *dear* Mike, how *marvellous* to see you again!' Fortunately, it was the last time we ever met.

1976 saw big changes in both BAOR and Osnabrück. First of all we had a new GOC in 2nd Division. Desmond Mangham was succeeded by Frank

Kitson whom I had known briefly as my Brigade commander in Belfast in 1971. Fortunately, despite his idiosyncrasies, I got on very well with him.

The big change in 1976, however, was a restructuring of I British Corps, which saw the abolition of the existing armoured and mechanized brigades. I wrote in the September 1976 edition of *Gateway*:

> On 1st September HQ 12 Mechanized Brigade and Osnabrück Garrison will change its name to HQ 5th Field Force and Osnabrück Garrison. This new title is only an interim measure and on 1st December two separate HQs will be established in Osnabrück. One HQ will be called HQ Osnabrück Garrison and the Garrison Commander, who will also be a Deputy Commander of the new 2nd Armoured Division, will continue to live in Talavera House. The second HQ will be called HQ 5th Field Force and will be located in the present Brigade HQ. 5th Field Force, which will be an air-portable formation, will have units located in Osnabrück and Münster and it will be commanded by a brigadier. Brigadier M. F. Reynolds becomes the first Commander of 5th Field Force and will continue to command Osnabrück Garrison. In December Brigadier Reynolds will be succeeded by two brigadiers – Brigadier J. Hopkinson will become the new Garrison Commander and Deputy Commander 2nd Armoured Division, and Brigadier R. Pascoe will command the 5th Field Force.

As one of the two Deputy Commanders of the 2nd Armoured Division, I was the designated Commander of Task Force (TF) Delta. This was basically a small brigade of variable size. The other Deputy Divisional Commander and commander of the other Task Force in the Division, TF Charlie, was Brigadier Desmond Langley, who had commanded 4 Guards Armoured Brigade in nearby Münster. He was a former Life Guards officer and a great character.

I won't bore the reader with the details of this restructuring except to add that the 5th Field Force (5FF) was responsible for Rear Area security. It later comprised 7th Regiment Royal Horse Artillery, 2 RTR, the Irish Guards, Staffords, 3 PARA and the necessary supporting units. Another officer claims he was the first commander of this Force but he wasn't. I quote from a letter from the Adjutant General, Sir 'Monkey' Blacker, dated 18 September 1975, following his visit to Osnabrück. Amongst other very complimentary things he wrote, 'I was glad to see how much you yourself were enjoying life – always a good thing'. He ended, 'My best wishes to you when you become the first commander of the 5th Field Force.'

With the approach of the end of the two Brigades of the 2nd Division – my own 12 Mechanized and Desmond Langley's 4 Guards – our thoughts turned to final parades. Desmond set the pace by putting on a spectacular formal parade with himself and all his staff officers mounted. The Major General London District took the salute and as Desmond handed the pennant of his Brigade to him for 'safekeeping until the Brigade is reformed', his horse farted and dumped a large pile of manure on the parade ground. Desmond, who had a great sense of humour, started chuckling as it did so and ended up roaring with laughter. So did all the spectators. When we got back to Osnabrück I decided that there was no way we could follow that and we would content ourselves with a lavish cocktail party. Everyone was very relieved when they heard of my decision and the party, to which we invited all the officers of 12 Brigade and all the important people in I British Corps, was a huge success.

From the beginning of September my life became extremely busy and quite complicated. Apart from my continuing Garrison responsibilities, I had to create and exercise HQ TF Delta, oversee the amalgamation of 23rd and 25th Engineer Regiments into a new Divisional Engineer Regiment, lose my Army Air Corps Squadron to a new Divisional Regiment, see my precious HQ and Signals Squadron, now under Bill Robins, split between 5FF and TF Delta, and set up the new Garrison HQ. To help me in these tasks I had two staffs – my old Brigade HQ staff under Mike Regan and a new 5FF staff of initially just three officers, Peter Irby and Willie McNair under Brian Elliot, its Chief of Staff. The gutting of an old school annex and the creation of the new Garrison HQ was overseen by my Brigade Chief Clerk, George Bartle, supervised by Mike Regan and approved by myself without any serious problems.

Part of the reason for the general restructuring of I Corps was to make the major HQs more 'lightweight'. They were to operate in tents rather than heavy vehicles. Fortunately, my TF Delta HQ was unaffected as we kept our APCs, but the overall requirement led to a most amusing incident involving me and Frank Kitson during an early CPX. General Al Hague, the American SACEUR, was due to visit TF Delta and Frank had felt it necessary to be present. Just before his arrival, however, we received an NBC warning and everyone had to don their NBC suits and respirators. Frank's ADC handed him his suit but it was a brand new one in a plastic bag with its interior coated with charcoal. When the all clear was sounded and Frank took off his suit he looked like an old-fashioned chimney sweep with his head and face covered in charcoal. The rest of us were alright because we knew the form and always wore old suits which had lost their charcoal. 'What am I going to do?' cried Frank, 'I can't meet

SACEUR looking like this!' 'Let me take you to my caravan General,' I said, 'You can have a shower there.' My caravan was a converted 4-ton lorry, complete with bed, shower, desk and chairs. All senior commanders had been equipped with such vehicles before the restructuring. 'What do you mean? You're not meant to have a caravan anymore. You're meant to be on light scales!' 'Well I've kept it Sir.' 'Well thank you – but for goodness sake, keep it out of sight, we don't want the Corps Commander seeing it!' After SACEUR's visit, which was a great success, I pointed out to Frank that I wasn't going to waste my Signallers' time by asking them to put up and take down a tent for me every time we moved, which was at least once every twenty-four hours. With my caravan I had only the driver and Corporal King looking after me. He took my point.

In late October my TF Delta took part in its first major exercises – KEYSTONE and SPEARPOINT 76. They lasted almost three weeks and went very well. Frank Kitson wrote on my last report:

> Brig Reynolds has been a very successful Brigade Commander and has skilfully pioneered the new role of Task Force Commander. He has got a great deal of tactical experience and thoroughly understands the function of all component parts of the Division. He is a practical man whose eye for ground and feel for time complements his theoretical knowledge.

During SPEARPOINT I had 2 RTR, the Staffords, the Cheshires (based in Münster) and 40th Field Regiment under my command. The CO of 2 RTR wrote afterwards:

> Thank you for the fun that all of us in the 2nd RTR Battle Group had on KEYSTONE and SPEARPOINT. I like to think that we did not forget professional matters but the fact that you took the lead that we should all enjoy it made the whole thing worthwhile. We were all delighted to be under your command.

And David Quayle of 40th Field wrote:

> It was a privilege to do my first BAOR exercise with a Commander and staff who so clearly knew what they wanted and how to achieve it. . . . A special word for your excellent Mess and the care with which I was always found the most comfortable accommodation.

On 25 November I was dined out by the WOs and Sergeants of my 12 Mechanized Brigade Signal Squadron. It was a superb occasion organised by the RSM, Jimmy Akehurst, with everyone in Mess Kit. I was reminded of the climax to the evening in a recent e-mail from Jimmy:

If you remember we organized a horse for you to ride out of Quebec Barracks on. To my surprise two horses appeared, one for you and of course the second for me. Having never ridden before, it only took a cigar to the rear end of my horse to set me up for what can only be described as a very basic back flip to land in the Sgts' Mess flower bed. Happy days!'

To this I replied:

If you remember, my horse got a cigarette up his rear end as well, but fortunately I could ride! Just as well as I only just managed to pull him up before the metal barrier outside the guardroom at the exit/entrance to Quebec barracks – otherwise he'd have tried to jump it, which on a concrete surface could have been a bit hairy!

I am not sure when, but sometime in November I received my next posting order. I was to be a student for a full year at the Royal College of Defence Studies (RCDS) in Belgrave Square, London. All the British students were colonels or brigadiers and it was therefore known as the 'School for Generals'. Anne and I were thrilled.

On 12 December I said a sad goodbye to my wonderful staff and the following day, after another sad farewell to Corporals King, Davidson and Norton, and Agnes and Giorg, Anne and I left Osnabrück. It had been a wonderful and very successful two years. Frank Kitson gave me an 'Excellent' final report and Dick Worsley, the Corps Commander whom I had come to know well, upgraded it to 'Outstanding'. And so I was able to send the promised signal to the DMO!

As a sad after-note to this chapter I must add that, in late 2008, I was able to make contact with the last Housing Superintendent in Osnabrück – a lady. She told me that there were no longer any British soldiers based there and that all the married quarters and most of the barracks had already been handed over to the Germans. They were all standing empty. The last one was due for handover in April 2009. I suppose that, with the collapse of the Soviet Union and the increase in global terrorism, major reductions in the number of troops in BAOR were inevitable, but no one could have foreseen this in 1976.

Chapter Twenty-one

Royal College of Defence Studies, London

We arrived back in England on 14 December 1976 and, once again, faced the problem of finding somewhere to live. I had been told that there were no quarters reserved for RCDS students and the only ones available in or near London were small flats in places like Putney or Kingston-on-Thames. Therefore, we decided to look outside the capital and settled for a Territorial Army (TA) quarter in Eastbourne, very close to Anne's mother and sister.

The house was one of four quarters built for the TA in the 1960s and was in the nice, western part of Eastbourne, near the 'Old Town', the 'Royal' Golf Course and just below the Downs. Although reasonably comfortable, it was a big 'come-down' after Talavera.

My first day at Seaford House, Belgrave Square, the home of the RCDS, was on 11 January 1977 and I knew immediately that I was going to enjoy my year there. Quite apart from the sumptuous surroundings, I was amongst friends. Of the ten British Army students I already knew five and, amongst the sailors, was surprised to find an old friend of Anne's family who had attended our wedding.

As well as the thirty British military students we also had eleven British civilian students – Foreign Office, Home Office, private sector – and thirty-five foreign and Commonwealth students. One big surprise for the College authorities was when the Americans nominated a woman as one of their students for our course – there had never been a female at Seaford House before. Knowing it might be a little embarrassing to have one woman amongst seventy-five men, someone quickly rustled up a British lady from the Department of Trade and Industry to keep her company.

My train journey to London was an hour and a half; however, the College was only a ten-minute walk from Victoria station and I was able to make use of the journey by reading and studying whatever subject was current at the time. Furthermore, since we didn't have to 'clock in' until 10 a.m., and often finished discussions and lectures at lunchtime each day, life was far from stressful. The working day (if you could call it that) usually consisted of a syndicate discussion, followed by a lecture by some expert. Occasionally there were further discussions after lunch but most of us, after perhaps a little research in the excellent library, would go home. In my case I was usually home by 4 o'clock.

I won't bore the reader with details of our studies, but the aim of the course was:

> To prepare senior officers and officials of the United Kingdom and other countries and future leaders from the private and public sectors for high responsibilities in their respective organizations, by developing their analytical powers, knowledge of defence and international security, and strategic vision.

There were four terms: 'The Elements of Power', 'The Contemporary Environment', 'Area Studies' (covering the whole world) and 'European Security'. Our Directing Staff comprised the Commandant, a charming admiral, and three two-star officers, one from each service, plus a civilian equivalent. The Course Handbook says: 'The Directing Staff act as tutors and councillors to their student groups, but lectures and seminars are conducted by outside experts drawn from the Government, the Universities and Professions, as well as from the Military.'

Although I am sure they were very interesting, I remember almost nothing of our discussions and lectures at the College and my outline diary of those days lists only visits and major events like the Queen's Silver Jubilee. It shows that, during our first two terms, we paid visits to 'the City' and to the HQs of the Metropolitan Police and ITN. We also attended a presentation and superb lunch at the Café Royal in Regent Street hosted by Sir Charles Forte, the head of Trust House Forte Ltd.

Later, in June and early July, the course broke up into four groups and paid formal visits to the Navy and RAF – in my case to the Royal Naval base at Faslane in Scotland and to the RAF at Coltishall. After that we were granted a full month's leave and Anne and I set off with Deborah to Plymouth to join Peter and Nicky Mason on their beautiful yacht *Nanice*. Peter had married Nicky nine years previously and he had invited us to sail with them off Devon. Apart from my own minor experiences on the Isle of Wight in 1953, it was the first time any of the Reynolds had been sailing. We sailed from Plymouth to Salcombe and back. Peter and Nicky could not have been kinder and we thoroughly enjoyed the experience.

One thing I had not been looking forward to at the RCDS was the requirement to write a dissertation of up to 10,000 words. As the Course Handbook put it, 'this paper is a personal intellectual challenge, and enables a Member to demonstrate his analytical calibre. It is an opportunity to research and analyze a subject deeply, to test conventional wisdom, and to arrive at conclusions pointing to a way forward.' My basic problem was that I couldn't think of a good and interesting subject. However, I came up with a way around it. In those days, probably as a result of my experiences at the Staff College, I was a better speaker than writer and, having learned that I was to be part of a Far East overseas tour in the September, I went to the Commandant and suggested that instead of a dissertation I was prepared to study the history of China, give a presentation on this before the tour and a second one describing the China of today on our return. To my surprise and delight he agreed, and to this day I think I am the only RCDS graduate who never wrote a dissertation. I gave my first lecture on 25 August and three weeks later set off with thirteen others on a five-week tour of the Far East – it was to be one of the most interesting experiences of my life. I had applied for the Far East tour because it included China and South Korea and, as I had fought against one in order to free the other, I was keen to visit them. Other groups went on tours of Europe, North America, Africa and the Middle East.

Our group was led by the senior civilian instructor at the College and comprised two naval captains, two air commodores, a civilian from the MoD, the British lady student, Greek and German air force colonels, a French naval captain, an Egyptian brigadier general and a German colonel who went on to command the Central Region of NATO. It could hardly have been a more varied and interesting group.

Our tour, which was full of surprises, took in most of the highlights of each country and, since it would make this chapter far too long to try to include them all, I will concentrate on the most memorable.

Our flight out to Hong Kong with the RAF was via Bahrain, where the temperature was 92 degrees, Colombo in Sri Lanka, one night in the Excelsior Hotel in Hong Kong and then a luxury flight with Cathay Pacific to Seoul in South Korea, including champagne with our breakfast and Chateau Mouton Baron Philippe 72 with our lunch.

I felt a little strange to be back in Korea and was certainly very surprised on the third day when I was extracted from our group and taken to the Korean Veterans' HQ where I had a medal pinned on my chest by a South Korean admiral in the presence of four South Korean generals. We were all made to feel very important with visits to the British Embassy, the United Nations HQ, the South Korean National Defence College and I US Corps HQ. In all these locations we were wined and dined and I always found myself at the top table and often on the right of the host.

With the help of a driver lent to me by the American Corps HQ, I managed to find the building which had been the American 121 Evacuation Hospital in 1952 where I had spent forty-eight hours after leaving the MASH and before being flown to Japan. It had changed but was still recognizable and brought back many memories – as did heli-copter flights to the 'Glorious Glosters' Hill' where we landed and were briefed on the famous battle, and then on to Panmunjon where we visited the HQ where the armistice talks had taken place. During these flights I was able to see clearly my old A Company position overlooking the Samichon valley, Hill 355, and as we flew along the demarcation line between North and South Korea, the exact area, now in the demilitarized zone, where I had been wounded. We also flew down to the industrial area of Pusan on the south coast and from there visited the nearby UN cemetery where I was able to find the graves of Watkins, Webster, Allman and, of course poor, brave Ketteringham.

After six wonderful days in Korea, we flew to Tokyo on 26 September. It had certainly changed since I had spent my five days' R & R leave there in 1952 – high-rise buildings and masses of people everywhere we looked. Kyoto was much more attractive. We travelled there on the Bullet Train and visited some amazingly beautiful places – a Shogun castle, a Shinto fortified feudal house, and a Buddhist temple on the first day and two more temples and two extremely beautiful gardens on the second. Then, sadly, we returned to Tokyo which we found once more to be hot and dirty with almost incessant rain. A very memorable incident occurred one night when a group of us, all Brits, were enjoying a very boozy time in the rooftop bar of the Marunouchi. There was a minor earthquake which surprised us but the liquor helped and we laughed it off despite the swaying of the hotel. However, we learned next morning that our Egyptian brigadier had panicked and had turned up in his pyjamas in the main lobby having run down the many flights of stairs.

From Tokyo we flew on to Peking (not Beijing in those days), the first Western military group to visit China after the death of Chairman Mao. Our first shock was to be driven down an almost empty twelve-lane highway into the centre of the city where we were accommodated in a newly-built, rather ugly hotel covered in red flags.

The following morning we were driven in eight cars through what looked like very deprived housing estates and past very old steam trains to a desert region surrounded by mountains, rather reminiscent of the Trucial Oman. This was the base of 6th Tank Division where we were greeted by a 100-man and woman Guard of Honour, all dressed in the same green Chairman Mao suits, with some carrying huge red flags and a few with large red drums. Then we were treated to a static display of equipment followed by lectures, including one by the wife of the Divisional Political Commissar who told us that officers' wives earned £12 a month for a six-hour, five-day week, plus one day for 'study'. Later we saw them sitting at industrial machines in a very noisy hangar-type building. After a very good lunch, including beer, schnapps and red wine, complete with many toasts to 'friendship' etc, we were seen off by the same Guard of Honour and driven to the Great Wall where we spent an hour and then on to the tombs of the thirteen emperors of the Ming Dynasty. That evening we had the first of many 'banquets', hosted this time by the Vice Chiefs of the General Staff and of the Air Force. The food was quite awful – hundred-year-old eggs, cold fish and duck, washed down by an evil drink called something like 'moo tie' and all interspersed with numerous speeches and toasts.

Shortly after 7 o'clock on our second day we were driven in cars to a huge square containing the Great Hall of the People, Chairman Mao's Memorial Hall and his Mausoleum. There were thousands of people, mainly Chinese but including some Westerners, waiting to enter the Mausoleum, but we were taken straight to the front of the queue where we paid our respects to his embalmed body! We then visited the Military Academy and were given descriptions of three Chinese military campaigns – 1948, 1949 and Korea October 1952 to July 1953; I had apparently been fighting in one of the 'Puppet Armies'! After a light lunch we were told we were free to walk about unescorted – at least officially – in the Peoples' Square which caused quite a stir since it was very clear that none of the hundreds of Chinese there had ever seen Western military uniforms before. They all stared at us as though we had come from Mars, particularly at me since, as a British brigadier in summer uniform, I had a red band round my hat, red stars and crowns on my shoulders and red epaulettes on my shirt collar. I think they thought I was a very high party official! We then enjoyed a fascinating and very memorable two-hour visit to the Forbidden City, the ancient Chinese imperial palace. I wrote in my diary that night: 'Drove through dark streets; no lights on any of the hundreds of bicycles; very, very few cars about; the Chinese look healthy with good teeth, few wear glasses; lots of spitting though!'

Our third day saw us flying in our private Chinese Trident jet, with a crew of ten including two hostesses, to the 38th Air Division's base about twenty minutes outside Peking. The Division had ninety F-6 aircraft (the Chinese version of the MiG-19) and, after a flying display which our RAF members said was very good, we had a chance to climb into the aircraft and have our photographs taken. Then on to a repair workshop and pharmaceutical factory manned by officers' wives who we decided needed a major lesson in basic hygiene. We left as we had arrived, to a huge guard of honour complete with a band of drums and cymbals. That evening we flew on to Shanghai where, after a twenty-minute drive through darkened streets, we arrived at the Jingiang Hotel on the edge of the Yangtze river. However, the Shanghai we visited bore little resemblance to the one of today with its modern skyscrapers. Our first evening there saw us entertained to a magnificent dinner by the Commander and Chief of Staff of the Shanghai Military Garrison with much drinking and the usual speeches. The following day was something of a revelation. After a visit to a shipyard where we were subjected to a talk by the Vice Chairman of the Revolutionary Committee, and during which he railed against 'The Gang of Four' and 'capitalist roaders', we drove through streets of incredible poverty to a Commune some twenty minutes south of Shanghai. It contained, so we were told, 27,000 people in 7,400 'homes', 46,000 pigs, 120,000 chickens and produced 274 tons of vegetables per day from its 13,000 hectares. Included in our tour through what can only be described as utterly squalid housing was a very unhygienic 'clinic' containing dental, maternity and acupuncture rooms. We returned to Shanghai along the Bund, the main waterfront, with its faded but magnificent old colonial mansions, banks and club houses. That evening we were given a 'western' meal for a change but then subjected to a two-hour film of Chou en Lai's funeral.

The following day, after another lecture on China's 'planned economy', we flew for two hours down to Kweilin where we stayed in a Government Rest House. Next morning we joined a large river barge and sailed downstream on the river Li Chiang to Yangshuo where we were shown round very beautiful pavilions and pagodas. The scenery everywhere was breathtakingly beautiful.

The next day we flew, again in our private Chinese Trident, down to Canton where we started with a visit to 'Chairman Mao's Peasant Movement Institute' for the usual propaganda talk, followed by a banquet with the usual toasts and lots of 'moo tie'.

We left Canton on 14 October in a luxurious carriage drawn by a steam locomotive through very attractive countryside and two hours later arrived in Hong Kong where we spent a pleasant and quite instructive three days before flying home. As a matter of interest the only skyscraper on the Island in those days was the Hong Kong Club. It had really been the 'trip of a lifetime'.

I gave my lecture on 'China Today' ten days after returning home. I backed it up with colour slides which I had taken myself and it was well received – so well in fact that it led to a nasty shock. A few days afterwards the Commandant announced that, as it was the fiftieth anniversary year of the RCDS as well as the Queen's Jubilee, she would be visiting the College and would attend one of our debates. He then announced that Brigadier Mike Reynolds would make the introduction and chair the debate. I was flabbergasted. I was also told that HM would be sitting just a few feet in front and to the left of the lectern from which I would conduct affairs. Fortunately all went well and the debate was lively and enjoyable. The morning ended with us all, including our wives, being presented to Her Majesty. The official photographs of her being greeted by the Commandant show her looking absolutely radiant.

Midway through my time at Seaford House I was told that my next job would be that of Divisional Brigadier of the Queen's Division, with a small HQ and staff, based with the Divisional Depot at Bassingbourn in Cambridgeshire. It involved being responsible for the manning of all nine battalions of the Queen's Division – those of the Queen's, Fusiliers and Royal Anglian Regiments. Initially I was quite looking forward to it but, as time went by, I came to the conclusion that there was little challenge in the appointment. Consequently, when I heard that the job of Deputy Adjutant General of BAOR was coming up, I asked to see the Military Secretary. I pointed out that I had been a successful Garrison commander in Osnabrück with responsibilities for conditions of service etc and would welcome a chance to continue in the same field on a larger 'playing field'. Fortunately for me, he accepted my argument and I got the job. If I hadn't I don't think I would ever have become a general.

Our last month at the RCDS was very busy with visits to the NATO HQ in Brussels, Berlin and, to my surprise, Osnabrück. The latter had been chosen as a major military garrison and it was very nostalgic to go back there and, again to my surprise, to be one of only three to stay in Talavera House. I had to attend a military demonstration but I made a point of not going round the garrison with the rest of the College and spent my time instead visiting old friends like the Station Staff Officer. I was very flattered and, to be honest very proud, when a fellow student told me that evening that one of the Estate Wardens had told him that 'Brigadier Reynolds really cared about the welfare of the soldiers and their families'.

I finished at Seaford House on 14 December and five weeks later Anne and I began a new life in Rheindahlen, near Mönchen-Gladbach in Germany.

Chapter Twenty-two

Senior Staff Officer in Germany

We arrived in Rheindahlen on 22 January 1978 and spent the first few nights in the Visitors' Mess whilst we sorted out our things in our quarter, one of the half dozen or so brigadiers' quarters on 'the patch'. It was really quite nice with a reasonable garden with woods beyond it and, being in a cul-de-sac, was very quiet with no traffic.

An MoD publication on JHQ Rheindahlen aptly describes its origin and what it was like in 1978:

> It was established in 1954, centralizing headquarters functions which at that time were scattered in several towns in Northern Germany, and functioned as the HQ of the Northern Army Group (NORTHAG), the British Army on the Rhine, 2nd Allied Tactical Air Force (2ATAF), and Royal Air Force (Germany). Rheindahlen was populated with British, American, German, Dutch and Belgian military personnel and in many cases their families. In appearance JHQ Rheindahlen was more like a medium-size town than a military base, consisting mostly of administrative buildings, living quarters, schools, shops, two cinemas and other areas typical of civilian towns. Many facilities existed in the complex. Shops, two NAAFI stores, NAAFI bar and restaurants for soldiers below the rank of sergeant, medical and dental centres, several primary schools, one secondary school, churches of all major denominations, separate messes for senior and junior officers, civilian school teachers and administrators, and of course for senior WOs and NCOs and the inevitable Thrift Shop.

Anne and I soon settled in and were privileged to have a daily cleaning woman and a full-time batman on loan from the 1st Battalion of my Regiment in Werl. His name was Smith, better known as Smudger and, although not particularly impressive to look at, being short and overweight, he was a safe pair of hands, did the boring work in the house and garden and was not a bad waiter at table. With petrol at £1.32 a gallon, whisky at £5.37 a litre, good wines at about £8 a bottle and champagne at less than £12 (all at today's prices), life promised to be very enjoyable – amazing how the price of wine has come down and whisky gone up in thirty years!

I was lucky in having an excellent staff in A Branch of HQ BAOR. The Manning side, under a lieutenant colonel, more or less ran itself and, apart from keeping a watching brief, I hardly got involved. The main part of the Branch, run by an excellent Colonel A, Brian Burditt, concerned itself with pay, allowances, conditions of service, the British Forces Broadcasting Service and even the introduction of British TV for our troops and families. This took up virtually all my time.

The two C-in-Cs BAOR during the time I was DAG were General Sir Frank King, whom I had known in Northern Ireland, and General Sir William Scotter. The officer I worked directly to was Major General (later General Sir) Roly Guy. I got on extremely well with all of them. Very sadly, they have all passed away.

Rather than risk boring the reader with the details of our work I will quote from my two Confidential Reports by Roly Guy covering my time in the HQ. In January 1979:

> Brig Reynolds has been the DAG at HQ BAOR for nearly a year. His main occupation has been with pay and Local Overseas Allowance (LOA). I have been much impressed by the advice he has given to the C-in-C on the line that should be taken over LOA to ensure the soldier in BAOR gets a fair deal. He has been tough and uncompromising about those aspects on which we cannot yield without seriously affecting morale. At the same time he has been judicious and realistic in his assessment of the limits to which we can go whilst retaining political credibility. . . . He has made it his business to get around and hear the views and opinions of the Divisional Commanders and also maintained a close liaison with the Ministry of Defence.

To this Bill Scotter added, 'We have been very lucky to have such a very competent DAG throughout a period of considerable strain on the 'A' side of the Army.'

And February 1980:

> It has been an eventful period on the 'A' side over the last year. We have seen introduced many improvements in our conditions of service and, after protracted and sometimes very difficult negotiations, the LOA problem was eventually satisfactorily resolved. We

have much to thank Brig Reynolds for over these successes. His imagination, hard work and determination contributed an enormous amount towards their achievement. I am also quite sure that the tough line he recommended in tackling the LOA problem and the tactic he advocated over the timing and implementation of the reductions in LOA, although unpopular in the MoD, were in fact the right ones, and undoubtedly they did much to lessen the adverse effect the LOA reductions might have had on morale out here.

I have to say at once though that it was the hard work of my staff officers, coupled with those on the RAF side, that ensured that we won the day over LOA. Amongst the 'many improvements' mentioned were twenty-four-hour radio programmes from the British Forces Broadcasting Service and the introduction of British TV in our major garrisons.

But what about our family life in Rheindahlen? Deborah was in her last term at St Mary's before going to the London College of Secretaries in Portland Place in September 1978. She had made it very clear that she didn't want to be 'buried in the country' like her sisters at Fryerning. Gabrielle was by now living in New York and having a wonderful time; however, she came home in April for the big event of 1978 which was Vicky's wedding to Corin on the 22nd. Peter and Nicky Mason very kindly lent us their delightful little house in Chelsea from which to launch this and, after detailed recces, Vicky chose St James's Church, Spanish Place, with the reception for 130 guests at the Basil Street Hotel in Knightsbridge. Gabrielle and Deborah were bridesmaids and everything went perfectly. Receptions in those days were very simple – none of today's sit-down meals and dances – they were just stand-up parties with champagne, canapés, wedding cake and the usual speeches. As the bride's father was expected to pay for everything, this was just as well.

Not long after arriving in JHQ I was surprised to find one of my captains from Osnabrück, Peter Crocker, being shown into my office by my excellent PA, Staff Sergeant Robinson. Peter, now a major in the Intelligence Division of the HQ, immediately suggested that we should run another PIED PEIPER Tour. 'But I can't do it all myself Brigadier, so this time you'll have to help!' I was happy to do so and we agreed that I would represent the German side of the story and he the American. In order to prepare the tours we decided it was essential to recce the ground again and work up our scripts. Accordingly we drove down to La Gleize sometime in late 1978 and were sitting in the café in the village square when we saw a wedding party come out of the church. Everyone came into the café and we were squashed into a corner. Suddenly I saw the former mayor of the village who had welcomed us on our first PIED PEIPER tour and I was pointing him out when his wife saw me. She came straight over and introduced herself, saying they would like to invite us to their house. I replied that this would be very nice and so began a wonderful friendship which has lasted to this day. I count Edouard and Marie-Berthe de Harenne amongst my very dearest friends. During my time in JHQ Peter and I ran two PIED PEIPER tours for HQ BAOR and one for HQ AFCENT.

Our holidays in our two years in Rheindahlen were some of our best. In June 1978 we set off for Lerici hoping it would still be beautiful and unchanged. Sadly it wasn't and, after only one night there, we drove west along the coast looking for somewhere nice. We eventually saw a little village called Spéracèdes perched on a hill above Grasse. There was only one small auberge but, when the owner opened the shutters, we looked down to see vineyards and trees stretching all the way to the Mediterranean some twenty miles away. The room was pretty basic but the food was excellent. Our days were simple, spent mostly at la Bocca on a lovely, unspoilt and uncrowded beach just west of Cannes. When the weather wasn't perfect, which it was most of the time, we visited Grasse, Nice and Cannes. We stayed a full three weeks.

In mid-September 1978 we took a two-week holiday in Antibes. Debs had already been there on holiday to help with the two little boys of an RAF couple also based in Rheindahlen and she had told us that the house they had rented was super. It was a beautifully converted fisherman's house within the ramparts, with the ground floor being the original boathouse. Our bedroom was on the top floor and, from a roof terrace above it, we had lovely views over the town. All the crowds had disappeared by that time of year, so we had an idyllic holiday.

June 1979 saw us back in Spéracèdes. This time we rented a lovely villa at the western edge of the village which we had found during our Antibes holiday. As well as having superb views towards the coast, it had a magnificent sun terrace and was large enough for Gabrielle and Deborah to join us, each with her own bedroom. Once again the weather was perfect and we stayed a full three weeks.

We arrived back in Rheindahlen to startling news. A letter was waiting for me from the Military Secretary telling me that I was 'to take over as Commander Allied Command Europe Mobile Force Land – AMF (L) – in June 1980' in the rank of major general and with my HQ in Sechenheim, near Heidelberg. He added, 'I am delighted you have been rewarded with a divisional command – and a very challenging and fascinating one it is too!' I could hardly believe it. I had been hoping for promotion but had expected to command one of the divisions in Germany, for which I was very well qualified. A short time later, I received a letter from Major General Sir Michael Fitzalan-Howard, Marshal of the Diplomatic Corps, congratulating me and telling me I was 'getting the best job in the Army'. He had been the first British Commander of the AMF (L) in 1965.

In September we set off for another three weeks in Antibes but this time we had a full house – Gabrielle, Deborah and the Masons who flew out to join us. With the news of my promotion and next appointment it was a very happy holiday.

On 3 March 1980, after a series of farewell parties, we left Rheindahlen and a day later moved into a temporary quarter in a very pleasant block of flats in Putney. I had arranged this as we had much to do before taking up my new appointment the following June.

Chapter Twenty-three
Marking Time in England

April 1980 proved to be a very busy month, starting with an interview with the Chief of the General Staff and followed a few days later by drinks in St James's Palace and lunch at the Turf Club with Michael Fitzalan-Howard. This proved to be not only an exciting meeting but also a very useful one. He told me not to accept the offer of an American quarter on a military 'patch' in Heidelberg, known as Patrick Henry Village, as he had done. As a commanding general, I was entitled to a 'residence' with ambassadorial standards of furniture and should demand this. I duly did so and was amazed to receive immediate agreement. Obviously, I couldn't go over to Germany to look for a 'residence', so I contacted the British staff in my future HQ and asked them to look for one for me.

The rest of April saw us looking for a flat in England. We had been married for twenty-five years and Anne said it was about time I bought her a base in England. I could hardly say no. Although we both wanted one in London my father warned against leaving one empty there for long periods whilst we were away in Germany – squatting was rampant at that time. We eventually settled on a very nice ground-floor flat with a beautiful walled garden in Eastbourne. It had the added advantage that Anne's mother and sister could keep an eye on it for us when we were away.

In May we paid a two-day visit to Sechenheim. I saw my new HQ, met my future staff and Anne and I agreed on the 'residence' the British element had been found for us. There was only one snag – it was brand new and wasn't finished. And there was another problem – it wasn't furnished. However, to our amazement, we were told that we could visit a Government 'Aladdin's Cave' in London, designed for Foreign Office personnel serving abroad, and choose all the furniture, and everything else the 'residence' needed from curtains and carpets to bed linen, cutlery and even pictures for the walls. It was an incredible experience and Anne was in her element.

On 8 June we crossed to Germany. A very exciting and fulfilling period of my life was about to begin.

Chapter Twenty-four

Two Star Commander in NATO

At a full ceremonial parade in Seckenheim, near Mannheim, on 11 June 1980, I stood in front of the Supreme Allied Commander Europe, US General Bernie Rogers, and was appointed Commander Allied Command Europe Mobile Force (Land). Speeches by Bernie Rogers, the US officer I was taking over from, and me followed, and then contingents from the seven nations contributing to the AMF (L) paraded before us complete with a marvellous forty-three strong band provided by the Italian Alpini. It was one of the proudest moments of my life – and indeed of Anne's as she stood on the saluting dais beside Bernie's wife. I was delighted to learn later from Admiral Bill Crowe, Commander Allied Forces Southern Europe, and later US ambassador in London, that he thought my speech was the best he had ever heard on such an occasion.

I remember little of my time in Seckenheim; firstly, because four months after I arrived there the AMF (L) barracks were handed over to the German Army and my HQ moved to Heidelberg ten miles away; and secondly, because in those four months I visited nine countries, introduced myself to all the senior NATO and national commanders in Western Europe, attended a CPX in Germany and participated in a major exercise in Turkey. This pace of events would continue for the whole of my NATO command.

What exactly was the AMF (L)? Without going into too much detail, it was a rapid reaction force designed to deploy to the flanks of NATO – Norway, Denmark, Italy, Greece and Turkey – as a deterrent and to display NATO solidarity in the event of a threat by the Warsaw Pact. If this display failed we were required to fight alongside the host nation forces in normal defensive operations. The force comprised parachute battalions from Belgium, Germany and the USA, and winter-warfare-trained battalions from Canada, Italy and the UK; each came with an artillery battery, a logistic support detachment and recce helicopters. Supporting these units were a British armoured reconnaissance squadron, a joint British and German helicopter squadron with six Wessex and six

Hueys, two signal companies (British and German), a British logistic support battalion, an American HQ Company and two field hospitals, one German and one Italian. The ski-trained British, Canadian and Italian battalion groups deployed to the northern flank with the Italian Field Hospital, whilst the American, German and Belgian battalion groups went to the southern with the German Field Hospital. Luxembourg also provided an infantry battalion which reinforced us in Denmark and, towards the end of my command, in Norway. My own HQ, with three dedicated light helicopters, the American HQ company, the armoured recce squadron, both signal companies (one radio and one line), the Force helicopter squadron and the logistic support battalion went to both flanks. Although not under my command, I could count on dedicated air support from recce, fighter and attack squadrons of the AMF (Air), again with squadrons from seven NATO countries including Holland.

Our residence in Wilhelm Leuschner Strasse, Mannheim, was a very nice, large house in a well-to-do suburb of the city and within walking distance of the Rhine. We were well off for staff for, as well as my ADC who lived in the 'Granny Annex' of the house, and the services of a full-time cleaning lady and a German air force driver for my Mercedes staff car, I had inter-viewed and selected a House Sergeant from the Regiment, Sergeant Cockram, and a full-time ACC cook, Corporal Taylor. They were all very nice and efficient. Sergeant Cockram ended up as House Butler in a Cambridge College and Corporal Taylor as a warrant officer. My first ADC, Lance Mans, was the son of a major general and Colonel of the Queen's Regiment; as I write this he is a brigadier responsible for NATO Special Forces in Afghanistan. He was a delightful companion and good at his job. Since three years was too long for a young officer to be away from Regimental duty, after eighteen months James Turk, also from my Regiment, took over. He was equally good.

The most important family event during my first year with the AMF (L) was Gabrielle's wedding to Austen. It happened soon after I took command and with a Guard of Honour of eight Scots Dragoon Guards and two pipers in full dress, plus Deborah as the chief bridesmaid, it was a huge success.

It was as well that we had a good house staff for in the relatively short periods I spent in Mannheim – only ninety-two nights in the first eight months – we did a lot of entertaining, including ten NATO generals in the first year. Fortunately, I was given a generous entertainment allowance by the British Army which offset most of the cost. And fortu-nately for Anne we discovered that when I was away she could fly home for nothing, care of the Canadians from their airbase at Lahr, only an hour's drive from Mannheim, to another air terminal they had at Gatwick airport.

Whilst on the subject of entertaining, Sergeant Cockram was soon nick-named Sergeant Cockup or Sergeant Cockers. Three instances will suffice. At one of our most important dinner parties, when guests included the US C-in-C Europe, General Fritz Kroesen, Sergeant Cockram came into the drawing room dressed in scarlet uniform and announced to Anne that, 'Madam, Dinner is served', I duly escorted Mrs Kroesen down the corridor to the dining room only to find it in total darkness – Cockers had forgotten to light the candles! On another occasion my ADC came into the study at about 10 p.m. and asked me to come outside as there had been an 'incident'. It transpired that Cockers, who had only recently learned to drive, had engaged the wrong gear in his car and instead of reversing out of our parking area into the road had driven forward straight into the garden. All I could see was the rear end of his car! Fortunately he was unhurt and, at my request, the Americans produced a recovery vehicle next morning and lifted his car out. Remarkably it was virtually undamaged. He was even luckier on the third occasion. He went home to bring his wife to pre-Christmas lunchtime drinks which we always organized for our staff. On the way he lost control of his car on an icy road and drove straight into the side of a brand new Mercedes causing a lot of damage and writing off his own car. Remarkably, the German police decided it was not Cockers' fault, but that of the owner of the Mercedes for parking on a sharp corner in those conditions. Believe it or not, Cockers was able to buy a new car with the money provided by the insurance company. Having said all this, we were very fond of him and he was an excellent House Sergeant.

Michael Fitzalan-Howard had told me that he had found it necessary to fight a major battle over his relationship with SACEUR. The US Chief of Staff at SHAPE had demanded that Michael should approach SACEUR through *him* but, as a 'commanding general', he had refused to do so and, fortunately, the SACEUR of the time had agreed with him. This meant I could ask to meet, write to or even telephone Bernie Rogers direct. Not only this, but I was in the unique position of having no British boss. The Deputy SACEUR, RAF Air Chief Marshal Sir Peter Terry, visited my HQ and my Force on exercise several times but I was never under his command.

Fortunately, I got on well with Bernie Rogers from the day we met. I had been told he had a very quick temper, but I saw nothing of this. He was always charming and cooperative with both me and my staff and he visited all our major exercises. By the end of our three years together we were very good friends.

Turning now to my HQ and staff, we soon settled into the top floor of an old Hitler block in Campbell Barracks in Heidelberg – the HQ of the US Army in Germany. As well as more than adequate office space we even had room for an all ranks' club where we held a weekly get-together and many 'Hail and Farewell' parties. My staff came from all the AMF nations and was headed by a Belgian colonel who proved to be a great travelling companion. My PA was a charming American, the wife of a serving US lieutenant colonel. The GI Branch (Personnel and Administration) was headed by a Canadian, G2 (Intelligence) by a British officer, G3 (Operations) by a German, G4 (Logistics) by an American, and the Chief Communications Officer was an Italian – all lieutenant colonels. I also had an Air Liaison Officer, a RAF Wing Commander. Although none of them went on to reach high rank they were all good officers and very pleasant companions, as were the twenty-five or so less senior officers and the clerical staff supporting them. The only discord we had was between my Belgian Chief of Staff and my German G3 who both displayed their national characteristics: the latter, for understandable reasons, disliked having to approach me through the former. After a 'head to head' meeting with me on one of our early exercises their relationship improved, but it was never as warm as I would have liked.

I attended an AMF (L) CPX soon after I took command. This took place in Germany about 100 miles from Seckenheim and I was appalled with what I saw. My predecessor, a paratrooper with no time for tracked vehicles, had mounted the HQ in small, wheeled vehicles with barely enough room in the back for one, let alone two staff officers and the necessary radios. There was no way the vehicles could be linked together. All staff officers slept in small tents which they had to erect themselves when they came off duty. There was no alternative HQ. After long discussions with my Chief of Staff and G3 and making detailed enquiries with the Americans, I discovered that American armoured, tracked, air-transportable, command vehicles were readily available. These could be linked together with fitted canvas screens to form a united HQ with electric lighting and, when necessary, with heating stoves. I then decreed that the only personnel allowed in Main HQ were those *on* duty; those *off* duty were to be located at an Alternate HQ, at least a couple of miles away, where they would sleep in tents erected and packed up by members of the US HQ Company. The Alternate HQ would always have two officers 'on watch' in case Main came under attack and could not operate effectively, in which case all off-duty personnel would man Alternate. These changes, which took a few months to implement fully, were met with great enthusiasm by everyone in the HQ – except the Americans in HQ Company who resented putting up tents for other people. They soon accepted the situation, however, and I became quite popular when I further decreed that just because the US Army allowed no alcoholic drinks when on exercise there was no reason why the rest of us should suffer in the same way. I therefore ordered that, if they wished, all ranks, including the Americans, could have two bottles of beer per day; I cleared this with General Fritz Kroesen. I then turned to my own situation. I wasn't happy sleeping in a tent which, with our frequent moves, involved two or three soldiers including Sergeant Cockram constantly putting it up and taking it down and laying on electric light and, on the northern flank, heating. Therefore I went to a huge US vehicle depot in nearby Pirmasens where I was able to choose a caravan with fitted bed, desk, chairs, battery-powered electric lighting and heating. Sergeant Cockram travelled in the cab with the American driver of the towing vehicle and I was well looked after with minimum effort. Cockers brought me my breakfast there, but otherwise I ate with my HQ staff in a tent attached to the HQ cookhouse. On the subject of food I should point out that, during the deterrence phase of each exercise, most contingents ate fresh food and for the combat phase their national combat ration packs – in the case of my HQ we had US C-rations. Interestingly, my Italian Alpini Battalion Group provided a half-litre of wine per man per day. The only problem we had with this system was in Turkey. I was told that my Americans were not allowed to eat the local fresh food; instead they would have their fresh food flown and trucked in direct from the US Sector in Germany or even direct from America. This was despite the fact that my German medical advisor, a colonel, assured me after visiting the local Turkish markets and abattoirs that their products were first class. The rest of the Force certainly enjoyed delicious meats, vegetables and fruit.

A very big change in my life, and indeed that of Anne's, occurred in September 1981. On the 15th a terrorist organization called the Red Army Faction (RAF) – known in its early stages as the Baader-Meinhoff Group – attempted to kill General Fritz Kroesen. They fired two RPG-7 rockets at his car as it crossed a bridge in Heidelberg. The first missed and the second hit but failed to explode. A few days later my ADC and I arrived at Frankfurt airport from a meeting in Denmark to find our aircraft surrounded by German policemen carrying machine guns. I was asked to leave the aircraft first, was bundled into a police Mercedes and driven home under heavy escort. I was told that raids on suspects' houses had revealed that I was Number 2 on the terrorists' hit list in the Heidelberg area. After that things moved very fast. Cameras connected to the local German police station were fitted in our house to cover all approaches, I was provided with an armoured BMW with bulletproof tyres and a

German police Porsche escort car and, within a few days, a Royal Military Police sergeant and three corporals with a Ford Granada arrived to act as a close protection (CP) team. They all carried 9mm pistols or small submachine guns and were highly trained in their role; one of them had recently been an escort to Maggie Thatcher. Not long after this the British provided an armoured Mercedes with a specially-trained driver and my NATO Mercedes staff car became a second 'chase car'. The five members of this team then moved into the 'Granny Annex' to our house enabling my ADC, to his delight, to move into a nice flat in Heidelberg. All this made a huge difference to the way we lived. I had to have at least two escorts with me at all times when outside my house or away from military premises and Anne had to have one with her whenever she left the house; we therefore had little privacy. Furthermore, German police constantly patrolled past the house, I was not allowed to wear uniform outside military premises and we had to take a different route to work and travel at different times every day. All this took a lot of getting used to, but there were always lighter moments and the team members, who changed every six months, were not only highly efficient but also delightful and a credit to their Corps and nation. Since I always had to have two escorts with me, the corporals were all trained as waiters and so, whenever we went to a dinner or drinks party, our hosts found themselves with a couple of free waiters.

This change of circumstances also affected our possessions. By this time we had a VW Golf GTi and a lovely 4.2-litre silver Jaguar. The GTi was fine, provided I had a 'chase car' with me, but I was told that I had to get rid of the Jag because it was the only one in the Heidelberg area and was right-hand drive. I sold it to a Danish count who lived in London.

When I was on duty, the CP team usually drove me to and from the UK and always within Germany, Belgium, Holland and Luxembourg. I always flew, either civil or military, to Norway, Denmark, Greece and Turkey, having free use of the VIP lounge at Frankfurt airport. Italy was a different matter. If it was northern Italy I usually went by road, but the Italians wouldn't accept a foreign CP team; instead they provided a Carabinieri escort which met me at the relevant border crossing. They were often motorcycle-mounted and whoever was driving, sometimes my ADC, sometimes my official driver or even on rare occasions me, had to keep up with them. It was very exciting as they would often 'perform' on their bikes, even standing on the saddles. The other place where I had a memorable escort was in the City of Luxembourg. I paid a visit to their Minister of Defence and was given an escort of police cars in front and behind my Mercedes with sirens blaring and all other traffic stopped to allow us to speed through the streets. The visit was also memorable for the fact that I spent the night in the castle in Diekirch where I slept in the bed once used by Marshal Foch in the First World War.

I mentioned that we did a lot of official entertaining in Mannheim and we had many visits by family and friends who not only wanted to see us but also the lovely city of Heidelberg and the Rhine, Neckar and Moselle valleys. Amongst our many guests in Mannheim were General Tonne Huitfeldt, Commander North Norway – who was to be my boss in my next job although neither of us knew this at the time – General Niels Rye Andersen, Commander Baltic Region, General Vittorio Santini, Commander Allied Land Forces Southern Europe and his wife, and General Sir Frank Kitson and his wife. The latter was now Commander UK Land Forces and my British units were under his command when they were at home. When I mentioned that I was a little puzzled why he had asked to come to see my HQ in Heidelberg and not in the field, he replied, 'Well Elizabeth wanted some jeans from the American PX, didn't she?!' The PX was the equivalent of our British NAAFI.

During my time in Heidelberg I arranged three AMF Study Days for my unit COs. In December 1980 the subject was Anti-Armour Operations and, as well as cocktail and dinner parties for all participants and their wives, we organized a dinner dance in the Officers' Club in Patrick Henry Village. In November 1981 the subject I chose for our Study Period was Operation GOODWOOD in Normandy in 1944 and, after showing the British Staff College excellent film of this operation, I was able, to everyone's amazement, to introduce two famous Panzer commanders who had taken part in the battle – Hans von Luck and Karl von Rosen. Earlier in the year I had attended the funeral service in Lahr of the wife of the Commander of Canadian Forces Europe; he was a good friend of mine. At the reception afterwards I met Major General von Rosen who was the German liaison officer to the Canadians. Recognizing the name, I asked him if he was the former commander of the Tiger II Company which had been part of 503rd Heavy Panzer Battalion at GOODWOOD. He smiled and said yes. I immediately thought of using this battle for my next Study Period and asked him if he would attend and answer questions. Again he said yes and asked if I would like Hans von Luck to come as well. I could hardly believe my ears. Von Luck was a very well-known Panzer commander who had commanded a *Kampfgruppe* of the famous 21st Panzer Division in the battle. He stayed in my house for two nights and we had a dramatic Study Period with the two Germans answering so many questions that we had to delay lunch by over an hour. To complete the Study Period we held our annual Ball in Heidelberg castle. Air Chief Marshal Sir Peter and Lady Terry came as guests and stayed with us. He wrote later, 'What a marvellous setting you contrived! And what a most impressive evening with so much friendship and good humour so obviously generated by everyone associated with your command. It is very encouraging for me and for Betty to be thought of as part of the AMF family.' We held another Study period in November 1982, again followed by a Ball in the Castle. And just to complete the picture of slightly unusual events, I ran two PIED PEIPER Battlefield Tours for the officers of HQ AFCENT during my time in Heidelberg – one in 1980 and another in 1982. Both times I stayed with Edouard and Marie Berthe de Harenne and held picnic lunches for the officers in the grounds of their lovely chateau.

During my three years in command of the AMF (L), we completed major exercises in Norway, Denmark, and Italy, and in both western and eastern Turkey. We also carried out detailed recces for our wartime role in all our contingency areas, including Greece, and completed artillery concentrations with live firing by thirty-six guns, supported by twelve heavy-lift helicopters, in Portugal, Belgium and Germany. On the major exercises we spent about five days practising our deterrence role and then usually about five days in the combat role with a live enemy – normally provided by the host nation, but, on a couple of memorable occasions, by US Marines and British Royal Marine Commandos. As the reader will have deduced I was very busy. I completed 155 fixed-wing international flights and 420 helicopter flights, ranging from short hops visiting units and carrying out recces on exercises, to one which took me from Denmark all the way back to Heidelberg. In my three years in command I visited Belgium twelve times, Paris four times for Western European Union meetings, Luxembourg three times, Portugal twice, Italy nine times, the USA once, Canada three times, Denmark five times, Norway six, Greece four and Turkey seven times – plus England no less than nineteen times! These visits were to meet the senior national and NATO commanders, discuss with them contingency plans, exercises and contributions to my Force and to visit my units in their home bases. I made many good friends during this time, especially amongst the senior commanders in Belgium, Germany, Denmark, Norway, Italy and Turkey. And to my amazement I found myself hosting King Olaf and Prince Harald of Norway, Queen Margrethe and Prince Henrik of Denmark and the Grand Duke of Luxembourg during their visits to us on various exercises. Just to complete the picture of my life during these three incredible years we managed to fit in two holidays in the South of France.

I won't attempt to describe my many visits to the various NATO countries and HQs in any detail, other than to say that I was completely spoiled by my hosts who without fail went out of their way to show me, and sometimes Anne, their national treasures. These ranged from ancient monuments, to churches, museums, art galleries and even famous restaurants. Just a few examples will suffice: a private, escorted visit to the Papal apartments and gardens and the Sistine Chapel in the Vatican, laying a wreath on Ataturk's tomb in Ankara, a visit to Mount Athos by helicopter, an audience with Queen Margrethe in the Amalienborg Palace in Copenhagen and the same with King Olaf in the Royal Palace in Oslo. Nor will I attempt to detail the many exercises in which I participated, but rather mention just a few of the highlights and more memorable events.

One of the most surprising exercises was in Turkish Thrace soon after taking command. A week before it was due to start the Chief of the Turkish General Staff, General Evren, had seized power in a coup d'état. We naturally expected the exercise to be cancelled but, to our amazement, it went ahead with his and NATO approval and I soon found myself standing next to him on a dusty hillside near Corlu. In order to give the reader some idea of the scale of this exercise it took three ships and sixty-six heavy transport aircraft lifts to deliver the AMF (L) to Turkey. The exercise went well and met with everyone's approval except mine. It had been planned in detail before I assumed command and I had been unable to change the outline or any of the details. I subsequently wrote to SACEUR:

> After you visited the Force in Turkey, we were honoured, as I am sure you know, not only by a visit by General Evren, but by the entire Turkish National Security Council. I am pleased to say that the Observers' Day which they attended was generally judged a success although I was personally far from happy with the tactics demonstrated. Through no fault of our own we showed, with a certain amount of professionalism I hope, how a small elite force could be decimated through wrong handling – a heliborne and foot mounted counter-attack in broad daylight against a prepared, mechanized enemy! This had been directed by the Turks under whose command we were operating. So be it, but I hope never again or for real.

*   *   *

My love of Italy and the Italians began with my first holiday when I was twenty-one and continued with numerous holidays there with Anne and the girls. It was, therefore, with great pleasure that I discovered that, as Commander AMF (L), I not only had north-east Italy as one of my contingency areas, with my superior NATO operational HQ located in

Verona, but also that my Italian Alpini contingent was based near Turin and my American Airborne Battalion Group in Vicenza. With many reasons to visit Italy, I took full advantage of this privilege. One of the most dramatic visits was to General Vittorio Santini's NATO HQ LAND-SOUTH in Verona in April 1981. It was located in the Palazzo Carli in Verona and we stayed in his apartment on the top floor. On the second night, Vittorio announced that we were going to have dinner in Signor Bolla's nearby Cantina. Signor Bolla was the head of Bolla wines and his Cantina was a huge cellar where we were surrounded by thousands of bottles of wine. Other guests included Count Bernini, General Carlo Dalla Chiesa, Head of the Carabinieri, and Brigadier Jim Dozier, the senior US general in that part of Italy. After a fantastic dinner of many courses, each accompanied by a different wine, Vittorio announced that, as it was a beautiful night, we would walk back to the Palazzo Carli through the narrow, beautiful streets of Verona. As we did so I mentioned to him that we – Dalla Chiesa, Dozier, me and indeed he himself – were presenting a very good target for the Red Brigade or other terrorist organizations. He told me to look in the shadows – sure enough, every few yards I detected a dark figure carrying an Uzi sub-machine gun. We were indeed well protected by the Carabinieri. Nevertheless, within a few months Dalla Chiesa had been murdered in Sicily and Jim Dozier kidnapped in Verona – fortunately he was rescued unharmed by the Carabinieri after forty-two days in captivity.

My memories of my four visits to Greece are mixed – mainly happy, but overshadowed by disappointment. On my first visit in 1980 to meet the Chief of Staff of the Greek Army, the Commander of the First Hellenic Army and all his Corps commanders, I was treated to the many wonders of Athens and Thessalonica, and following this I was able to carry out helicopter recces of all our contingency areas on the borders of Bulgaria and Yugoslavia (now Macedonia). These were equally fascinating. However, due to political problems the AMF had not exercised in Greece for nine years and most people in NATO were pessimistic about it ever doing so again. After my recces I wrote to SACEUR:

> The Greek Army would obviously like to see the AMF (L) exercising in Greece as soon as possible, but it is equally clear that the decision to allow us back into Greece will be a political one. It is my own view that the best chance of holding an FTX in Greece in 1982 is to divorce my exercise from DISPLAY DETERMINATION [a major NATO exercise which was to include the Turks]. This will avoid any possible difficulties with the Turks. The Greek COS agrees with me.

In December 1981 I returned to Greece with my unit commanders and staff to recce our planned deterrent operations and possible combat options. Again I wrote to SACEUR:

The Greeks could not have been more cooperative and open and obviously hope that our FTX in north-east Greece planned for next September will go ahead. However, the general view, forcibly expressed by the Commander of B Corps, was that by making a fuss the Turks are getting too much of the NATO 'cake' and it is time for Greece to get in on the act. They feel that your country and mine are more sympathetic to Turkey than we are to Greece.

In mid-August we completed the Commanders' recce for the planned FTX in Greece. The preparations went well and it promised to be a first-class exercise culminating in three AMF (L) Battalions joining the Greek airborne forces in a multi-national parachute drop. Sadly it was not to happen. I wrote to SACEUR again:

Naturally we are all very disappointed that APEX EXPRESS was cancelled [by the Greek government] at the last moment. It caught us very much by surprise as we had no idea there was a serious problem on the air side [this was to do with the status of Lemnos which the Greeks insisted on including in the scenario]. It was particularly sad that the cancellation came at such a late date, resulting in wasted expenditure of some 56 million Belgian Francs. We shall, however, continue our efforts to finalize our operational plans for Greece.

This we did the following spring, culminating with me signing a Bilateral Agreement with the Greek Chief of Staff for cooperation between the Greek Armed Forces and the AMF (L). So ended my Greek odyssey.

My memories of Denmark are all happy ones except for one embarrassing incident. One of the more amusing happenings occurred in September 1981. We were carrying out a full-scale FTX (AMBER EXPRESS) in southern Zealand and I was suddenly told that Queen Margrethe was going to visit us. I immediately looked at the map for a suitable venue, spotted a beautiful house and estate in a suitable place called Kragerup and told the US major responsible for deploying and running the HQ in the field, George Basso, to ask the owner if we could locate our HQ in the barns and stables there. The owner told him to get lost! However, when I told George to go back and tell him that his Queen was due to visit us, his attitude completely changed and I was immediately invited for drinks to discuss the details. Strangely, although the owner, Erik Dinersen, was a Gentleman of the Royal Bedchamber, he had never met his Queen. The visit was a great success culminating in a champagne reception in the main house. It transpired that Eric was a very wealthy man whose estate included a beautiful indoor swimming pool and a superb collection of vintage motor cars. After the royal visit he was very generous with his hospitality, allowing many AMF (L) officers to use the facilities of his estate and visit his car museum. Erik and his charming wife and I subsequently became good friends and we met again by sheer accident the following year during visits to Troy and Ephesus in Turkey.

AMBER EXPRESS proved quite a stressful exercise. The day before Queen Margrethe's visit, I received twenty-one senior visitors, including the NATO Commander Northern Europe, my old friend General Sir Anthony Farrar-Hockley, and the Chiefs of Defence of Denmark, Italy and Belgium. Despite these distractions, the exercise went quite well and a heliborne attack by the enemy, Royal Marine Commandos, on three bridges we were defending was judged by Tony Farrar-Hockley, who happened to be in the area at the time, to have been a complete failure with heavy loss – especially when I ordered a counter-attack by my Italian Alpini Battlegroup against the remnants. However, the Marines got their revenge the following day. Sometime after dark, and having checked that all was well throughout my area of responsibility, I decided to retire to my Alternate HQ and get some sleep. A final call to my Chief of Staff at Main HQ revealed that all was quiet although some helicopters had been heard in the area. My suspicions were aroused and I ordered George Basso to put everyone on alert. Sure enough, within half an hour all hell broke loose. The Marines had landed nearby and launched a quick attack on my Alternate HQ. The next thing I knew was a young Marine captain entering my caravan and telling me I was his prisoner. I congratulated him but pointed out that this was my Alternate, not my Main HQ. I told him that I was not prepared to go with him as his prisoner but that in fairness I would take no further part in the exercise for twelve hours. Then, in his presence, I spoke to my Chief of Staff at Main and confirmed my agreement, telling him to take command for the next twelve hours. Honour was thus satisfied.

I greatly enjoyed all my visits to Norway and became very fond of the country and its people. All our exercises were north of the Arctic Circle and I was greatly privileged in seeing the spectacular countryside of that beautiful country by the best means of all – a helicopter. One flight was particularly memorable: I was flown by one of the Norwegian Divisional commanders, a trained helicopter pilot and a close friend, from Tromso, across Finmark to Kirkenes near the border with the then Soviet Union. Finmark is more or less completely flat and has little vegetation and, as dusk fell, one could see only the odd light here and there every kilometre or so. I asked my friend what on earth people did for a living that far north; he replied 'you have to love your wife a lot!'

Amongst other privileges I enjoyed in Norway were staying in a very luxurious wooden cabin in the mountains belonging to the King and having reindeer to eat at a dinner party with King Olaf, Bernie Rogers and all the senior Norwegian generals. Our major exercise took place there in March 1982 when the temperature plunged below minus 30C. The US Marines were our enemy. I knew that they were not ski-trained and that, with their abundance of helicopters, they would launch an airborne assault. After a careful study of the ground, I decided there was only one place where they could land to achieve their aim and sited my British, Canadian and Italian battlegroups accordingly, well dug-in and with plenty of artillery and air support. At the end of the exercise the umpires agreed that the attacking force would have been decimated. The Marines had their revenge though. After the exercise the Norwegians put on a 'shrimp party' in which a small rowing boat is filled with shrimps and, after dipping them in mayonnaise, one eats nothing else and drinks nothing but aquavit and beer. At the start of the evening a Norwegian officer demonstrated how non-Norwegians always take off the head, shell and legs of a shrimp before eating it. He then showed us how to eat it the Norwegian way – whole and straight into the mouth! I knew I would have to make a speech of thanks and, fortunately for me, my Royal Naval adviser, Commodore Michael Clapp (who was in charge of the British amphibious ships in the Falklands conflict shortly after our exercise), nudged me and said he had just tried it and it wasn't that difficult. At the end of my speech, after the toast to our hosts, I therefore ordered all AMF (L) officers to stand and to take a shrimp and eat it the Norwegian way. Everyone was horrified, but after much laughter we all managed it. However, the commander of the US Marines in his thank-you speech went one better – at the end of it he ordered all US Marines to 'take two shrimps and eat them!'

My last exercise was in eastern Anatolia in Turkey in June 1983. It was a very large FTX and would climax with me handing over command of the AMF (L) to a Canadian. The AMF (L) had never exercised in eastern Turkey before due to the difficulties in getting there and the expense involved. However, I had argued that if it was a designated NATO contingency area it was essential that we exercised there and understood the problems involved. My determination finally won the day and, in an address to all AMF (L) officers immediately before the exercise started, the new C-in-C US Army Europe, General Glenn Otis, said, pointing at me, 'Without this officer this exercise would never have happened.'

The preparations for the very aptly named Exercise ADVENTURE EXPRESS had started nine months earlier in September 1982 with a recce of both the exercise area, which was only some 100 miles from the border with the Soviet Union, and the proposed site for the Change of Command parade near Sarikamis. We began with a visit to Ankara and then moved on to Erzurum where I was greeted by a very large Guard of Honour, the Mayor and heavy security. In Sarikamis I was greeted by the Regional Governor, the Mayor and what looked like half the population of the town. The recce itself, however, was not without its difficulties for the Turks had earmarked a completely unsuitable piece of ground for our staging area for the deterrence phase of the exercise and only after a lot of argument were we given one which was easily accessible and not likely to flood in wet weather. In the process of finding somewhere more suitable and recceing the combat phase of the exercise, I was able to see much of the magnificent countryside of eastern Anatolia.

On 4 June 1983 I flew with my senior staff to a US airfield near the port of Mersin on the southern coast of Turkey. Our heavy equipment had been shipped there rather than airlifted direct to the exercise area in order to save money. From Mersin it was moved by train to Erzurum. All this was quite exciting and, as well as seeing another fascinating part of Turkey, I was able to visit Tarsus, the scene of the first meeting between Mark Antony and Cleopatra and birthplace of Saint Paul.

ADVENTURE EXPRESS started on 7 June, lasted twelve days and was a great success. I had already hosted Sir Peter Terry (DSACEUR) two days before it ended and then, on the final day, I had to leave command of the AMF (L) to my Chief of Staff and G3 and host Joseph Luns, the Secretary General of NATO, Bernie Rogers, the US and Turkish ambassadors to NATO, the Turkish Minister of Defence, the Turkish Chief of the Army Staff and the Turkish Army commander. They had also come to see the Change of Command parade which took place thirty-six hours later. Bernie Rogers arrived nearly an hour early for this and so he and I and my successor, Alan Christie, rested in the 1878 Russian Czar's hunting lodge before going on parade. The parade itself had been rehearsed during the deterrence phase and, as well as a march past by contingents of all seven of the countries contributing to the AMF (L), accompanied by the huge band of the Third Turkish Army, there was a drive past by the British Recce Squadron and the Force artillery and fly past by all my helicopters. It was a superb display and I was very proud. A British *Daily Mirror* newspaper reporter, Revel Barker, who had covered many of our exercises during my time in command, interviewed Bernie at the reception which followed the Parade and I was very proud and slightly embarrassed when the latter said, 'Anything you write about this man wouldn't do him justice'. I found the Parade quite an emotional affair. When I said goodbye to a particular Turkish general who commanded the Division in the Sarikamis area and with whom I had become particularly friendly, I have to admit there were tears in my eyes. I flew back to Erzurum in one of my HQ US helicopters, flown by an officer I had come to know well. I told him that I wanted to land and take off one more time in order to make it 420 take-offs and landings during my time in command. He told me that this had already been arranged and, to my great surprise, then landed at the Main AMF (L) helicopter base where all the pilots and ground crews were on parade saluting me. Again I had tears in my eyes. That night I had dinner with my entire staff and the following morning they and Alan Christie were at the airport to say goodbye as I took off for the last time to fly to Ankara, Istanbul, Munich and so to Mannheim. It had been an incredible three years.

In a final letter to me before I handed over command, Bernie Rogers wrote:

> Congratulations! I am delighted to hear that you have been appointed a Companion of the Order of the Bath, which justly recognizes the exemplary manner of your command these past three years. Your unique Force has amply reflected those high ideals envisioned at the birth of the Alliance. This, in no small measure, is due to your outstanding leadership, vigor and diplomacy. This national recognition most appropriately acknowledges the contribution you have made.

I don't know if Bernie ever knew it, but I was told later that I had been in line for a knighthood for my performance with the AMF (L). It would have been most unusual for one major general to be knighted in a single year, let alone two, and in the event the only two-star knighthood awarded in 1983 went to the Garrison Commander of the Falkland Islands after they had been recaptured from the Argentineans.

Chapter Twenty-five

NATO International Military Staff
– Brussels

Seven months before the end of my command of the AMF (L) I was informed that my next appointment would be Assistant Director, Plans and Policy Division, NATO International Military Staff (IMS) in Brussels commencing on 1 July 1983. I was not pleased and demanded an interview with the Military Secretary, Roly Guy, whom I knew well and who had been my immediate superior in HQ BAOR. I told him that as this would be my last job I thought it only fair and proper that I should serve my last two years in the UK where I could look for a civilian job and buy a house convenient to it. I pointed out that I had spent the last sixteen out of nineteen years abroad and even soldiers normally spent their last posting in the Army at home. To my surprise, he told me that I had been selected for this job in Brussels as a stepping stone to taking over the three-star post of my future boss – the Director of the NATO International Military Staff (DIMS). This would be coming up in fourteen months and, if the NATO Military Committee selected me, I would be promoted to the rank of lieutenant general, leading in those days to an automatic knighthood. I could hardly go on arguing and said I would be honoured to accept the nomination.

Brussels sounded quite fun and, at least, was nearer than Mannheim to our flat in Eastbourne and we could both get back to the UK easily. The only problem was that, as so often had happened during my career, there was no quarter with the job and we would have to find somewhere to live. Accordingly, I took a week's leave in March 1983 and, after four days, we found a superb apartment more or less in the centre of Brussels and only a short drive from HQ NATO. It was on the floor below the penthouse in a modern block on the elegant Avenue Tervuren and very close to Place Montgomery. There were many excellent shops and restaurants within walking distance. It had a large entrance hall, a very spacious drawing room, large dining room, small breakfast room off a well-equipped kitchen, a master bedroom with en-suite bathroom and a small balcony looking west over some attractive rooftops and quiet streets, two further bedrooms, a large bathroom and a small utility room. It also had a large garage and cave in the basement. The charming owners lived in a farmhouse near the Waterloo battlefield. The owner of the penthouse above us was an extremely wealthy man, Baron Aldo Vastapane (*alias* Mr Martini-Belgium), who was rarely there so we heard no noise. The next problem, however, was that, apart from carpets and a beautiful marble dining-table, the apartment was unfurnished. I asked if we could take some of our Mannheim furniture with us rather than see it all go back to London but, to my horror, I was told that it (like my knighthood!) was to be shipped to the Falklands for use by the new military governor. We were allowed to take the curtains for our new apartment and some small items like side tables but otherwise had to accept normal G-Plan furniture. Amazingly, the apartment seemed to lend itself to this and, with Anne's magic touch and our own 'bits and bobs', we soon had it looking very attractive indeed. Everyone who came there was impressed.

We arrived in Brussels on 3 July and, after a night in the excellent Belgian Officers' Club, moved into our apartment. We had said a very sad farewell to our wonderful staff in Mannheim and our close protection team. However, we were entitled to a daily 'help' and, because I was still a potential terrorist target, I was given a staff car with a full-time, specially-trained driver. Corporal Firth served me very well for our three years in Brussels. I was the only two-star officer at NATO HQ with this privilege.

I will not attempt to describe the organization of HQ NATO in 1984 in any great detail. Under the North Atlantic Council, which comprised the Permanent Representatives (Ambassadors to NATO) of all the members of the Alliance, were the Defence Planning Committee (DPC), the Nuclear Planning Group (NPG) and the Military Committee (MC) – NATO's senior military authority. Its members were nominated generals from each member state (MILREPs). The executive body of the Military Committee, the IMS, comprised five divisions – Intelligence, Plans and Policy, Operations, Communication and Information Systems and Logistics. I found myself as head of the Plans and Policy Division (P&P). The NATO Secretary General when I arrived was Alfred Luns whom I had met only recently in Sarikamis in Turkey. The Chairman of the Military Committee during all my time in Brussels was also a Dutchman, General Cor De Jager; his Deputy was an American, Lieutenant General 'Bo' Williams. The DIMS was a charming Norwegian, Tonne Huitfeldt. I had known him well in Norway. Of course, he had no idea that the British planned to nominate me as his successor. Fortunately, I got on very well with all my HQ NATO superiors, and also with the British MILREP to the MC, Admiral Sir Tony Morton. I had known him in 1969 in Londonderry when he was the Captain of HMS *Sea Eagle*. I was sad to see him leave when he handed over to an Army general six months after I arrived.

My deputy in the P&P Division was an excellent German brigadier who sadly died suddenly at the beginning of 1984. His successor, also a German brigadier, was equally good. My Divisional staff comprised some thirty colonels, lieutenant colonels and majors from all the member countries; they worked on the various aspects of NATO plans and policy. The focus of all our work was the Cold War and I will not bore the reader with details that are well recorded elsewhere. On the personal side I had a Dutch colonel as my Military Assistant (MA) and a British lady as my PA. She had been in the job for a long time and, unfortunately, shared an office right outside mine with another British PA who served my Deputy and MA. They talked incessantly and I soon became very irritated by their behaviour. They hardly looked up when I arrived in the morning and the best response I got was a fairly cold 'good morning'. My coffee was served without a smile or comment. After a couple of weeks of this I had had enough and asked my PA to come and sit down. I told her that I was not prepared to be treated like this and that I expected a nice smile and 'good morning General', or 'Sir' or even 'Mike' on arrival. I also told her I would like my coffee served with a smile and not banged down with some of it in the saucer. She was devastated but it did the trick and we were soon on excellent terms. She even came to our house in Eastbourne for lunch long after I had retired.

Shortly after our arrival in Brussels we were invited by the Belgian Chief of Defence, Maurice Gysemberg, to a superb dinner in a elegant room at the top of the Memorial Arch known as Cinquantenaire – it was only a 'stone's throw' from our apartment. Maurice had been a close friend at the RCDS in London. Other guests included Bernie and Anne Rogers and the US Ambassador to Belgium, who later became Ambassador in London. After dinner Bernie took me to one side and told me he was delighted to have a friend at HQ NATO and he was sure I would support him getting his ideas and plans accepted by the MC. I assured him I would try.

Our work load in P & P was not heavy and initially I found it rather boring. My day started at 9 o'clock and ended, for security reasons, at 4.30 when all the files were locked away. Unlike my brother officers who did not have the luxury of a car and driver, I normally went home for lunch, although on occasions I joined my civilian and military colleagues in the senior officers' restaurant in the HQ. On the work side I had to attend a DIMS conference every Monday morning when each Divisional

Director brought everyone up to date on what was happening in his Division. I also had to attend weekly MC Committee meetings and less frequent DPC meetings, sitting behind the Chairman and DIMS ready to brief them if someone asked an unexpected question on plans or policy. They rarely did. However, I got a nasty shock on 5 December 1984 when the German Minister of Defence asked when 'The Conceptual Military Framework' (CMF) would be ready. This was designed, as I soon discovered, to specify how Europe would look from a military point of view in ten years' time. The Minister went on to say that, without guidance from NATO, he could hardly be expected to frame a coherent defence policy for his country. The Secretary General asked the Chairman of the MC for an answer; he asked DIMS who then looked at me. I had never heard of it! The Minister was told that a firm answer would be given the following week, but he demanded that, as far as he was concerned, he expected the completed CMF document within six months. I eventually discovered that work on the CMF had been going on in my Division for a quite long time, but the German officer responsible had no sense of urgency over its completion and I had never been briefed about it. This was all very embarrassing, not only for me, but for DIMS and the Chairman of the MC who were also unaware of it. Anyway, after many apologies, I got hold of one of my best officers, a German air force colonel, Michael Vollstedt, who later became a general, and told him he had to complete the CMF within four months and, if I was happy with it, I would personally spend the final two months 'managing it' through the NATO system. The latter involved numerous meetings with national representatives but we achieved it and, to everyone's great relief, the CMF was completed on 25 April and passed by the MC, ready to present to the DPC, on 21 May. Little did anyone realize that the concept presented would be completely outdated within five years. The fall of the Berlin Wall and the collapse of the Soviet Empire in 1989 were totally unforeseen.

Shortly after we completed work on the CMF, Tonne Huitfeldt retired and was replaced as DIMS, not by me, but by a Belgian air force lieutenant general. How did this come about? On 9 April 1984 the UK MILREP had written to the MC as follows, 'The United Kingdom Authorities wish to nominate Major General M. F. Reynolds, UKAR, for the post of Director, International Military Staff. He would be appointed in the rank of Lieutenant General.' Five months later the MC held a meeting in Porto in Portugal during which they were to select the new DIMS. I was naturally rather apprehensive, particularly since my Dutch MA and several of the members of the MC with whom I had become very friendly – namely the Belgian, German, Italian and Spanish – had told me that they could not understand why the British MILREP was not canvassing for me as other MILREPs were doing for their candidates. I learned later that mine did not think it was his business to do so! Anyway, I had to be in support of DIMS and the Chairman at the MC meeting and so flew out to Porto with Anne. We had a very pleasant four days until I learned that I had *not* been selected to be the next DIMS. I was not present when the MC chose the new DIMS and it is more than possible that the main factor that swayed the decision against me was the fact that, three weeks after the Porto meeting, Alfred Luns was to hand over to Lord Carrington as Secretary General. To some it was unacceptable to have a Brit as Secretary General and another as head of the IMS. Naturally I was extremely disappointed but, as it turned out, Anne and I were able to enjoy the rest of our time in Brussels and I got on well with the new DIMS. Looking back, it is clear that if I had become a NATO three-star officer I would have been uniquely qualified to go on to a four-star NATO appointment. And what would those four-star appointments have been? Either DSACEUR in Mons, Belgium, or Commander Northern Europe in Oslo. But it was not to be.

One of the most enjoyable things about my appointment in Belgium was the chance it gave me to travel within NATO. As well as Trilateral meetings in Munich, Ankara, Athens and the Hague, I was able to visit and lecture at the NATO Defence College in Rome, the NATO School in Oberammergau and even fly to Norfolk, Virginia, for a conference held by the Supreme Allied Commander Atlantic. On that occasion I was privileged to have lunch on the amphibious assault ship USS *Nassau* and go to sea in the nuclear submarine USS *Phoenix*.

In November 1983 I was summoned to Buckingham Palace to receive my CB from the Queen. Anne and Deborah came with me. I had first seen Her Majesty close to on parade at Sandhurst, then at the RCDS and now for my award. On all these occasions she looked quite lovely and I have never ceased to admire her.

At beginning of 1984 I was chosen by the Colonels of the Queen's, Fusilier and Royal Anglian Regiments to be the Colonel Commandant of the Queen's Division. This was an honorary post as the Queen's Divisional HQ at Bassingbourn, although technically *my* HQ, was run on a permanent basis, as described in a previous chapter, by the Divisional Brigadier. Apart from visits to some of the battalions of the Regiments, my basic responsibility was to chair the quarterly meetings of the three Regimental Colonels and, if necessary, represent their views and recommendations to the Director of Infantry. It was not an arduous appointment.

The most memorable occasion during my time as Colonel Commandant was Beating Retreat on Horse Guards in June 1985 by the massed bands and Corps of Drums of the Queen's Division and the Pipes and Drums of our two affiliated Ulster Defence Regiment Battalions – a total of seven Bands, eight Corps of Drums and two Corps of Pipes and Drums. It was a four-night programme, superbly organized by a young Queen's major, Mike Jelf. Since we needed to be in London for the whole of this period, Peter and Nicky Mason again very kindly lent us their house in Chelsea. On 10 June I took the salute at the final rehearsal and found myself standing on the same dais used by the Queen when she takes the salute on her annual Birthday Parade. It went well, but when the leading Drum Major, whom I knew well, asked for permission to 'march off', I surprised him by saying that it had been good except for the thirteen Drum Majors whose mace drill was uncoordinated and that he should rehearse them next morning in Wellington Barracks. He was devastated but did so and all was well from then on. Anne had been able to watch my parade from the Major General's Office above Horse Guards and afterwards we were able to entertain some of our closest friends there. On each of the three following nights I stood on the same dais with the Colonels of the three Regiments of the Queen's Division and those they had asked to take the salute: Margaret Thatcher, the Duke of Kent and Queen Elizabeth, the Queen Mother. Afterwards on each night we proceeded to the Banqueting Hall in Whitehall for drinks and canapés. Two of these were very memorable – Maggie Thatcher, who never drew breath and hardly listened to anyone, and the Queen Mother, who was utterly charming and stayed twice as long as expected. When I had suggested that she should have a rug round her knees on the saluting dais she replied that it was a very kind thought but she would prefer to sit on it so that she could see better.

Other memorable occasions during my tenure were representing the Chief of the Defence Staff in Brussels for the Fortieth Anniversary celebrations of the liberation of Belgium, and flying to Gibraltar to visit a Battalion of the Queen's Regiment and, after inspecting the Guard of Honour, having lunch with the Governor, Sir David Williams.

Returning to our life in Brussels, it was highly social. As well as going to and giving many drinks parties, we hosted at least one dinner party a month during our three years, and numerous lunch parties. The dinners included many of the MILREPs, DIMS and even one or two ambassadors. Since Brussels is one of the gastronomic capitals of the world we were spoiled with choice for excellent restaurants. Our regular favourite, where we shared many happy evenings with friends and family, was Jacques, a superb seafood restaurant in the port area.

Needless to say, most of our family came to stay with us during these three very happy years. Even my parents, in their mid-eighties, drove out to stay and Gabrielle and Austen and Deborah were regular visitors. Victoria and Corin came to stay for a quick visit just before leaving for Hong Kong where he was to serve with the Gurkhas. This allowed us to fly out to stay with them for a fascinating twelve-day holiday at the end of 1984. Numerous old friends came to stay as well, including Peter and Nicky Mason, Edward and Louise Clowes and Mike and Anne Doyle. We were a good stopping-off point for friends on their way to and from continental Europe. And it was whilst we were in Brussels that I was able to organize another 12 Brigade Reunion of my old staff from Osnabrück days. It was a huge success and included lunch in our apartment, a tour of the Waterloo battlefield and a superb dinner in the Belgian Officers' Club, the Club Prince Albert, where they all stayed.

Living in Belgium allowed me to renew my interest in the Battle of the Bulge and, in late 1985, I chanced to meet a Belgian historian, Gerd Cuppens, who told me that a number of Waffen-SS veterans were planning to retrace their December 1944 steps through the Ardennes and asked if I would like to join them. I could hardly believe my ears, but sure enough, on 1 and 2 October, I was able to join a group of eleven former members of Hitler's Bodyguard Division – the 1st SS Panzer Division, *Leibstandarte Adolf Hitler*, in the area where they had fought forty-one years before. They ranged in rank from regimental commander to tank commander and driver and it was fascinating to hear the story from the 'other side of the hill'. Also present were Cuppens, someone driving him whom he introduced as his nephew, and a German Bunderswehr reservist colonel, Wolf Mauder, with whom I became very friendly and who helped me a lot with my subsequent researches into the actions of *Kampfgruppe* Peiper. However, a short time after this meeting I was shocked when my MA brought a copy of a Dutch magazine called *Knack* into my office and showed me a photograph of myself with the Waffen-SS veterans under the heading 'NATO general accompanies SS Veterans as they re-conquer the Ardennes'! It transpired that Cuppens' so-called 'nephew' was nothing of the kind but was a journalist. I was furious and told my PA to call Cuppens and tell him I wanted nothing more to do with him. I then rang Wolf Mauder to tell him and he passed on the news to the German veterans. Everyone was equally angry. Just as embarrassing for me was the fact that I had to go in and show the magazine to both the DIMS and the Chairman of the MC. The latter, being a Dutchman, would almost certainly have been shown the magazine by someone. However, they were both very understanding and fully accepted my explanation of how it had happened: that I was merely pursuing my interest in the Battle of the Bulge and had been misled. As a result of this debacle, Peter Crocker and I ended up conducting the Chairman and most of the MC on a PIED PEIPER tour in June 1986, shortly before I left Brussels. I had already done tours on my own for forty members of the IMS and the Deputy Chairman of the MC and several senior American officers in October 1985 and April 1986 respectively.

In April 1986 Anne and I returned to England to look for a house for our retirement. Fortunately, we found almost exactly what we wanted only a short distance from our flat in Eastbourne. One never gets *exactly* what one wants, but we certainly got 90 per cent.

Our last couple of months in Brussels were hectic with farewell lunches and dinners, one of the nicest being given in our honour by an old friend from Staff College days, Ted Burgess, who was now General Sir Edward Burgess, DSACEUR. Others by DIMS, the Chairman of the MC and the Belgian Chief of Defence were equally enjoyable.

On 3 July I attended my last MC meeting where I was thanked and congratulated on a job well done by the Chairman. It was the end of my professional military career; although I was sad about this I had been able to come to terms with it. I could look back on not only a very successful career but also a very happy one. Many years later I was given a copy of the curriculum vitae sent to the IMS in 1984 by the Ministry of Defence supporting my nomination as DIMS. I had never seen it before and only when I read it did I realize how much I had achieved. It was one of the sparks that led to these memoirs. It read:

> Major General Reynolds is an infantry officer with unusually wide experience both as a Commander and Staff Officer. As a young officer he saw service in Germany, Korea, where he was severely wounded, and in the Middle East. As a Commander he has commanded at all levels from Company, through Battalion, to Mechanized Brigade in the Central Region of Allied Command Europe and in addition held an active service command in Northern Ireland. His academic ability is evidenced by the facts that he graduated second from his course at Military Academy, obtained direct and immediate entry to the Staff College and was an outstanding student at the Royal College of Defence Studies in London where he was selected to chair a very important debate in the presence of HM Queen Elizabeth II. As a Staff Officer, Major General Reynolds has worked in semi-technical appointments in War Gaming and Operational Requirements and in the Operations environment at a senior level during real operations in Northern Ireland and in

NATO. As a one-star general officer he was Head of Personnel Matters in the British Army in Germany for two years. Major General Reynolds can truly be described as a NATO soldier. He has served as an exchange officer for two years in Canada; he has served in the 1 (BR) Corps of NORTHAG as a Battalion and Brigade Commander, been an ACOS G3 in HQ AFCENT in the Netherlands, taken part in and organized the annual LIVE OAK Tripartite Exercise and most significantly, and perhaps uniquely, held NATO Command *and* Staff appointments at two-star level. As a Major General he commanded with distinction the AMF (L). This brought him into close contact with all the major NATO Commands and Principal Subordinate Commands in Europe, as well as most NATO MoDs and USAREUR. He was of course under the personal command of SACEUR. As COMAMF (L) he exercised direct command of contingents from seven NATO countries and completed major FTXs in Norway, Denmark, Italy, Eastern and Western Turkey, detailed recces in Greece and artillery concentrations in Germany, the UK, Belgium and Portugal. He was widely held in very high regard in this appointment, particularly his sensitivities to national views and feelings, his positive approach to problems and above all his ability to get the best out of those under his command.

On 4 July 1986 I crossed the Channel for the last time as a serving officer. My official retirement date was 8 October 1986 which gave me three months in which to decide what to do after the Army. I should add that, by now, our family had grown considerably. By mid-1983 Victoria and Corin had Katie and Harry; and Gabrielle and Austen had Thomas and Henry by the time we left Brussels.

Chapter Twenty-six

Retirement

In early September 1986 I was told that the Chief of the General Staff wished to thank me for my service and say goodbye. Accordingly, on the 16th, I entered the Ministry of Defence for the first time in my life. I have always been very proud of the fact that I was never a 'Whitehall Warrior'. General Sir Nigel Bagnall was charming and, after saying he was sorry that I had never been under his direct command and that I might have gone further if I had been, he thanked me for all I had done for the Army and my country.

By this time I had decided that I would not start another full-time career. Having reached near the top of one tree I was not prepared to start at the bottom of another. I had been offered a number of jobs, including resident Governor of the Tower of London. However, I had no wish to be 'sent to the Tower' or live in the east end of the City. Nor was I tempted with offers of being chief executive in a number of charities. In all cases they meant renting accommodation in London or commuting daily, wearing a suit and tie every day, and putting up with a small staff and a secretary who had usually been in the job for many years. No, after looking at my ex-military friends I realized that the ones who seemed to be the healthiest and happiest were those who had not taken a full-time job after leaving the Army. I was also aware that the two I knew best, a colonel and my old friend Brigadier Tony Baxter, had smaller pensions than me and that neither had the benefit of a private income. If they could manage and be happy, there was no reason why I couldn't do the same.

But how would I fill my time and occupy my brain if I did not get a full- or even a part-time job? The first six months were easy for, whilst continuing to live in our flat in Eastbourne, we were fully occupied getting our new house and garden, only some half a mile away, the way we wanted them. In those days all regular soldiers, sailors and airmen were entitled to a six weeks' 'resettlement course' of their choice. I knew one officer who chose an 'orchid growing' course, but I chose 'House Maintenance' and so was able to do quite a lot of the basic decorations myself; that said we had to employ professionals to make major alterations to the house and garden. It all went very well, however, and on 5 December we moved in. Our whole family came to stay for a very merry Christmas. There were now nine of them but, as the house had five bedrooms, there was no problem.

As a result of my PIED PEIPER tours for the IMS and MC I had become quite well-known as an expert on the Battle of the Bulge and the first quarter of 1987 saw me making visits to the Dutch Army Staff College in the Hague, the NATO Defence College in Rome and the American War College in Carlisle to lecture on the subject. By the end of that year I had completed five PIED PEIPER tours for British, American and NATO audiences which were so successful that I decided to offer myself to various NATO and British Army organizations, formations and units as a guest speaker on the subject. I told them that I was not prepared to organize the tours, but I would offer them advice on accommodation and other administrative matters. I would also arrange if they wished it, which most of them did, a superb dinner at the end of each tour in an excellent restaurant in La Gleize. The owner, Louie, and his partner, Maggie, were great hosts and they, with his mother, Mama, who always gave me a full kiss on the lips whenever we met, and a very attractive girl behind the bar, Arlette, made sure every evening was a huge success. Between 1987 and 2000 I appeared as the guest speaker on forty-one PIED PEIPER tours, for a total of over 1,500 officers and senior ranks. They were usually for British units and Brigades but they included tours for SHAPE, HQ BAOR, HQ NORTHAG, I British Corps and even the German MoD. I always stayed with my dear friends Marie-Berthe and Edouard de Harenne and with their usual generosity they allowed us to have a picnic lunch in the grounds of their Chateau and, on more than one occasion when the weather was inclement, to have lunch in their drawing and dining rooms.

One of the most memorable tours was when Wolf Mauder asked me to join him on a tour for former members of *Kampfgruppe* Peiper. This happened in June 1991 and we conducted ten veterans along the route they had taken forty-seven years before. It was fascinating and I learned a lot more about their actions.

Although I was quite busy with battlefield tours, I should mention that Anne and I were able to enjoy some wonderful holidays – India, the Nile, the Danube, Russia, Sicily and Tunisia, to mention some of the more interesting ones. I was also able to enjoy some wonderful sailing holidays with Peter and Nicky Mason off Cornwall, the west coast of Scotland and off Norway and Sweden.

In July 1990 the problem of my own personal security returned to disturb our lives. That month Ian Gow, my local Member of Parliament, was killed by a bomb placed under his car at his home in a village near Eastbourne. It was the work of the Provisional IRA. Ian had been in our house for a drink only a few weeks before and, shortly after his death, two Special Branch officers visited me and, having discovered that I had also been on the IRA, and indeed other 'hit lists', wanted to know why I had not told them of my presence in Eastbourne. I explained that I was 'ex-Directory', did not use my rank and generally kept a low profile when at home. This they accepted, but they insisted that a security check should be carried out on our house, told me that occasional police patrols would keep an eye on the property and gave me a codename and number I could call if I was suspicious of anything or anyone. My codename was 'Owl'. About six months later a car with a Northern Ireland number plate parked outside our house and, when it had not moved after a couple of days, I rang the number and said, 'This is Owl.' 'Who?' came the reply. 'Owl.' 'Who?' 'Owl – this is my codename and I've been told to call this number if I have a security problem!' 'Oh, hang on!' And so it ended amicably and they checked the car which was found to be harmless. That was the only potentially serious incident we had.

A major influence on my retirement occurred in 1989 when I was asked to take over as Colonel of The Queen's Regiment. I was very honoured and thoroughly enjoyed the first eighteen months, visiting the three Regular and three Territorial Battalions of the Regiment in Great Britain, Germany, Cyprus and Northern Ireland. I was also about to enjoy many of our affiliations, including those with our Canadian Regiments, the Haberdashers' Livery Company and with two Royal Navy ships. Other highlights of my Colonelcy were being received and honoured by our Allied Colonels-in-Chief. Queen Margrethe of Denmark, whom I came to know quite well, made me a Commander First Class of the Order of the Dannebrog in 1990, and Queen Beatrix of the Netherlands made me a Knight of the House of Orange in 1992.

In 1990, however, the Government announced an 'Options for Change' policy and the fun came to an end. This was a major restructuring of the British armed forces aimed at cutting defence spending following the end of the Cold War. It came as a great shock to everyone in the Regiment and in the counties of south-east England where we recruited. To our utter disbelief we were told that we were to be amalgamated with the Royal Hampshire Regiment which had only one regular battalion, and was a Regiment with which we had nothing in common. Needless to say, we decided to fight this injustice and, with support from many influential people, including MPs, and especially from the Associations of our founding Regiments, we all, past and present, came together to try to ensure the survival of the Queen's. However, despite all our efforts, culminating in a very well-attended march on 10 Downing Street to hand in a petition, we lost the battle and, on 9 September 1992, the amalgamation took place and my Colonelcy, and with it my military career, ended. What particularly disappointed and angered me was the refusal of the Chief of the General Staff, General Sir John Chapple, to give me any reasons for the decision to amalgamate my Regiment with the Royal Hampshires which I could read out to my officers and men. I was shocked to receive the following written reply to my request, 'It is not in the interests of the Army that further explanations of the reasons behind the choices should be made, and I regret therefore that I shall not be giving you an answer.' It seems that once again vested interests rather than justice had won the day! My only consolation came a few years later, when a former Chief of the Defence Staff, Field Marshal the Lord Bramall, at a dinner in Armoury House, pointed at me and told those at the table, 'No one could have done more to try to save his Regiment than this officer.' It is perhaps of further interest that none of the four Regiments in which I served as an officer, The Queen's Royal, The Royal Norfolk, The Queen's Royal Surrey and The Queen's, still exists – a sad reflection on the demise of the British infantry over a period of just thirty-three years – 1959 to 1992.

Although my active military career was over, my interest in military history was as strong as ever and by way of a fortunate accident I was about to start a second career. It began when a PIED PEIPER tour I attended in July 1993 went horribly wrong. The coach turned up two hours late, it rained all day and the Belgians had closed for repairs some of the roads I wanted to take the coach down. At the end of the day I announced that I was getting too old for this sort of thing – I was sixty-three – and would be giving up battlefield tours. I later relented and did six more, the last being in 2000, but at the time I really meant it and it was only after several friends told me that it would be a tragedy to waste all the knowledge I had gained that I agreed to start writing it down with the intention of giving it to the Army for use as a training aid. When I mentioned this to my old friend Peter Mason he immediately said I should turn it into a proper book and he would introduce me to a senior executive of Hodder and Stoughton, the well-known publishers. This he did and I was told my writings certainly had potential but needed a specialist publisher. He then put me in touch with Jamie Wilson of Spellmount Publishing and the rest is history. In a short time Jamie and his wife Beverly became close friends and, after the success of my first book, *The Devil's Adjutant*, he asked me to write another book, and then another – and so it went on until I had written six books on the Second World War. I had again been very fortunate – I had accidentally found a second career which continues to this day and, in the process, had become an internationally-known military historian and author – even to the point of being asked by Steven Spielberg to join him and Tom Hanks on the film set of *Saving Private Ryan*! And since I always insist on seeing the places where the fighting I describe took place, I have been able to enjoy fascinating visits to Hungary, the Czech Republic, Slovakia, Slovenia, Sicily and Morocco. I could hardly have chosen a more enjoyable and fulfilling second career. Another surprise has been the number of individuals and battlefield tour operators that have followed my lead in taking people along the PIED PEIPER route, not to mention one or two who have 'borrowed', to put it politely, some of the things I wrote in *The Devil's Adjutant* and in the brochure issued to everyone who attended our PIED PEIPER tours!

Epilogue

My father often used to say to me, 'You were born lucky!' and he was right. I had a very happy childhood and exciting teenage years with wonderful parents, a successful military career and ended my active life as a relatively well-known author. Even being wounded in the Korean war actually turned out to be a blessing in disguise – if I hadn't been wounded I would never have met my wife and had three lovely daughters, six grandchildren and three great-grandsons; and disappointments such as not being selected for further promotion in 1985 proved to be for the best. If I had been promoted, I would never have been able to enjoy over twenty-five years in retirement and write seven books. Yes, I lived through some wonderful years and can say with a smile, 'Yes, those were the days'. I have been very fortunate.

Index